T0313925

Matching with Transfers

The Gorman Lectures in Economics
Richard Blundell, Series Editor

A series statement appears at the end of the book

Matching with Transfers

The Economics of
Love and Marriage

Pierre-André Chiappori

Princeton University Press
Princeton and Oxford

Copyright © 2017 by Princeton University Press

Published by Princeton University Press,
41 William Street, Princeton, New Jersey 08540

In the United Kingdom: Princeton University Press,
6 Oxford Street, Woodstock, Oxfordshire OX20 1TR

press.princeton.edu

Jacket art: *The Marriage of the Virgin*
(*Sposalizio della Vergine*),
by Raphael, 1504, oil on board, 170 × 118 cm.
Brera Art Gallery, Milan, Italy / Mondadori Portfolio /
Electa / Paolo e Federico Manusardi / Bridgeman Images

All Rights Reserved

ISBN 978-0-691-17173-9

Library of Congress Control Number: 2016959113

British Library Cataloging-in-Publication Data is available

This book has been composed in Minion Pro

Printed on acid-free paper. ∞

Typeset by Nova Techset Pvt Ltd, Bangalore, India
Printed in the United States of America

1 3 5 7 9 10 8 6 4 2

To Kristina,
My perfect match

Contents

Preface

In 2012, University College London (in the person of Richard Blundell) asked me to give the 2013 Gorman Lectures on a subject of my choice. The topic was quite clear in my mind: the 2013 Gorman Lectures would be devoted to matching theory in general, and to matching with (perfectly or imperfectly) transferable utility in particular. I had been working on matching with transfers for several years, and was starting to better understand some of the basic issues; time had come to put these ideas together, and the Gorman Lectures would provide a perfect opportunity.

Although I have worked in various fields, I am mostly a family economist, by which I mean that the economics of the family have always been my major interest. During the years I spent working on the topic, from both theoretical and empirical perspectives, I acquired several insights, one of which is of particular importance: power matters. In a typical household, husband and wife cannot be expected to agree on everything. And whenever they do not totally agree, the distribution of "power" (or "influence" or "bargaining positions" or any other related notion) between them does have an impact on the outcome: who has the final say matters a lot for what will be decided. Not much of an insight, you may think—it sounds like basic common sense. And I would certainly agree with that. But for an economist trained in the 1970s, such a statement was something of a heresy. Standard approaches had accustomed us to thinking of households as perfectly harmonious and homogeneous entities, where differences in tastes or objectives could be omitted and the decision processes could safely be summarized by the fiction of a well-behaved family utility function that would be maximized under budget constraints. This "unitary" approach had several advantages; notably, it allowed one to directly transpose the tools and results of standard consumer theory at the household level, without having to develop an entirely new theoretical framework. At the same time, however, it was offering a highly specific—and I believe deeply biased—representation of household decision processes, whereby unanimity was the rule, and the notion of power (or "empowerment") of the various agents was either irrelevant, or at the very least exogenously given and unresponsive to changes in the environment.

Retrospectively, one cannot help to be amazed by the naiveness of this view—which is perfectly illustrated by the following anecdote. A friend and colleague of mine was working on program evaluation in a developing country, and was trying to understand the role of family decision processes in the impact of the program.

Unlike many, he was convinced that a crucial consequence of the program—whereby some cash payments were made *to the mother*, conditional on children attending school and regularly visiting a doctor—was a change in the respective powers within the couple; indeed, he later found, thanks to a very careful statistical analysis, that the expenditure patterns of the additional income provided by the program was quite different from what would have been expected had the supplement resulted from, say, an increase in the husband's wage. However, my friend, a very serious social scientist, did not want to let any prejudice taint his empirical analysis. He therefore decided, in addition to the specific statistical tests aimed at checking the validity of his hypothesis, to directly collect the subject's views on that issue; in practice, he asked one of the women he interviewed whether the fact that the money was paid to her, not her husband, made any difference at all. The outcome was spectacular, although maybe not exactly what he had hoped for. "All of a sudden," he later told me, "I felt I had lost all the prestige associated with my position of a professor in a prestigious university abroad, whose expertise was required by no less than the federal government. She just could not believe I could ask such a stupid question. 'Of course it does make a huge difference—what on earth do you think' she replied—and then she basically declined to continue the conversation."

Indeed, the conclusion itself—whom the money is paid to matters for how it is spent—does not seem that unexpected. After all, in most countries family benefits are paid to the wife, not the husband—and there is little reason to believe that this choice is not deliberate. If anything, the surprising thing is that economists spent so much time assuming the opposite and referring to the unitary framework, which, by its very nature, *imposes* that paying a benefit to the husband or the wife cannot possibly make any difference. A few decades later, the profession's view has largely changed. Accumulated empirical evidence has shown that the so-called income-pooling property of the unitary approach—whereby only total income matters for household behavior, not the identity of the recipient—provided a very poor description of reality.[1] From a theoretical perspective, we now know how to model "collective" households (i.e., households where the distribution of power between spouses has an impact on behavior) without giving up such

---

[1] Several papers have shown that, controlling for total income, the share of income coming from the wife has an impact on the structure of household expenditures (Thomas 1990, Browning et al. 1994, and many others); see Browning, Chiappori, and Weiss (2014) for a survey. Two of the most convincing pieces of evidence are provided by Duflo (2003), who studies elderly benefits in South Africa and concludes that the same transfer has drastically different impacts on the health of female grandchildren depending on whether it is paid to the grandmother or to the grandfather, and Attanasio and Lechene (2014), who exploit the random structure associated with the *Opportunidades* program in Mexico to show that the money paid by the program to the mother is spent differently than other sources of income.

essential requirements as generality, testability, or empirical tractability. These are important achievements; it is fair to say that our understanding of family decisions is much richer and much more complex, but also much more realistic than it used to be.

As always with research, however, new progress raises new questions. Once we have established that power matters, one issue becomes prominent—namely, where does power come from, and how can it be redistributed? This is a huge (and hugely difficult) question, on which much has been said; not only (actually not principally) by economists, but also by sociologists, ethnologists, historians, and other social scientists (and even by evolutionary biologists). Still, we want to consider this question as economists, using the tools of economic theory. And matching models are, for that purpose, one of the most useful tools in the box.

This intuition dates back to the pioneering work of Gary Becker. In his seminal 1973 paper, Becker wrote: "...theory does not take the division of output between mates as given, but rather derives it from the nature of the marriage market equilibrium" (p. 813).

The operative word, here, is clearly "equilibrium". Becker's intuition is that marriage patterns can be analyzed as stemming from an equilibrium realized on a specific "market," the market for marriage. Consequently, the standard tools of market equilibrium can be invoked to understand the nature and, more importantly, the evolution of these patterns. In this view, the allocation of power (or resources) within the couple can be seen as a "price" that clears the market. In particular, this allocation is, by construction, fully endogenous, and may vary in response to exogenous changes in market conditions. What we have here, in other words, is potentially a full-fledged theory of the determination and evolution of power allocation within the family.

This is not to say that the market for marriage can be analyzed just like any other market—say, the market for milk or iron ore. There is not much difference between two gallons of milk or two tons of iron ore of different origins; mostly, very little is lost by considering milk or iron ore as homogeneous products. Not so, definitely, for marriage: no two individuals are identical, and individual-specific traits play a crucial role on this market. This is precisely why matching models are so useful in that context: they are explicitly designed to analyze trades on "products" that are intrinsically heterogeneous. In a matching game, each player is defined by a set of "characteristics," and a particular combination of characteristics typically makes each player unique. In addition, tastes differ. Not only do different persons exhibit a different combination of characteristics, but each person tends to value the respective traits of potential mates in a specific way. There is no such thing as the "value" of a particular characteristic, such as education or physical attractiveness; what we have instead is the value of a particular trait *for a particular person*. As a consequence, and to push the market analogy a little, there is certainly no such thing as the "price of men" (or of women) on such a market: even if we accept the notion of a price, we must recognize that each woman and each man will typically have her or his own 'price', reflecting his or her unique traits. Matching models (or hedonic models—the two, as we shall see, are largely equivalent concepts) are designed precisely to study markets of this type.

As it may be clear by now, this book will present matching theory from a specific perspective—namely, its applications to the economics of the family. This emphasis, however, is largely idiosyncratic; it reflects my own interests and motivations. Matching theory can be (and has been) applied to a host of different topics in economics, from the labor market to the price of housing and from credit relationships between a bank and its borrowers to the allocation of CEOs to firms. In any context where heterogeneity is a crucial aspect, matching models may potentially provide deep insights; my hope is that the present book, albeit centered on family economics, will help clarify this fact.

Acknowledgments

This book primarily reflects two major influences on my work. Gary Becker is the founding father of the economics of the family; as I mentioned above, some of its most fundamental insights—including the notion that the distribution of power can be analyzed as an equilibrium phenomenon—are present very early in his work. In addition, I had the privilege of being Gary's colleague and friend; I have had many opportunities to benefit not only from his amazing sharpness, but also from his no less amazing intellectual generosity. James Heckman is another towering figure. I remember presenting my ongoing work on collective models of the household to Jim for the very first time while I was visiting the University of Chicago in the fall of 1992. He immediately mentioned the importance of understanding the generation of power allocation—and then came the suggestion: "You should consider using matching theory." It is fair to say that his warm support has accompanied my work ever since.

The aim of this book is to summarize a collective intellectual endeavor that started with the path-breaking contributions of Koopmans and Beckman (1957), Shapley and Shubik (1972), and Becker (1973), and that has attracted and still attracts many outstanding minds. I had the privilege to work and/or hold discussions with several of them; a nonexhaustive list would include Joseph Altonji, Orazio Attanasio, Eduardo Azevedo, François Bourguignon, Yann Brenier, Martin Browning, Guillaume Carlier, Yeon Koo Che, Eugene Choo, Monica Costa Dias, Vincent Crawford, Flavio Cunha, Daniela Del Boca, Ivar Ekeland, Raquel Fernandez, Christopher Flinn, Alfred Galichon, John Geanakoplos, Marion Goussé, Roger Guesnerie, Yinghua He, Marc Henry, Ali Hortacsu, Murat Iyigun, Nicolas Jacquemet, Sonia Jaffe, Navin Kartik, Fuhito Kojima, Scott Kominers, Jeanne Lafortune, Valerie Lechene, Jacob Leshno, Ilse Lindenlaub, Qingmin Liu, Corinne Low, Shelly Lundberg, Georges Mailath, Maurizio Mazzocco, Robert McCann, Costas Meghir, Roger Myerson, Derek Neal, Lars Nesheim, Georg Nöldeke, Sonia Oreffice, Brendan Pass, Luigi Pistaferri, Robert Pollak, Andrew Postlewaite, Climent Quintana Domeque, Philip Reny, Jean Marc Robin, Bernard Salanié, Larry Samuelson, Sam Schuhlofer-Wohl, Robert Shimer, Steven Shore, Aloisius Siow, Robert Townsend, Alessandra Voena, Simon Weber, Yoram Weiss, and Bill Zame. In addition, I have had opportunities to present various aspects of the work to several audiences; I would particularly like to thank participants at Yale University (where I was invited to give the 2015 Koopmans Lectures), the University of Chicago (where I gave several minicourses on the topic), and of course my PhD students at Columbia for their comments. I am particularly indebted to Ivar Ekeland, Costas Meghir, Bernard Salanié, and Yoram Weiss for deep and illuminating discussions; to Richard Blundell for his support while writing this book (not to mention his help in choosing the title); to two anonymous reviewers for several useful suggestions; and to Sen Li and Qingmin Liu for carefully reading a first draft of the manuscript. A large part of my research has been funded by the NSF (Grant 1124277), whose support is gratefully acknowledged. Last but not least, Sarah Caro, Kathleen Cioffi, and Hannah Paul from Princeton University Press as well as Wendy Washburn, the copyeditor, and Jim Curtis, the indexer, have been extremely helpful throughout the process.

Errors are unfortunately mine, though.

Matching with Transfers

1

Introduction: Matching Models in Economics

Matching models can be (and have been) applied to a host of contexts, from finance to the labor market. In this book, however, I shall mostly illustrate my arguments with examples coming from family economics. And I shall start with two related puzzles that are directly related to family formation (and dissolution) and to intrafamily allocation, although their scope is obviously much larger. One has to do with the increase in inequality in the US in recent decades, and the other with some remarkable trends in gender-specific demand for higher education.

1.1 Motivation: Two Puzzles

1.1.1 Inequality

Rising inequality has been one of the most striking features of the recent decades. In the US, according to Kenworthy and Smeeding (2013), the Gini coefficients of both pre- and after-tax income distributions grew by 10 percentage points between 1979 and 2007 (from 0.39 to 0.49 and from 0.35 to 0.45, respectively). Similarly, the pre-tax income share of the top 10% of the US income distribution, which remained below 35% during the three decades following World War II, sharply increased from the early 1980s on, reaching 50% in 2010 (Saez 2013). Rising inequality is a complex phenomenon that has several causes, from skill-biased technological change to globalization. But one of these causes—although probably not the dominant one—is directly linked to family economics. Indeed, several papers have argued that some long-term demographic trends have affected the evolution of inequality; chief among these trends are the rise of single-parent families and an increase in assortative matching for existing couples.[1]

These demographic effects, whose exact magnitude is still discussed, unavoidably generate some difficult questions about the concepts at stake. An increase in assortative matching is not easy to define. We must first define the trait we should concentrate on: are we talking about education? wages? income? Income is probably a disputable choice, if only because it is obviously endogenous—the same matching patterns may exhibit strikingly different assortativeness in income if

---

[1] For instance, according to Greenwood et al. (2014): "if people matched in 2005 according to the 1960 standardized mating pattern there would be a significant reduction in income inequality; i.e., the Gini drops from 0.43 to 0.35" (p. 352).

some exogenous shock affects spouses' labor supply and participation in the labor market. Human capital is a better choice, since it can reasonably be considered as (at least partly) given when people enter the marriage market; note, however, that the impact of human capital investments on matching prospects may play a central role in agents' decisions regarding education (more on this later).

Second, while any increase in the percentage of single people has a mechanical impact on our *measures* of inequality, the economic reality behind the estimates is harder to assess. Consider a couple with annual income equal to \$30,000—well above the poverty level.[2] Assume, now, that the couple divorces; we have two singles with respective incomes \$12,000 and \$18,000—one of which is below the poverty threshold. According to standard measures, both poverty and inequality have increased. Still, and even if we ignore the role of public consumptions and economies of scale, the actual *change* in economic inequality must unavoidably depend on the inequality that prevailed *within* the pre-divorce couple. Standard inequality measures systematically ignore this inequality; in order to compare income across families of different composition, they use equivalence scales, which essentially amounts to assuming fair intracouple distribution.[3] That, however, does not mean that intrafamily inequality does not exist; in fact, it has been argued that such issues should play a central role in both the measure of inequality and the definition of policies aiming at reducing it.[4] An immediate difficulty, however, is that intrafamily inequality is notoriously hard to measure. As we shall see, matching models may in many cases provide a very useful tool for this purpose.

Third, the mere notion of "increase in assortativeness" is somewhat vague. In recent decades, women's education has changed drastically; for instance, the percentage of women aged 30 to 40 with a postgraduate degree has surged from 3% to more than 11% over the last 40 years. A mechanical effect of this increase is that highly educated men are more likely now to marry a highly educated wife. But are the observed changes in matching patterns only due to the mechanical effects of variations in the distributions of male and female education? Or did preferences for assortativeness also increase over the period? More fundamentally, how can such "preferences for assortativeness" be defined, and how can we measure their variations?

1.1.2   *Demand for Higher Education*

As I just mentioned, one of the salient trends in recent decades is the increased investment in education by women and the closing (actually reversing) of the gap

---

[2] According to the US Census Bureau, in 2014 the poverty threshold was equal to \$15,853 for a childless couple and \$12,316 for a childless single.

[3] See, for instance, Chiappori (2016).

[4] See, for instance, Chiappori and Meghir (2015).

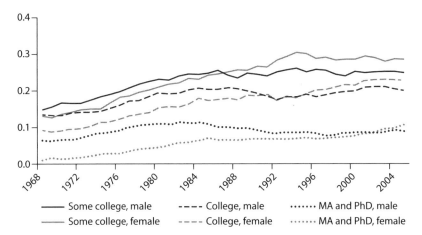

Figure 1.1. Educational attainment in US of spouses by husbands' year of birth (Chiappori, Iyigun, and Weiss 2009).

in schooling between men and women. Goldin and Katz (2008) show that, starting with the 1970 birth cohort, women have attained higher college graduation rates than men in the United States. They find similar reversals in 15 OECD countries.

Figure 1.1, borrowed from Chiappori, Iyigun, and Weiss (2009), describes the time trends in levels of school completion for men and women, aged 30 to 40, for the United States. As can be seen, the proportions of women with some college education, college completion, and advanced degrees (M.A., Ph.D.) have increased much faster than the corresponding proportions for men. By 2003, women had overtaken men in all of these three categories.

A particularly interesting feature pointed out by this graph is the asymmetry between genders regarding demand for higher education over the last few decades. Consider the percentage of individuals with a postgraduate degree, in dotted lines. That the labor market reward for graduate education has been increasing over the last four decades (and particularly at the end of the twentieth century) has been abundantly documented. When the return on some investment (here in human capital) sharply increases, one would expect the demand for such investment to surge. Indeed, we see that the percentage of women with a postgraduate degree more than trebles over the period—from about 3% in the mid-1970s to more than 11% in the mid-2000s. But no such increase is visible for men; if anything, the corresponding proportion slightly *declines* over the period.

These features raise two broad questions. First, how can we explain this puzzling asymmetry? In other words, how is it that men and women, faced with the same incentives, react in totally opposite ways? Second, and probably more importantly, what will be the long-term consequences of these evolutions? Changes in female education, labor supply, and earnings have been nothing short of dramatic over the period in the US but also in almost all developed countries, and actually in many intermediate or developing economies as well. It is hard to believe that such a landslide will not have deep and lasting effects on the distribution of powers within households, therefore ultimately on household behavior. This impact may be particularly important in developing countries, where we have considerable evidence that intrahousehold distribution of decision power strongly affects actual choices, including for such crucial issues as investment in children's human capital (health, education, etc.).

The two examples just described—and many others—share a common feature: they cannot be discussed without referring to an explicit model of household behavior formation, dissolution, and decision making. We need to understand the determinants of assortative matching (which factors make people more likely to marry their own kind, and how do these factors—or their impact—vary across time?), household formation and separation (why did the number of singles increase so drastically over the period?), and intrafamily allocation of resources and decision power. The purpose of this book is precisely to provide a framework in which these questions can be analyzed from both a theoretical and an empirical perspective.

1.2   Matching Models: Main Features

Matching models exist in various versions. All of these present some common characteristics, but they also differ in many respects. While a detailed presentation of the various models will be offered in the next chapter, it is useful to briefly recall their main features.

1.2.1   Absence of Frictions

First of all, matching models assume a frictionless environment. This means that, in the matching process between, say, firms and CEOs, each firm is assumed to have free access to the pool of all potential CEOs, with perfect knowledge of the characteristics of each of them, and conversely. In other words, matching models disregard the cost of acquiring information about potential matches, as well as the role of meeting technologies of all sorts (from social media to head hunters and from clubs to pure luck).

As always, an assumption of this kind is but a simplification of the infinite complexity of real-life processes. The question is whether such a simplification is acceptable. While the answer can only be case-specific, two general remarks can be made. First, the relevance of a frictionless setting largely depends on the question under consideration. A labor economist who is mostly interested in the dynamics of unemployment may be rightly reluctant to use a frictionless framework for modeling the matching of workers to jobs: there is a general consensus that a large fraction of unemployment results from various frictions on the labor market, and a search model should probably be preferred. If, however, the main issue is the allocation of specific individuals to specific tasks—say, which type of CEO ends up heading which type of firms—then a frictionless context may be more acceptable: while it is probably true that firms may not have a perfect knowledge of the pool of available CEOs, the resulting bias may be of second order, and neglecting it may be fully appropriate.

Second, the size of the market, as well as its structure, may have an impact on the relevance of a particular framework. Matching within a small community, in which individuals know each other, may be closer to the frictionless reference than in a very large market. Even with large populations (say, the "market for marriage" in a region of the US), one may want to concentrate on a very specific aspect involving a small number of broad categories (say, matching by education, broadly defined by four or five possible levels); then one may, for the sake of simplicity, disregard other individual traits and consider that two spouses with the same education are perfect substitutes. In such a context, neglecting frictions may be admissible.[5]

In the end, the choice of a specific model (frictionless matching versus search or other) should be driven, at least in part, by empirical considerations: what are the main stylized features of the situation we want to investigate, what types of frictions are more likely to matter, what importance should they represent, and last but not least which version fits the data best. It is therefore crucial to (i) deeply understand the meaning and implications of the various models under consideration, including their auxiliary hypothesis and apparently mundane details; and (ii) keep in mind the issues related to the empirical implementation of the various concepts at stake.

1.2.2   Are Transfers Relevant?

Within the family of frictionless matching frameworks, a second and crucial distinction relies on the role of transfers. The issue, here, is whether a technology exists that would allow one to transfer utility between agents participating to a matching process. Whether such transfers are possible makes a fundamental difference, because, when available, they allow agents to *bid* for their preferred mate by accepting the reduction of own gain from the match in order to increase the partner's. The exact nature of these bids depends on the context and may not take

---

[5] One could add that a small but important literature considers the issue of convergence of search equilibria to stable matchings of the frictionless framework when search frictions become negligible. The issue is quite complex, as one can find examples where the limit of search equilibria fails to be efficient (see, for instance, Lauermann and Noldeke 2014 for the non-transferable utility case, and Atakan 2006 for the transferable utility context).

the form of monetary transfers; in family economics, for instance, they typically affect the allocation of time between paid work, domestic work, and leisure; the choice between current and future consumption; or the structure of expenditures for private or public goods. Still, the possibility of utility transfers enables agents to negotiate, compromise, and ultimately exploit mutually beneficial solutions.

Not surprisingly, the existence of transfers between agents is one of the main factors structuring the matching literature. One polar framework (the so-called nontransferable utility—from now on NTU—model) assumes that transfers are not possible: there is simply no technology enabling agents to decrease their utility to the benefit of a potential partner. As a result, a match between two agents, say *a* and *b*, generates a gain for *a* and a gain for *b*, and these two gains are fixed; it is not possible for *a* to reduce her utility in order to increase *b*'s.

In the alternative context, in which transfers are possible, a match creates a total surplus that has to be divided between agents; and an equilibrium must specify not only matching patterns—who is matched with whom—but also the supporting division of the surplus. In other words, the division, between partners, of the gain created by a match is *exogenous* in an NTU context (it is part of the definition of the matching problem), whereas it is *endogenous* when transfers are freely available.

When transfers are possible, a polar setting (based on transferable utility, from now on TU) postulates, moreover, that the transfer technology has a very striking property: it allows the transfer of utility between agents *at a constant "exchange rate,"* so that, for a well-chosen cardinalization of individual preferences, increasing my partner's utility by one "utile" (i.e., unit of utility) has a cost of exactly one utile for me, irrespective of the economic environment (prices, incomes, etc.). In that case, a given match generates some total gain, and moreover the division is such that individual utilities always *add up* to the total gain. Technically, the Pareto frontier, which represents the set of utility pairs that are just feasible given resource constraints, is a straight line with slope -1 irrespective of the constraints; the latter can only affect its intercept. Alternatively, a more general version (often called ITU for imperfectly transferable utility) allows for transfers, but recognizes that the exchange rate between individual utilities is not constant and is typically endogenous to the economic environment.

In practice, the choice of a particular model has to be based on its relevance for the context under consideration. In a pioneering study, Roth (1984) has studied the allocation of residents to hospitals; consecutive work has led to major improvements in the National Resident Matching Program (Roth and Peranson 1999). Similar advances have resulted in improved mechanisms for kidney exchange (Roth, Sönmez, and Ünver 2004) or the allocation of students to public schools (Abdulkadiroglu and Sönmez 2003). In these examples (and several others), transfers are excluded, either by regulation or because of the prevailing institutional constraints. In other cases, although transfers do take place, they are not endogenous to the matching mechanism, but determined outside of it; one may think, for instance, of the marriage market in society ruled by very rigid social norms. In all such cases, the relevant model belongs to the NTU family.[6] The large literature on the NTU matching game has been abundantly described, particularly in Roth and Sotomayor's excellent monograph (1990) and in the more recent survey of Hatfield and Kominers (2011).

The present book concentrates on the opposite situation, in which transfers are possible and endogenously determined (or at least constrained) by the equilibrium conditions. Many (if not most) real-life examples of matching involve transfers. Employers and workers match, and the resulting agreements involve wages, which are transfers from employers to employees; agents meet on markets to trade commodities and services, and these exchanges are based on prices and payments; individuals and households enter in risk-sharing agreements, which support transfers from the lucky to the unlucky; and so on. A prominent example is the marriage market, which will be abundantly discussed in this book. One can certainly write models in which intrahousehold transfers are not feasible; but these require very strong (and actually grossly counterfactual) assumptions. For instance, they must rule out the presence of private consumptions; otherwise, changes in the allocation of private consumptions between spouses de facto result in utility transfers. Even if all commodities are public—in the sense that they are always simultaneously consumed by both spouses—one must assume either that there exists a unique consumption good, or that household members have exactly the same preferences regarding their consumptions; if not, then again changing the consumption bundle varies the distribution of utility between spouses, which is formally equivalent to a transfer.

The main differences between NTU and TU (or ITU) frameworks will be discussed in detail in the next chapter. Let me illustrate it on a simple example. The introductory puzzles discussed above stress the importance of assortative matching—that is, whether people tend to marry their own kind, and why. Consider the simple case in which individuals differ by a single trait—say, physical

---

[6] Lastly, endogenous transfers typically require some minimum level of commitment between agents. A somewhat extreme example is provided by Lundberg and Pollak (2003), who consider a BIM (bargaining in marriage) framework in which no commitment is possible at all. In a BIM world, any promise I may make before marriage can (and therefore will) be reneged upon minutes after the ceremony; there is just no way spouses can commit beforehand on their future behavior. Moreover, "upfront" payments, whereby an individual transfers some money, commodities, or property rights to the potential spouse conditional on marriage, are also excluded. Then the intrahousehold allocation of welfare will be decided after marriage, irrespective of the commitment made before. Marriage decision will therefore take the outcome of this yet-to-come bargaining process as given, and we are back to an NTU setting in which each partner's share of the surplus is fixed and cannot be altered by transfers decided ex ante. This point will be discussed later (see section 3.5).

attractiveness. When do we expect beautiful people to marry beautiful people? The answer depends on preferences (obviously), but also on the nature of the matching game. In an NTU framework, one just needs to assume monotonicity of preferences: if everyone prefers a better-looking spouse, then at the equilibrium (the exact nature of which will be discussed later on) matching will be perfectly assortative on physical attractiveness. The intuition is clear: the best-looking woman will select the best-looking man, and he will accept; then the second-most-beautiful woman will choose the second-most-beautiful man (who happens to be the best looking among available men), who will accept, and so on.

When transfers are possible, however, the logic is quite different; in fact, it is easy to construct examples in which, although preferences are still monotonic (so that everyone still prefers a better looking spouse), the equilibrium matching is actually *negative assortative* (so that the worst-looking man marries the best-looking woman, and so on). To see why, note that the driving force behind realized matching is the bidding game implicit in the process. The "winner" is not the most attractive person, but simply the highest bidder; attractiveness does play a role, but can always be compensated for by a large enough transfer. The question that determines assortative matching, therefore, is the following: even though everyone would prefer a better-looking spouse (therefore willing to bid more to attract one), *how does this additional willingness to bid vary with the person's own attractiveness*? If less-good-looking men are more eager to match with a beautiful spouse (say, because they are richer, therefore more able to bid high), the outcome could be negative assortative.

Of course, whether beautiful people marry their own (or not) is not of much interest, at least for an economist. In the present book, I shall mostly concentrate on more explicitly economic traits, such as education, income, and human capital. But the basic logic will be similar: the drivers of assortative matching are fundamentally different in games with and without transfers. If anything, the mechanisms involved will be more complex in the presence of transfers, as we shall see in some details.

From an applied perspective, thus, the main distinction is between models that involve transfers and models that do not. Theorists, however, sometimes refer to a different classification. Namely, they distinguish TU models from all other models, thus gathering NTU and ITU frameworks within the same category—which, in a somewhat confusing way, is often referred to as NTU models. This distinction is justified by the very specific, theoretical status of the TU model; as we shall see below, it is the only one for which stability—the main equilibrium concept—is equivalent to surplus maximization. It follows that the conceptual tools used to analyze TU models are often very specific; for instance, there exists a close relationship between matching models and a class of mathematical problems known as *optimal transportation* (or *Monge-Kantorovitch*) problems, and this relationship is unique to the TU framework. On the contrary, both NTU and

ITU models often refer to a similar methodology, particularly to variants and extensions of the basic Gale-Shapley algorithm.[7]

Throughout this book, and for the sake of clarity, I shall nevertheless stick to the tripartite distinction NTU-TU-ITU. In particular, the NTU label will be exclusively applied to situations in which utility *cannot* be transferred between agents.

1.3   Matching and the Household

1.3.1   Household Behavior: Existing Models

As I said earlier, an important motivation for the study of matching models is their applications to family economics. It may therefore be useful to briefly summarize the state of the art in that field.

The Unitary Model

Historically, the most commonly used model of household behavior has been the static unitary model. The main assumption implicit in this approach is that households behave as single decision makers, independently of the number of household members. As a consequence, the unitary approach characterizes the decisions of married couples about consumption, labor supply, and household production in the same way it characterizes the decisions of people living on their own. This assumption is equivalent to postulating that the household's preferences can be represented using a unique utility function that does not depend on prices, incomes, or any exogenous factor, independently of the number of household members.

The unitary model is a natural starting point for modeling household behavior, since it makes the model tractable, simple to test, and easy to estimate. Whether it is a good description of household behavior is, however, a different question altogether. A strength of the unitary model is that it generates testable implications that can be used to answer that question. Thus, a well-known implication of the model is that the demand functions it generates have specific properties. One is that the corresponding Slutsky matrix (i.e., the matrix of *compensated* price effects on demand) should be symmetric and negative semidefinite. These properties have been tested and generally rejected.[8] A second testable implication is *income pooling*. In the unitary model, individual nonlabor incomes y^1 and y^2 impact household behavior only through the budget constraint and only as the

---

[7] See, for instance, subsection 3.1.9 below.

[8] See, for instance, Lewbel (1995), Browning and Chiappori (1998), Dauphin and Fortin (2001), Haag, Hoderlein, and Pendakur (2009), Dauphin and Fortin (2001), and Kapan (2010).

sum $y = y^1 + y^2$. As a consequence, after controlling for total nonlabor income y, individual nonlabor incomes y^1 and y^2 should not affect household decisions: what matters is total income, not the source of its different components. The income-pooling property has been thoroughly tested and generally rejected, since individual nonlabor income affects household behavior in ways that go beyond the effect of total income on budget constraint.

A possible reason for the rejection of income pooling is that the unitary model aggregates individual preferences in a way that is not consistent with the data. It is plausible that households make actual decisions by assigning higher weight to the preferences of members that are perceived to be more important or, equivalently, have more power within the household. The power of a person in a group is generally influenced by her or his outside options, which in turn depend on a collection of variables, such as individual income, wealth, wages, and human capital. If this is the case, households aggregate preferences in a way that depends on all those variables. In the unitary model, this possibility is ruled out since individual preferences can only be aggregated by using some fixed household index, which must be independent of any additional variable.

The Collective Model

The limitations of the unitary representation have become increasingly clear;[9] an alternative representation has emerged, usually referred to as the "collective model" (Chiappori 1988, 1992). Collective models of the household explicitly recognize that households generally consist of several individuals who may have distinct utilities. This recognition implies that the intrahousesold decision process plays a key role in determining behavior. Collective models assume that household decisions are efficient in the sense that they are always on the Pareto frontier. Remember that the *Pareto set* is defined as the set of utility pairs that are reachable within the household (through adequate transfers and coordination of decisions). The Pareto frontier is the frontier of that set; that is, if an outcome is located on the Pareto frontier, then it is not possible to further increase an agent's well-being without reducing that of someone else. Said otherwise, the efficiency assumption requires that, whatever decision is made, no alternative decision would have been preferred by *all* agents.

This axiomatic nature is a distinctive feature of collective models. They do not rely on specific assumptions on the way household members achieve an efficient outcome, such as Nash bargaining (which I will discuss later on). They simply assume Pareto efficiency, which is satisfied if for any decision the household makes, there is no alternative choice that would have been preferred by all household

---

[9] See, for instance, Alderman et al. (1995).

members. While the assumption of Pareto efficiency is undoubtedly restrictive, collective models are sufficiently general to include as special cases most of the static models used to study household behavior. A nonexhaustive list includes the unitary model, but also models based on cooperative game theory (for instance, Nash-bargaining models of household behavior, pioneered by Manser and Brown 1980 and McElroy and Horney 1981), including more recent formulations (for instance, the "separate sphere" model of Lundberg and Pollak 1993) or models based on a market equilibrium, as proposed by Grossbard-Shechtman (1993), Gersbach and Haller (1999), and Edlund and Korn (2002).

In practice, efficiency has a simple, technical translation: a decision is efficient if and only if it maximizes a weighted sum of members' utilities. The corresponding weights are called the Pareto weights; they may, in principle, depend on prices, individual income, and any variable that may affect individuals' respective bargaining positions. In particular, Pareto weights have a natural interpretation in terms of respective decision *powers*. The notion of power in households may be difficult to define formally. Still, it seems natural to expect that when two people bargain, a person's gain increases with the person's power. This somewhat hazy notion is captured very effectively by the Pareto weights: for any *given* cardinalization of utilities, the larger a person's Pareto weight, the larger that person's utility at the end of the decision process.

The collective theory of household behavior is by now well understood. In particular, we now have a set of necessary and sufficient conditions that fully characterize demand functions stemming from a collective framework (Chiappori and Ekeland 2006). Moreover, conditions have been derived under which individual preferences and the decision process can be recovered from the observation of household behavior (Chiappori and Ekeland 2009a,b); these conditions take the form of a "exclusion restrictions," since they require that, for each agent, there exists at least one commodity this agent does *not* consume (while other agents do).

A crucial property of the collective approach, however, is that it takes the household as given. In a typical, collective approach, both household composition and intrahousehold allocation of power are exogenously given; what the collective theory does is (i) derive necessary and sufficient conditions characterizing the demand functions generated by such a framework, and (ii) provide conditions under which the sole observation of household behavior is sufficient to *identify* the model—that is, to uniquely recover individual preferences and the decision process (as summarized by the Pareto weights associated with some specific cardinalizations of individual utilities). The next step, obviously, would be an "upstream" theory that would *endogenize* both household composition ("who marries whom?") and the resulting intrahousehold allocation of power. To reach that goal, two main paths have been followed by the literature: bargaining models and matching models. I will briefly discuss the first option; the remainder of this book will be devoted to the second.

Noncooperative Models

Before that, let me briefly mention an alternative family of models based on the notion that individuals do not always agree on the various decisions a household has to make, and that the resulting decision process is systematically conflictive, in the (strong) sense that spouses fail to cooperate even when cooperation would be beneficial for all. Specifically, while recognizing that the existence of public consumption within the household is a strong motivation for household formation, noncooperative models assume that spouses, when deciding how much they would be willing to spend on public expenditures, always disregard the benefits their partner would derive from these. Technically, individuals thus play a noncooperative game of private provision of the public goods. A precise description of these models is beyond the scope of this book; the interested reader may, for instance, refer to Browning, Chiappori, and Weiss (2014). Let me just mention two points. First, a recent literature has shown some surprising (and largely counterfactual) consequences of noncooperative models. For instance, whatever the number of public goods consumed by a two-person, noncooperative household, there can be at most one goods to which both spouses contribute; all other public goods are exclusively funded by one of the spouses. Moreover, whenever such a jointly contributed good exists, then household demand exhibits a strong version of the income-pooling pattern discussed above: a (small) redistribution of resources across spouses has no impact whatsoever on either public or even individual consumptions.

Second, very few papers in the matching literature actually use noncooperative models; besides their counterfactual predictions, such models do not seem fully consistent with the efficiency properties implied by TU matching. However, an interesting exception is provided by a recent article by Del Boca and Flinn (2014), who use marital sorting patterns as "out-of-sample" information to assess whether household behavior is efficient or not. Their approach develops a likelihood-based metric to compare marriage market fits under the two alternative behavioral assumptions of efficiency and inefficiency. Empirical estimation on a sample of households drawn from the Panel Study of Income Dynamics finds strong evidence supporting the view that household behavior is (constrained) efficient—a further validation of the collective approach.

1.3.2   Bargaining Models of the Household

A natural tool to formalize the endogenous genesis of individual powers within the household is cooperative game theory.[10] The approach, here, is axiomatic: given

---

[10] For a more detailed presentation, see Browning, Chiappori, and Weiss (2014).

the context of the game, theory provides a way to determine the outcome based on some properties that the solution concept must satisfy. The "context" is defined by two components: individual preferences on the one hand and *outside options* (or *threat points*) on the other hand—the latter representing the utility an individual would receive should no agreement be reached.

Bargaining models assume that the outcome of the decision process is Pareto-efficient. Clearly, if no point within the Pareto set can give the agents at least their threat points, then no agreement can be reached, since at least one member would lose by agreeing. In the opposite case, both agents can gain from the relationship; then an agreement will be reached, and the goal of bargaining models is to analyze how threat points influence the location of the chosen point on the Pareto frontier.

While bargaining models seem to provide a natural solution to our problem—how should we endogenize Pareto weights?—they still require two choices to be made: selecting a bargaining solution concept and defining the threat points.

Choosing the Bargaining Solution

I will start with the solution concepts. The most commonly used bargaining solution was proposed by John Nash in the early 1950s. Nash derived this solution as the unique outcome of a set of axioms that any "reasonable" solution must satisfy. Some of the axioms are uncontroversial (and, as a matter of fact, are shared by all commonly used bargaining solutions). One is individual rationality: an agent will never accept an agreement that is less favorable than his or her threat point. Another is Pareto efficiency, as discussed above. A third mild requirement is invariance with respect to affine transformations:[11] if both the utility and the threat point of an agent are transformed by the same increasing, affine mapping, the prediction about the equilibrium outcome of cooperation does not change. Note, however, that a nonlinear transform will change the outcome; that is, Nash bargaining requires a *cardinal* representation of preferences.

The last two axioms are more specific. One is symmetry; it states that if utilities and threat points are permuted between members, then the outcomes are simply switched. Natural as it may sound, this assumption may still sometimes be too strong. In many socioeconomic contexts, for instance, male and female roles are by no means symmetric. Fortunately, Nash bargaining can easily be extended to avoid the symmetry assumption.

The last and crucial axiom is independence. It can be stated as follows. Assume that the set of available opportunities (the Pareto set) shrinks, so that the new Pareto set is within the old one, but the initial equilibrium outcome is still feasible;

---

[11] An affine mapping is of the form $f(x) = ax + b$.

then the new equilibrium outcome will be the same as before. In other words, the fact that one member misses some opportunities that she had before does not affect her bargaining position with respect to the other member. This requirement alone implies that the Nash solution maximizes some function of the utilities of the two partners. Actually, Nash shows that the only outcome compatible with these axioms maximizes the product of individual "gains," the latter being defined as the difference between a person's utility when reaching an agreement and the person's threat point.

While Nash's bargaining concept is often used, it is by no means the only one. An alternative concept, proposed by Kalai and Smorodinsky (1975), replaces independence with the following *monotonicity* property. Consider two bargaining problems such that (i) the range of individually rational payoffs that player *a* can get is the same in the two problems, and (ii) for any given, individually rational utility level for player *a*, the maximum utility that player *b* can achieve (given the Pareto frontier) is never smaller in the second problem than in the first. Then player *b* should do at least as well in the second problem as in the first. In other words, if one enlarges the Pareto set by inflating *b*'s opportunities while keeping *a*'s constant, this change cannot harm *b*. Kalai and Smorodinsky prove that there exists a unique bargaining solution that satisfies all the previous axioms except for independence, which is replaced with monotonicity, and formally characterizes the corresponding solution.

Lastly, Nash himself suggested that one should provide noncooperative foundations to the bargaining solutions derived from axioms. The most influential framework is the model of Rubinstein (1982), in which players make alternating offers until one is accepted. When time matters through a constant discount factor, there exists a unique, subgame perfect equilibrium of this noncooperative game, which is characterized by the requirement that each player should be indifferent with regard to accepting the current offer or waiting for an additional round and making an offer that the opponent would accept. Binmore, Rubinstein, and Wolinsky (1986) have analyzed the link between these noncooperative formulations and the axiomatic approaches. Specifically, they study a model in which the bargaining process may, with some probability, be *exogenously* interrupted at each period. This model has a unique, subgame perfect equilibrium; moreover, if one allows the time interval between successive offers in both models to decrease to zero, then the equilibrium converges to the Nash bargaining solution.[12]

The main message of this brief review is that the choice of a bargaining solution concept is neither innocuous nor obvious; for instance, whether, when describing household decision processes, the independence axiom sounds more "realistic" than the monotonicity one is probably open to discussion.

---

[12] For a more complete discussion of two-person bargaining, see Myerson (1991, ch. 8).

Choosing the Threat Points

Next, how should one translate the abstract notion of "threat point" in the particular case we are considering—i.e., household bargaining? A first point is that the corresponding choice is crucial. Indeed, a result due to Chiappori, Donni, and Komunjer (2012) states that *any* Pareto-efficient allocation can be derived as the Nash bargaining solution for an ad hoc definition of the threat points. This implies that any additional information provided by the reference to bargaining theory must come from specific hypotheses on the threat points—that is, on what is meant by the sentence: "no agreement is reached."

Several ideas have been used in the literature. One is to refer to divorce as the "no agreement" situation. Then the threat point is defined as the maximum utility a person could reach after divorce. Such an idea seems well adapted when one is interested, say, in the effects of laws governing divorce on intrahousehold allocation. Another interesting illustration would be public policies such as single-parent benefits or the guaranteed employment programs that exist in some Indian states; Haddad and Kanbur (1992) convincingly argue that the main impact of the program was to change the opportunities available to the wife outside marriage, with potential consequences on intrahousehold inequality, even (and perhaps mostly) for couples who eventually did not divorce. However, choosing divorce as the threat point is probably less natural when minor decisions are at stake: deciding who will walk the dog is unlikely to involve threats of divorce.

A second idea relies on the presence of public goods, and the fact that noncooperative behavior typically leads to inefficient outcomes. The idea, then, is to take the noncooperative outcome as the threat point: in the absence of an agreement, both members provide the public good(s) egotistically, not taking into account the impact of their decision on the other member's welfare. This version captures the idea that the person who would suffer more from this lack of cooperation (the person who has the higher valuation for the public good) is likely to be more willing to compromise in order to reach an agreement. A variant was proposed by Lundberg and Pollak (1993), who postulate that each public good belongs to the "separate sphere" of one of the spouses, who, in the absence of an agreement, becomes the unique decision maker for the corresponding expenditures.

There is, however, something deeply unsatisfactory with any of the previous choices. Start with the model based on private provision of public goods (or its separate spheres variant): it only considers outside options *within* marriage. This is acceptable for minor issues, much less so when considering consequential choices. Divorce is a crucial aspect of family economics, if only because nearly half of all marriages end in divorce. It seems unwise to disregard it: among the "outside options" a spouse is likely to consider in case of a serious disagreement on a very important issue, switching to a new partner can hardly be dismissed prima facie. Granted, divorce threats are unlikely to determine who will walk the dog. Then again, who will walk the dog is not the most fascinating problem economists would want to understand. And when it comes to really substantial decisions—fertility, choice of a job, choice of a location, etc—divorce issues just cannot be easily omitted.

What about, then, models adopting divorce as a threat point? The problem here is that these models typically adopt an exclusively local approach, when a global perspective would be needed. In the end, what matters is not the possibility of divorce by itself, but the utility each spouse can expect to have after divorce (this is the technical definition of a threat point in this context). But the latter, in turn, depends on many aspects: the probability of remarriage, the likely characteristics of the new spouse, and also the (expected) distribution of powers within the new couple. The last point is obviously problematic: it implies that in order to predict the distribution of powers within any given couple, one needs to know the distribution of powers in all other couples, including future and potential ones.

For an economist, a situation of this type is by no means unfamiliar. After all, we cannot predict the wage structure that will prevail in a given firm without knowing the wage distribution in the rest of the economy, precisely because this distribution impacts the outside options of both parties. In other words, these are market-wide phenomena, and they can only be addressed at the market level—the "global" perspective that I was alluding to.

The problem is especially serious when we want to address issues that, by nature, are global. Assume, for instance, that we want to model the impact on intrahousehold decision processes of a reform of the legislation governing divorce. For any given couple, the reform will modify the spouses' outside options—i.e., utilities in case of divorce—in a number of ways. For instance, it will typically affect actual divorce decisions; but this impacts what could be called the "market for remarriage" by changing the number and profiles of divorcees looking for a new partner. In turn, such changes alter all aspects of the costs and benefits of divorce—the remarriage probability, the set of potential new spouses, and ultimately the distribution of powers. In this context, an analysis of the consequences of the reform can only be performed at a global level: what is needed is a characterization of the new equilibrium that may emerge after the reform.

To summarize: if one is to take seriously the idea that divorce should be considered as a reference threat point for modeling bargaining within marriage—as I think one should—then only a "general equilibrium" model of matching on the marriage market can be expected to generate the desired outcome. This intuition is by no means new. The abstract of the seminal, 1973 paper by Gary Becker, published in the *Journal of Political Economy*, starts with the following two sentences:

I present in this paper the skeleton of a theory of marriage. The two basic assumptions are that each person tries to do as well as possible and that the "marriage market" is in equilibrium.

Becker's work was obviously imperfect (although it amounted to much more than a "skeleton"). The model he used was far from general; some of the simplifying assumptions he made would be frowned upon today. Matching theory has made considerable progress since then, both on theoretical and empirical fronts; it is only fair to say that the technicalities of modern approaches exceed (and sometimes contradict) those of Becker's initial contribution. But for all these advances, the main conclusions have essentially confirmed Becker's vision, and particularly the central intuition of his 1973 paper—namely, that the division of surplus (or of power) between spouses could be derived from the nature of the marriage market equilibrium. The remainder of this book will illustrate how such a derivation can work.

1.4   Content

Large numbers of contributions have been devoted to matching theory in recent decades. Matching has become a huge field, and I will certainly not try to cover all of it in this short book. In particular, and as the title of the book indicates, I will exclusively consider matching models in which transfers between agents are possible. Therefore, I will not cover the literature on matching with NTU. Several reasons motivate this choice. One is that the two families of models—with and without transfers—are, in many respects, quite different; many of the intuitions that emerge from an NTU framework would not be robust to the introduction of transfers. Another reason is that my primary interest is family economics, a context in which transfers are usually crucial; analyzing household decisions under the maintained assumption that there is no way a husband and a wife can transfer utility between them, although technically possible, does not sound too promising. Last but not least, the literature on NTU matching has already been covered, notably by Roth and Sotomayor's (1990) excellent monograph, as well as in several subsequent surveys (for instance, Hatfield and Kominers 2011).

A second limitation is that I will exclusively analyze bipartite (or one-to-one) matching models, i.e., models in which agents from two distinct populations (say, men and women) match by pair. In particular, I will not consider frameworks involving either many-to-one or many-to-many matching. Again, these are less relevant for the type of applications I will consider, including the marriage market. Also, these models raise specific problems (for instance, a stable matching may not always exist) that would be outside the scope of this short essay. The cost of this choice is that many interesting questions will be largely left aside. For instance, I will not spend much time discussing the links between matching and auction or general equilibrium theory; even in the field of family economics, I will not consider issues such as polygamy, although some of the results could be extended to this question.

Throughout the book, I will mostly adopt what could be called an "applied theory" perspective. That is, although I will present and discuss the main theoretical results underlying the approach, I will mostly consider how these abstract concepts can be used to represent and think about real-life issues; the reader interested in more technical aspects can refer to the recent monograph by Galichon (2015). Similarly, I will not discuss in depth the technical issues related to the econometric implementation of matching models; again, the interested reader can refer to existing surveys such as Graham (2011) and Chiappori and Salanié (2016). Moreover, matching models with transfers can involve either finite or continuous distributions of agents. The main results apply to both settings. However, I will put a particular emphasis on continuous models, in which agents' characteristics are drawn from an absolutely continuous and atomless distribution; for many applications, this context is both richer and more tractable.

Lastly, I will mention a few applications of matching models to such real-life issues as the empowerment effect of abortion legalization or the surge in women's demand for higher education. The choice is purely idiosyncratic, and reflects both my own interests regarding economic issues and my unavoidably incomplete knowledge of the large number of models that have been developed over the last two decades. As I said earlier, matching with transfers is a booming field, which I could not dream of covering in this short essay. If, however, some readers are convinced of both the importance of the issues at stake and the practical usefulness of matching models to address them, then this book will have achieved its goal.

2

Matching with Transfers: Basic Notions

2.1 Bilateral, One-to-One Matching: Common Framework

Let me first introduce the notations that I will use throughout the book. I consider two compact, separable metric spaces $\bar{X}$, $\bar{Y}$, which, for the sake of convenience, will be respectively referred to as the space of female and male characteristics—although other interpretations (workers and firms, lenders and borrowers, etc.) are obviously possible. The corresponding vectors of characteristics fully describe the agents; i.e., for any $x \in \bar{X}$, two women with the same vector of characteristics x are perfect substitutes for the matching game (and similarly for men). In what follows, I will routinely say "woman x" or "Mrs. x" for "woman endowed with the vector of characteristics x".

These spaces are endowed with measures F and G, respectively; both $F(\bar{X})$ and $G(\bar{Y})$ are finite. In what follows, I shall assume that the spaces are finite-dimensional; specifically, $\bar{X} \subset \mathbb{R}^n$ and $\bar{Y} \subset \mathbb{R}^m$, endowed with a Borel measure. Note, however, that the spaces may be *multidimensional*—that is, $n \geq 1$ and $m \geq 1$ in general.

Since we will consider matchings between men and women, two technical difficulties arise. First, some agents may remain unmatched. In order to capture this situation within the same global notation, a standard trick is to "augment" the spaces by including an isolated point in each: a dummy partner $\emptyset_X$ for any unmatched man and a dummy partner $\emptyset_Y$ for any unmatched woman. Therefore, from now on, we consider the spaces $X := \bar{X} \cup \{\emptyset_X\}$ and $Y := \bar{Y} \cup \{\emptyset_Y\}$. The point $\emptyset_X$ (resp. $\emptyset_Y$) is endowed with a mass measure equal to the total measure of $\bar{Y}$ ($\bar{X}$). In particular, it is possible (although not efficient in general) to consider a matching in which all women (all men) remain single, by posing that they are all matched with $\emptyset_Y$ ($\emptyset_X$).

The second difficulty is related to the mere definition of a "matching". The underlying intuition is pretty clear: we want each woman to be associated to one man at most, and conversely for men. The natural translation could be to define a matching as a mapping ϕ from X to Y (or alternatively, a mapping ψ from $X \cup Y$ to itself of order two, i.e., such that $\psi(\psi(t)) = t$, as in Roth and Sottomayor 1990). As it turns out, this is not too convenient when the spaces X and Y are continuous. A notation like $y = \phi(x)$ explicitly assumes that all women with the same vector of characteristics x are matched with the same type of man, defined by the vector y. But this is just too restrictive; we also want to be able to consider situations in which two women with identical x are matched to men with different characteristics—say, y and y' (although, in practice, there may be more than two potential spouses). Such a situation is sometimes called "randomization", because one interpretation is that both women are matched with either y or y' with positive probabilities, say, p and $p' = 1 - p$.[1] Allowing for randomization is crucial: as we will see, there exists examples in which the *unique* equilibrium matching requires randomization for an open subset of characteristics.

We therefore define a matching as a *measure h* on $X \times Y$; intuitively, one can think of $h(x, y)$ as the probability that x is matched to y in this matching. Note that this definition implies conditions on the measure h. Intuitively, if, for some given x, we add up $h(x, y)$ for all potential spouses of x (including the dummy husband $\emptyset_Y$), we must end up with the total number (or the total density, in the continuous case) of women with characteristics x, as defined by the measure F. Technically, the constraint is thus that the *marginals* of h on X and Y are F and G, respectively; formally:

$$\int_{y \in Y} dh(x, y) = F(x) \quad \text{and} \quad \int_{x \in X} dh(x, y) = G(y). \qquad (2.1.1)$$

A point that will become very important later on is that this constraint is *linear*. Emphasizing the linear aspects of the problem is another, crucial advantage of the formulation in terms of measure.

Finally, a matching is *pure* if the support of the measure is included in the graph of some function ϕ—that is, if for almost all (x, y), $h(x, y) = 0$ unless $y = \phi(x)$. In other words, purity prohibits randomization: if the matching is *pure*, then there exists a mapping ϕ such that $y = \phi(x)$ almost everywhere.

2.2   The Three Types of Models

While the previous framework is common to all (bipartite, one-to-one) matching models, other features are specific to each of the three types of models described above. They relate to both the statement of the problem and the definition of a solution—i.e., of an equilibrium.

2.2.1   Defining the Problem

In all cases, the fundamentals of the problem under consideration include the two spaces X and Y, together with the corresponding measures. But they also involve

---

[1] Note that this interpretation is by no means the only one; alternatively, one can consider that among all women with characteristics x, a fraction p are (deterministically) matched with y and the remaining $p' = 1 - p$ are (deterministically) matched with y'. From our perspective, these interpretations are exactly equivalent, and we will not try to distinguish between them.

a definition of the outcome of each possible match, and that definition is specific to each type of model.

Starting with the NTU case, the matching of $x \in X$ and $y \in Y$ generates *two* utilities, one for each spouse—say, $u(x, y)$ and $v(x, y)$. Indeed, remember that the utility for Mrs. x of being matched with Mr. y (as well as that of Mr. y for being matched with Mrs. x) is exogenously given; both are part of the statement of the problem. Note also that u and v are defined over the entire set $X \times Y$; that is, individual utilities are defined for any possible match, and also for singlehood ($u(x, \emptyset_Y)$ being the utility of x when single, and similarly for $v(\emptyset_X, y)$). Finally, one can see that only the *ordinal* representation of utilities—i.e., the structure of individual *preferences* over potential mates—matters. Replacing $u(x, y)$ with $\Phi[u(x, y), x]$ for some mapping Φ that is strictly increasing in its first argument does not change the game.

The TU case is different. Here, what is given is *one* function, say $S(x, y)$, representing the *total* gain generated by the matching. How this gain will be divided between the spouses is now endogenous, therefore part of the solution. The TU assumption simply means that for any matched couple, what she gets and what he gets add up to the surplus they generate. Technically, the match defines a Pareto frontier, the equation of which is

$$u(x) + v(y) = S(x, y). \tag{2.2.1}$$

Here, $u(x)$ (resp. $v(y)$) is the utility she (he) obtains, and is generally called the (male or female) *payoff function*; its exact value (or equivalently the location of the chosen point on the Pareto frontier) is defined, or at least constrained, by the equilibrium conditions. As before, the gain may be defined for singlehood; however, we may, without loss of generality, normalize it to zero[2] by posing

$$S(x, \emptyset_Y) = S(\emptyset_X, y) = 0 \; \forall x, y. \tag{2.2.2}$$

With this normalization, S can be interpreted as the *surplus* generated by a marriage—over and above whichever utility levels the spouses could achieve when single. Note, however, that this leads to a corresponding interpretation for u and v; namely, $u(x)$ represents the *additional* utility that x derives from marriage, over and above what she could get as a single (and the same interpretation is obviously valid for $v(y)$).

---

[2] As we shall see below, there is a standard distinction between the *gain* from marriage, defined as the maximum sum of utilities any given pair can achieve, and the *surplus*, which is the difference between the gain generated by the matching of x and y and the sum of utilities that x and y could respectively achieve as singles.

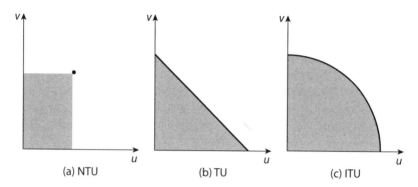

Figure 2.1. Shape of the Pareto frontier (solid) and set (shaded)

Unlike the NTU case, what matters here is the *cardinal* representation of
S. Replacing $S(x, y)$ with $\Phi(S(x, y))$, where Φ is strictly increasing (but not
necessarily affine), will in general change the outcome of the game.

Lastly, the ITU case generalizes the TU framework by relaxing the linearity
assumption in (2.2.1). Again, there exists a feasibility constraint that limits the pair
$(u(x), v(y))$ of utilities that x and y could reach if matched together. However, this
constraint is not assumed linear; rather, its equation is of the type

$$u(x) = H(x, y, v(y)), \qquad (2.2.3)$$

where the function H is decreasing and concave in v. As always, equation (2.2.3)
requires a particular, cardinal representation of individual utilities.

A natural representation of these three cases uses the Pareto frontier they each
generate. The Pareto set is defined as the set of pairs of utilities that a given couple
may reach (as a function of their respective characteristics). The Pareto frontier is
the subset of the Pareto set consisting only of points that are not strictly Pareto-
dominated; it is usually represented in a two-dimensional graph, with u on the
horizontal axis and v on the vertical one.

Figure 2.1 represents the Pareto frontier (solid line) and the Pareto set (shaded
area) in each of the three cases described. In the NTU context (a), the set and its
frontier boil down to a point. In the TU case (b), the Pareto frontier is a straight
line with slope -1; this is the distinctive characteristic of the TU case. Lastly, in the
ITU framework (c), the matching of x and y generates again a continuous Pareto
frontier. But the latter is no longer a straight line; it is a decreasing, concave curve
(equivalently, the Pareto set is convex).

In the most general version of the models, only minimal assumptions are made
on the functions (typically, upper semicontinuity and boundedness). In practice,
however, stronger properties (e.g., differentiability) may be required for some of
the results.

To summarize, a matching problem is defined

- in the NTU case, by two sets X and Y, with their measures, and two functions u and v mapping $X \times Y$ to $\mathbb{R}$;
- in the TU case, by two sets X and Y, with their measures, and one function S mapping $X \times Y$ to $\mathbb{R}$;
- in the ITU case, by two sets X and Y, with their measures, and a function H mapping $X \times Y \times \mathbb{R}$ to $\mathbb{R}$.

2.2.2 *Defining the Solution*

Similar differences appear in the definition of an equilibrium. In all cases, the basic equilibrium concept is *stability*. A matching is stable if

- no matched individual would rather be single;
- no pair of individuals would *both* like being matched together better than their current situation.

In other words, stability implies robustness to unilateral and bilateral deviation: a matching is stable if one cannot find either an individual or a pair of individuals who would gain from deviating. It follows that any matching belonging to the core of the game must be stable; otherwise, a deviating couple would be a blocking coalition. Conversely, any stable match is in the core; the intuition for this result is that, given the structure of the game, the only meaningful deviations are by individuals or pairs, so a matching that is robust to such deviations is robust to any deviation (see Alkan and Gale 1990).

Nontransferable Utility

In practice, however, the translation of stability differs with the type of model. Starting with NTU, a matching is stable if one cannot find x, y, x', y' such that $h(x, y') > 0$, $h(x', y) > 0$ and

$$u(x, y) \geq u(x, y'), \quad v(x, y) \geq v(x', y), \tag{2.2.4}$$

with one inequality at least being strict. Indeed, that would imply that x and y are matched with some other mate (resp. y' and x') with positive probability, but strictly prefer being matched together. Note that this property implies that in case of randomization (i.e., x being matched to both y and y' with positive probability), it must be the case that $u(x, y) = u(x, y')$ (if, for instance, $u(x, y) > u(x, y')$, then the previous property is violated for $x = x'$). In particular, for any stable matching, let $u(x)$ (resp. $v(y)$) denote the utility reached by Mrs. x (Mr. y). Then it must be the case that

$$u(x) = \max_{z \in Y}\{u(x, z)|v(x, z) \geq v(z)\}$$

and

$$v(y) = \max_{z \in X}\{v(z, y)|u(z, y) \geq u(z)\}.$$

Transferable Utility

We now consider the TU case. Here, defining a matching requires not only choosing a measure on $X \times Y$ (which defines "who is matched with whom"), but also determining, for couples who are matched with positive probability, how the surplus will be shared. Technically, we need to define two functions $u(x)$ and $v(y)$ such that

$$u(x) + v(y) = S(x, y) \qquad (2.2.5)$$

for any (x, y) belonging to the support of h (i.e., such that $h(x, y) > 0$, implying that x and y are matched with positive probability; mathematically, the equality (2.2.5) should hold "h-almost everywhere", meaning that the measure, *by h*, of a set of couples for which it is not satisfied must be zero). Here, $u(x)$ (resp. $v(y)$) is the utility reached by Mrs. x (Mr. y) at this particular matching; it is often called the *payoff* of Mrs. x (Mr. y). Equation (2.2.5) simply states that whenever a couple is matched with positive probability, the sum of what they each get equals the total surplus they generate.

In turn, stability can be stated as a property of the payoff functions u and v. Specifically, the matching is stable if and only if these functions satisfy:

$$u(x) + v(y) \geq S(x, y) \quad \forall(x, y) \in X \times Y. \qquad (2.2.6)$$

To see why, assume for a moment that one can find $(x, y) \in X \times Y$ such that this inequality is not satisfied—i.e., such that

$$u(x) + v(y) < S(x, y).$$

For one thing, x and y cannot be matched with positive probability (otherwise we would have an equality). Moreover, they would both benefit from being matched together: the surplus they would generate, $S(x, y)$, would be sufficient to provide *both* of them with more utility than they currently have. But that would be a violation of stability. Conversely, it is easy to see that whenever a measure h, the marginals of which are F and G, and two functions u and v are such that (2.2.5) and (2.2.6) hold, then the matching thus defined is stable.

Finally, an equivalent way of stating this property, which is quite useful in various applications, is the following: if a matching is stable, the corresponding functions u and v, from X to $\mathbb{R}$, and from Y to $\mathbb{R}$, respectively, must be such that

$$u(x) = \max_{z \in Y}\{S(x, z) - v(z)\} \tag{2.2.7}$$

$$\text{and } v(y) = \max_{z \in X}\{S(z, y) - u(z)\}, \tag{2.2.8}$$

the max being reached in each case for potential spouses (possibly including the dummy one) to whom the individual is matched with positive probability.

This form has an interesting interpretation. Think of $v(y)$ as the "price" woman x must "pay" (in terms of the share of the surplus she is giving away) to attract man y. This price is husband-specific (it depends on y), but not wife-specific: *any* woman must pay (or "bid") $v(y)$ to attract man y, and conversely any woman who is willing to bid that amount can attract man y (in other words, the price $v(y)$ clears the "market" for men with characteristics y). Obviously, the same interpretation applies to $u(x)$ as the price of x.

Then (2.2.7) is a standard, utility maximization problem: Mrs. x simply chooses the match that maximizes her utility. The latter consists of the surplus generated, $S(x, y)$, which depends on all attributes of both spouses and may include match-specific components, from which one should substract the utility to be received by the spouse. The crucial point, here, is that if $v(y)$ is a price, then x behaves as a price-taker: she considers that price as given and maximizes her utility conditional on the price schedule (i.e., the prices of all possible mates). In other words, the underlying reference of matching models is a perfectly competitive framework.

Imperfectly Transferable Utility

The last case—ITU—is a direct extension of TU to nonlinear Pareto frontiers. Again, a matching must now be defined as a measure h and two payoff functions u, v such that

$$u(x) = \Phi(x, y, v(y)) \quad \forall(x, y) \in \text{Supp}\,(h), \tag{2.2.9}$$

where Supp (h) denotes the support of the measure h. Similarly, stability now requires

$$u(x) \geq \Phi(x, y, v(y)) \quad \forall(x, y) \in X \times Y, \tag{2.2.10}$$

which is equivalent to

$$u(x) = \max_z\{\Phi(x, z, v\,(z))\} \text{ and } v(y) = \max_z\{\Phi^{-1}(z, y, u\,(z))\}, \tag{2.2.11}$$

Note that the interpretation of $v(y)$ as the price of y still applies; in particular, we are still (implicitly) in a competitive context where agents are price-takers. The main difference is that x's utility is no longer linear in that price.

To summarize:

- In the NTU case, a matching is defined as a measure h on $X \times Y$, the marginals of which are F and G; it is stable if conditions (2.2.4) are satisfied.
- In both the TU and ITU cases, a matching is defined by a measure h on $X \times Y$, the marginals of which are F and G, *and* two functions u and v, mapping X and Y to $\mathbb{R}$, respectively, that satisfy (2.2.5) in the TU case and (2.2.9) in the ITU case; it is stable if u and v also satisfy (2.2.6) in the TU case and (2.2.10) in the ITU case.

3

Matching under Transferable Utility: Theory

Let me now concentrate on the TU case.

3.1   Definition and First Properties

3.1.1   Formal Definition

We start with a formal definition of the transferable utility (TU) property.

Definition 1 *A group satisfies TU if there exists monotone transformations of individual utilities such that the Pareto frontier is a hyperplane*

$$u(x) + v(y) = S(x, y). \tag{3.1.1}$$

This definition suggests a few comments. First, TU is a property of a *group*—not of an individual. As we shall see, it requires specific features of individual preferences, but also some common features for all utilities in the group. Secondly, TU is an *ordinal* property; there must exist a *transformation* of individual utilities such that (3.1.1) is satisfied. TU is a property of preferences; in particular, it does not require linearity or quasilinearity of the utility function. An important consequence is that the TU framework may in some cases be relevant for such issues as risk sharing between risk-averse consumers (which in an expected utility context requires a concave cardinal utility); I shall discuss this point later on.

3.1.2   TU as an Ordinal Property

The ordinal nature of the TU restriction has consequences that should be understood. Consider the example of a couple consuming several commodities and facing a budget constraint. Fix the values of prices and incomes, and choose a particular representation of individual preferences—say, utilities U and V for the wife and the husband, respectively. The Pareto frontier for these representations takes the form

$$U = \Phi(V),$$

where Φ is decreasing and concave. Now, it is always possible to change the cardinal representation of V to generate a linear Pareto frontier. Indeed, just take

$$\tilde{V} = 1 - \Phi(V), \tag{3.1.2}$$

which is an increasing transform of V (therefore represents the same preferences); then the frontier is

$$U + \tilde{V} = 1.$$

Does it mean that all pairs of utility have the TU property? Of course not. The key point, here, is that the Pareto frontier (therefore the function Φ) depends on prices and income (e.g., boosting income typically increases the Pareto set). This means that the cardinal representation needed to generate a linear Pareto frontier in (3.1.2) will vary with the particular price-income bundle under consideration. In contrast, the TU property would require the existence of cardinal representations satisfying (3.1.1) *for all values of prices and income*—and that is a much more demanding property.

Another aspect of the ordinal nature of the TU property can be seen on a simple, comparative statics exercise. Consider a couple whose preferences satisfy the TU property; i.e., for some well-chosen cardinalization, the Pareto frontier of the couple, when facing prices p and endowed with total income y, is a straight line with slope -1, described by the equation

$$u + v = S(p, y). \tag{3.1.3}$$

In particular, if we compare two different price-income bundles, say (p, y) and (p', y'), only three cases are possible: $S(p, y) > S(p', y')$, $S(p, y) = S(p', y')$, or $S(p, y) < S(p', y')$. In the first case, the Pareto frontier $\mathcal{P}$ corresponding to (p, y) is interior to the frontier $\mathcal{P}'$, corresponding to (p', y'); for any point on $\mathcal{P}$, there is a point on $\mathcal{P}'$ that strictly dominates it. The same is true, *mutatis mutandis*, in the third case; and in the second case, $\mathcal{P}$ and $\mathcal{P}'$ are equal—the two Pareto frontiers (and sets) exactly coincide. What cannot happen, however, is that the two frontiers intersect in some point(s) without being identical everywhere.

Assume, now, that we change the cardinalization of the respective utilities in some arbitrary way. This, obviously, will change the shape of the Pareto frontier; in particular, the equations of the new frontiers, say $\bar{\mathcal{P}}$ and $\bar{\mathcal{P}}'$, will no longer have the simple, additive form (3.1.3). The crucial point, however, is that what we just said about comparative statics remains valid. Indeed, the fact that two Pareto frontiers intersect is an *ordinal* property—it means that there exists a point on $\bar{\mathcal{P}}$ and a point on $\bar{\mathcal{P}}'$ between which *both* spouses are indifferent, and indifference is ordinal. We conclude that under TU, whatever the cardinalization, either the

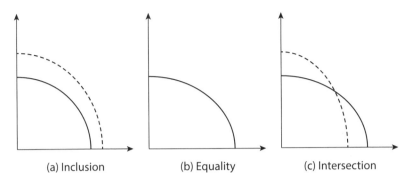

Figure 3.1. Possible and impossible patterns for Pareto sets under TU.

Pareto sets corresponding to two different, price-income bundles coincide, or one is totally included in the other—but the frontiers cannot intersect. The conclusion is illustrated in figure 3.1; under TU, both a and b are possible, but c is not.

This property, in turn, has an important implication—namely, that the choice between the two bundles (p, y) and (p', y') does *not* depend on the distribution of power within the pair, because agents are always *unanimous* regarding the best choice (obviously, the one that generates the largest Pareto set), provided they can freely renegotiate: they will always end up on a point located on the exterior Pareto frontier, no matter what the property rights may have been. In other words, there is a complete divorce between the couple's choice of a price-income bundle (and generally its choice between any two possible options), on the one hand, and the allocation of the resulting gains on the other hand: the former is entirely driven by efficiency considerations (just choose the larger Pareto set), whereas the second depends on the property rights on the surplus. This property lies at the core of several results in micro theory and notably of the various versions of the so-called Coase theorem; of particular importance for family economics is the Becker-Coase theorem, whereby changes in laws governing divorce cannot affect divorce probability.

3.1.3   Specific Assumptions on Preferences

What assumptions on preferences are needed to get the TU property? We first need a model of household behavior that accounts for individual preferences—i.e., that does not a priori merge them into the fiction of a unique household utility; the notion of household utility is perfectly acceptable, but only if it is *derived* from specific assumptions on individuals. Throughout the book, I will use a standard version of the collective model of household behavior, as described above.[1]

---

[1] See subsection 1.3.1.

Using the same notations as before, let us thus consider a two-person household that can consume n private and N public goods. Again, private consumption of good k by agent i is denoted q_i^k, while the household's (public) consumption of good K is denoted Q^K; agents are egoistic, so that their utilities are of the form $u_i(q_i, Q)$. Commodities can be purchased at prices $(p^1, \ldots, p^n)$ and $(P^1, \ldots, P^N)$ for the private and public goods, respectively; Y denotes the household's income, so that the budget constraint is

$$\sum_{i,k} p^k q_i^k + \sum_K P^K Q^K = Y.$$

Now, what assumptions do we need to make on these utility functions for the TU property to hold? The answer is provided by Chiappori and Gugl (2015). We need, first, to recall the notion of conditional indirect utility (CIU), initially introduced by Blundell, Chiappori, and Meghir (2005). Assume that the household's consumption decision takes place in two stages. At stage 1, the household decides on the quantity of each public good to be purchased, $Q = (Q^1, \ldots, Q^N)$, and how to allocate the remaining income $Y - \sum_K P^K Q^K$; thus, 1 receives some amount ρ_1 and 2 gets $\rho_2 = Y - \sum_K P^K Q^K - \rho_1$. Here, $\rho = (\rho_1, \rho_2)$ is called the *conditional sharing rule*. At stage 2, agents each decide on their private consumption, under the budget constraint

$$\sum_k p^k q_i^k = \rho_i \quad \text{for} \quad i = 1, 2.$$

Blundell, Chiappori, and Meghir (2005) show that this interpretation of the household decision process can be adopted without loss of generality; for any process that always generates an efficient outcome, there exists a conditional sharing rule such that the household behaves as if it was following the two-stage process just described.[2] Now, the CIU describes the maximum utility an agent can get during the second stage as a function of the vector of public consumptions, the prices of the private goods, and his conditional sharing rule. In other words, the CIU of agent i is the value of i's second-stage maximization program:

$$v_i(Q, p, \rho_i) = \max_{q_i} u_i(q_i, Q) \quad \text{under} \quad \sum_k p^k q_i^k = \rho_i. \tag{3.1.4}$$

---

[2] Note, however, that the converse is not true: a two-stage process of this type will not generate efficient outcomes unless the choices of public consumptions and the intrahousehold redistribution are linked by the well-known Bowen Lindahl Samuelson condition.

Chiappori and Gugl (2015) show the following result: a necessary and sufficient condition for TU is that (a well-chosen cardinalization of) the CIU of each agent be affine in the sharing rule

$$v_i (Q, p, \rho_i) = a_i (p, Q) + b_i (p, Q) \rho_i$$

and that, moreover, the coefficients b_i be identical across agents:

$$b_1 (p, Q) = b_2 (p, Q).$$

A well-known example of such preferences is the generalized quasi-linear (GQL) form introduced by Bergstrom and Cornes (1983), which requires that there exist strictly increasing functions F_i, A_i, and b_i such that

$$u_i (q_i, Q) = F_i \left[A_i \left(q_i^2, \ldots, q_i^n, Q \right) + q_i^1 b_i (Q) \right], \quad i = 1, 2, \tag{3.1.5}$$

with, moreover, $b_i(Q) = b(Q)$ for all i. When $b(Q) = 1$, we have the standard, quasilinear (QL) form. GQL is much more general; in particular, unlike the QL restriction, it does not require all income elasticities but one to be zero. The ACIU (for affine CIU) of Chiappori and Gugl further generalizes GQL by allowing the replacement of q_i^1 with a 1-homogeneous function of $\left(q_i^1, \ldots, q_i^n \right)$ in (3.1.5). For instance, preferences of the form

$$u_i (q_i, Q) = F_i \left[A_i \left(q_i^{m+1}, \ldots, q_i^n, Q \right) + \left(\sqrt[m]{q_i^1 \ldots q_i^m} \right) b(Q) \right], \quad i = 1, 2 \tag{3.1.6}$$

satisfy ACIU, and boil down to GQL for $m = 1$.

The form (3.1.5) guarantees the TU property for all Pareto-efficient allocations such that $\rho_i > 0$ for all i. This fact is easy to check. The first-stage allocation program can be written as the maximization of a weighted sum of CIUs:

$$\max_{Q, \rho} v_1 (Q, p, \rho) + \mu v_2 \left(Q, p, Y - \sum_K P^K Q^K - \rho \right). \tag{3.1.7}$$

Consider, now, an efficient allocation satisfying $\rho_i > 0$ for all i. Then first-order conditions with respect to the conditional sharing rule ρ give

$$\frac{\partial v_1}{\partial \rho} = b (p, Q) = \mu \frac{\partial v_2}{\partial \rho} = \mu b (p, Q).$$

It follows that $\mu = 1$; i.e., with ACIU preferences, efficiency plus positive private expenditures require the maximization of the *sum* (instead of the weighted sum) of utilities—which is exactly the TU property. Then the surplus is the value of this program—i.e., the maximum level of total utility attainable under the budget constraint.

Intuitively, the amounts allocated for private consumptions can be used to transfer utility between agents. A crucial property of TU is that such transfers operate at a constant "exchange rate"; i.e., that (for well-chosen representations of preferences) the marginal utility of each dollar spent on private expenditures is always equal across agents. The ACIU form has precisely this property, since the marginal utility equals $b(p, Q)$ for all members. This argument also explains why the ACIU form is necessary: there must exist a representation such that the marginal utility of private consumption is always the same for all agents, which implies that (i) it does not depend on individual *levels* of private expenditures (hence the affine form), and (ii) it is the same for all agents. This is exactly what the ACIU form achieves.

In summary, under TU—or equivalently when preferences satisfy ACIU with positive private consumption for all partners—the household's decision process is

$$\max u_1 (q_1, Q) + u_2 (q_2, Q) \tag{3.1.8}$$

under the household's budget constraint

$$\sum_{i,k} p^k q_i^k + \sum_K P^K Q^K = Y.$$

Coming back to the two-stage representation, at stage 1 the household jointly solves the program:

$$\max_{Q,\rho} v_1(Q, p, \rho) + v_2 \left(Q, p, Y - \sum_K P^K Q^K - \rho \right) \tag{3.1.9}$$

which determines the vector Q of household public consumption and the allocation $\left(\rho, Y - \sum_K P^K Q^K - \rho \right)$ of the amount devoted to private consumption between the spouses; then, at stage 2, individuals each choose their vector of private consumption, conditionally on the vector Q, by solving (3.1.4). Since preferences satisfy ACIU, program (3.1.9) can be written as

$$\max_Q a_1(p, Q) + a_2(p, Q) + b(p, Q) \left(Y - \sum_K P^K Q^K \right), \tag{3.1.10}$$

which shows that the choice of public goods is independent of the allocation of private consumption—a property that is specific to the TU setting.

3.1.4 The Sources of Heterogeneity

Now, what is not explicitly mentioned in these equations, but remains implicitly crucial, is that agents are heterogeneous, and this heterogeneity is summarized by a vector of characteristics—x for women and y for men. In practice, heterogeneity can take various forms. It can affect preferences; that is, the utility of Mrs. x is $u(q, Q, x)$, and her indirect utility is

$$v_i(Q, p, \rho_i) = a(p, Q, x) + b(p, Q)\rho_i$$

(and similarly for men). Note that b cannot vary with x (it must be the same for all agents to guarantee TU).

Alternatively, x and y may represent male and female income. Then $Y = x + y$, and the previous maximization becomes

$$\max u_1(q_1, Q) + u_2(q_2, Q) \tag{3.1.11}$$

under the constraint

$$\sum_{i,k} p^k q_i^k + \sum_K P^K Q^K = x + y.$$

An important and widely used implication of this form is the following. Remember, first, that under TU, program (3.1.11) can be written as

$$\max_Q a_1(p, Q) + a_2(p, Q) + b(p, Q)\left(x + y - \sum_K P^K Q^K\right), \tag{3.1.12}$$

which is just a restatement of (3.1.10). Let $G(x, y)$ denote the value of this program. Then G has three crucial properties:

1. It only depends on the sum $x + y$:

$$G(x, y) = \Gamma(x + y). \tag{3.1.13}$$

2. It is *increasing* in the sum $(x + y)$, therefore in both x and y.
3. It is the max of a family of linear, increasing functions in $x + y$; as such, it is *convex* in $x + y$. Together with (3.1.13), convexity implies that

$$\frac{\partial^2 G}{\partial x \partial y} = \Gamma''(x + y) \geq 0,$$

implying that G is *supermodular*. We shall see later several crucial implications of this property.

Of course, individuals do not necessarily match on income (or on income only). Another possibility is that individuals differ in the prices they face for some goods; that is typically the case when agents match on wages (or human capital), as in Chiappori, Costa Dias, and Meghir (2017). Or they may match on tastes, race, religion, physical attractiveness, and a host of other characteristics. Moreover, heterogeneity can actually be *multidimensional* and encompass several or all of these components.

We can now introduce some definitions. The *marital gain*, $G(x, y)$, is defined as the (common) value of programs (3.1.8), (3.1.9), and (3.1.10); in other words, it denotes the maximum total utility the household can achieve when married. The *surplus* $S(x, y)$ is the difference between the marital gain and the sum of utilities individuals could achieve as single; this is needed to maintain the normalization of the surplus of singles to zero. The payoffs $u(x)$ and $v(y)$, which are part of the definition of a matching, must therefore be understood as the share of total surplus respectively received by Mrs. x and Mr. y, over and above their utility as single. Alternatively, one can recover the total utility $\bar{u}(x)$ of Mrs. x when married: this is the sum of the payoff $u(x)$ and x's utility when single. Total utility $\bar{v}(y)$ of Mr. y is defined similarly.

3.1.5   A TU Model Is Unitary

An important property of TU models is that the household behavior they describe belongs to the "unitary" family, in the sense that the household's *aggregate* behavior can be seen as resulting from the maximization of a single (household) utility function. This is clear from (3.1.8), which is simply the maximization of a well-behaved utility (which happens to be the sum of two individual utilities) under a budget constraint. That is, the household maximizes a price-independent utility under budget constraint; its behavior is identical to that of an individual whose utility would be the sum of individual utilities. In particular, household *aggregate* demand for private as well as public goods is the same for all Pareto-efficient allocations—although *individual* private consumptions typically differ across various efficient allocations.

In other words, a distinctive property of the TU framework is that all Pareto-efficient allocations are associated with the same aggregate consumptions of all commodities. Changes along the Pareto frontier—which obtain when individual powers vary while agents keep making efficient decisions—correspond exclusively to different allocations of some or all of the private commodities between members, out of a total consumption vector that is identical for all allocations. This feature can be assessed differently according to the viewpoint adopted. On the positive side, TU introduces a clean separation between issues related to efficiency and those related to power. Efficiency determines the household's aggregate behavior, irrespective of powers; conversely, the exact amount consumed by each member is pinned down by power relationships. This property is widely used in several models, including Becker's seminal contributions. The cost, obviously, is that any impact of powers on aggregate demand (in particular on the demand for public goods) is assumed away. If, for instance, one investigates how changes in the husband's and wife's respective powers, caused (say) by variations in the distributions of male and female education, affect the household's expenditures on children, then a TU model is not an adequate framework—an ITU formulation would be more appropriate. Still, most of the time, the TU approach provides, at the very least, a useful benchmark; and in many cases a model based on TU is sufficient for the purpose under consideration.

3.1.6 An Example

We now provide an example of preferences that are not GQL, but satisfy ACIU (and therefore TU). This example is directly borrowed from Chiappori and Gugl (2015). Consider the following preferences:

$$u_m\left(Q, q_m\right) = \frac{a(Q)}{\Gamma_m} \prod_{k=1}^{n_1} \left(q_m^k - e^k\right)^{\gamma_m^k} + \beta_m\left(Q, q_m^{n_1+1}, \ldots, q_m^n\right), \quad m = h, w,$$

(3.1.14)

with

$$\sum_{k=1}^{n_1} \gamma_m^k = 1 \quad \text{and} \quad \Gamma_m = \prod_{k=1}^{n_1} \left(\gamma_m^k\right)^{\gamma_m^k}.$$

The conditional indirect utility of m is defined by

$$v_m\left(Q, p, \rho\right) = \max_q \frac{a(Q)}{\Gamma_m} \prod_{k=1}^{n_1} \left(q_m^k - e_m^k\right)^{\gamma_m^k} + \beta_m\left(Q, q_m^{n_1+1}, \ldots, q_m^n\right) \quad (3.1.15)$$

under

$$\sum_{k=1}^{n} p_k q_m^k = \rho.$$

The maximand in (3.1.15) is separable in $\left(q_m^1, \ldots, q_m^{n_1}\right)$; therefore, the program can be solved using two-stage budgeting. Define

$$\varrho = \sum_{k=1}^{n_1} p_k q_m^k; \tag{3.1.16}$$

then $\left(q_m^1, \ldots, q_m^{n_1}\right)$ must solve

$$\max_{\left(q^1, \ldots, q^{n_1}\right)} \prod_{k=1}^{n_1} \left(q^k - e_m^k\right)^{\gamma_m^k}$$

under (3.1.16), which gives

$$q_m^k = e_m^k + \frac{\gamma_m^k}{p_k} \left(\varrho - \sum_{i=1}^{n_1} p_i e_m^i\right).$$

The first stage is, therefore,

$$\max_{\varrho, q_m^{n_1+1}, \ldots, q_m^n} \left(a(Q) \prod_{k=1}^{n_1} (p_k)^{-\gamma_m^k}\right) \left(\varrho - \sum_{i=1}^{n_1} p_i e_m^i\right) + \beta_m \left(Q, q_m^{n_1+1}, \ldots, q_m^n\right)$$

under

$$\varrho + \sum_{k=n_1+1}^{n} p_k q_m^k = \rho.$$

The maximand is quasi-linear in ϱ; assuming that $\varrho > 0$, this implies that $\left(q_m^{n_1+1}, \ldots, q_m^n\right)$ only depends on (p, Q):

$$q_m^k = \phi_m^k(p, Q) \quad \text{if} \quad k \geq n_1 + 1$$

so that

$$\beta_m \left(Q, q_m^{n_1+1}, \ldots, q_m^n\right) = B_m(p, Q) \quad \text{and}$$

$$\varrho = \rho - \sum_{k=n_1+1}^{n} p_k q_m^k = \rho - C_m(p, Q).$$

Finally, we get

$$v_m (Q, p, \rho) = a(Q) \prod_{k=1}^{n_1} (p_k)^{-\gamma_m^k} \rho$$

$$+ B_m(p, Q) - a(Q) \prod_{k=1}^{n_1} (p_k)^{-\gamma_m^k} \left(C_m(p, Q) \sum_{i=1}^{n_1} p_i e_m^i\right),$$

which has the ACIU property for all prices if and only if $\gamma_w^k = \gamma_h^k$ for $k = 1, \ldots, n_1$. The corresponding Pareto frontier is therefore defined by

$$u_w + u_f = K(p, P, Y),$$

where

$$K(p, P, Y)$$
$$= \max_Q \left[\begin{array}{l} a(Q) \prod_{k=1}^{n_1} (p_k)^{-\gamma^k} \left(Y - \sum_k P^k Q^k \right) + \sum_{m=w,h} \left(B_m(p, Q) \right) \\ -a(Q) \prod_{k=1}^{n_1} (p_k)^{-\gamma^k} \left(C_m(p, Q) \sum_{i=1}^{n_1} p_i e_m^i \right) \end{array} \right].$$

In particular, we see the following:

- For $k \leq n_1$,

$$q_m^k = e_m^k - \frac{\gamma^k}{p_k} \left(\sum_{i=1}^{n_1} p_i e_m^i \right) + \frac{\gamma^k}{p_k} (\rho_m - C_m(p, Q)).$$

Therefore, the household aggregate demand for good k is

$$q^k = \sum_m q_m^k$$
$$= \sum_m \left(e_m^k - \frac{\gamma^k}{p_k} \left(\sum_{i=1}^{n_1} p_i e_m^i \right) - \frac{\gamma^k}{p_k} C_m(p, Q) \right) + \frac{\gamma^k}{p_k} \left(\sum_m \rho_m \right).$$

- For $k \geq n_1 + 1$,

$$q_m^k = \phi_m^k(p, Q) \quad \text{if} \quad k \geq n_1 + 1.$$

Therefore,

$$q^k = \sum_m q_m^k = \sum_m \phi_m^k(p, Q) \quad \text{if} \quad k \geq n_1 + 1.$$

Different efficient allocations correspond to different values of the conditional sharing rule (ρ_m, ρ_f); but for all of them the sum $\sum_m \rho_m$ is the same, since

$$\sum_m \rho_m = Y - \sum_k P^k Q^k.$$

This confirms that the household's aggregate demand is the same for all efficient allocations.

3.1.7   Extensions

Altruism

In the preceding presentation, agents are assumed egoistic: they only care about their own (private and public) consumption and disregard their spouse's welfare. However, this setting can be extended to allow for altruism—or, to use the term coined by the literature, for *caring*. To see why, assume that each member welfare is a weighted sum of both spouses' utilities; that is, i considers

$$W_i(q, Q) = u_i(q_i, Q) + \gamma_i^j u_j(q_j, Q), \quad i \neq j.$$

Here, γ_i^j represents the weights of j's utility in i's welfare.

As above, efficiency requires that the couple maximizes a weighted sum $W_1 + \mu W_2$; here, the maximand is thus

$$W(q, Q) = \left(1 + \mu \gamma_2^1\right) u_1(q_1, Q) + \left(\mu + \gamma_1^2\right) u_2(q_2, Q),$$

which is a weighted sum of the members' utilities. By the same argument as above, if the u_i are of the ACIU form, the weights must be equal

$$1 + \mu \gamma_2^1 = \mu + \gamma_1^2$$

and the couple maximizes

$$W(q, Q) = \left(1 + \mu \gamma_2^1\right) [u_1(q_1, Q) + u_2(q_2, Q)],$$

which is equivalent to the program above.

Labor Supply and Domestic Production

Secondly, one can readily introduce labor supply and domestic production within this setting. Consider a model in which a public good is produced using the spouses' time as an input. For expositional simplicity, we omit other public goods and other inputs (including them is straightforward but notationally cumbersome). Specifically, assume that the public good is produced according to the production function $Q = f(t_1, t_2)$, and that the household maximizes a weighted sum of utilities under the budget and time constraints

$$\sum_{k,i} p^k q_i^k = w_1 \left(T - L_1 - t_1\right) + w_2 \left(T - L_2 - t_2\right) + y_1 + y_2$$

and

$$L_i \geq 0, \quad t_i \geq 0, \quad L_i + t_i \leq T, \quad i = 1, 2.$$

Here, L_i, t_i, w_i, and y_i respectively denote i's leisure, domestic production time, and wage and nonlabor income, and T is total time available.

Again, one can write conditions under which the TU assumption is satisfied; efficiency then requires that the household maximizes the sum of utilities; the household program is therefore

$$\max_{q,t,Q} u_1 \left(q_1, L_1, Q\right) + u_2 \left(q_2, L_2, Q\right)$$

under the budget and production constraints. And, again, the surplus will typically be the value of this program. Note that, in this context, matching is bidimensional in general, because agents differ by their wages and their nonlabor income. In particular, wage heterogeneity requires a slight modification of the ACIU condition to guarantee TU; specifically, the CIU of agent i must be of the form

$$v_i \left(Q, p, w_i, \rho_i\right) = a_i \left(p, w_i, Q\right) + b(p, Q)\rho_i,$$

where the coefficient b cannot depend on i's wage.

3.1.8 Testable Implications

The TU assumption generates two types of testable predictions, relating either to the form of individual preferences or to the implications for aggregate behavior. On the first front, Chiappori (2010) derives a set of necessary and sufficient conditions for an individual demand function to derive from preferences of the GQL form; Chiappori and Gugl (2015) extend these results by providing corresponding conditions for the more general, ACIU form (which is necessary and sufficient for TU). These results are complemented by a "revealed preferences" characterization in Cherchye, Demuynck, and De Rock (2014). Broadly speaking, the idea is to consider the demand for private goods *conditional* on the level of public goods, and exploit the specific properties due to the affine form of the (conditional) indirect utility. Although the level of public good consumption is clearly endogenous, it can be instrumented using the corresponding prices. This characterization can also be translated into conditions relative to the Marshallian (as opposed to conditional) demand.

Regarding household behavior, the main implication is that, as mentioned earlier, the TU framework implies a unitary model; i.e., the household can be described as maximizing a single (price-independent) utility function under budget constraint. The main implication is that the demand function will satisfy income pooling and Slutsky symmetry and negativeness. There exists a number of tests of these properties in the literature; the reader is referred to Browning, Chiappori, and Weiss (2014) for a detailed presentation. In addition, the specific form of individual preferences required for the ACIU property to obtain has implications for household demand; these are characterized in Chiappori and Gugl (2015).

3.1.9 A Bridge between NTU and TU: From Gale-Shapley to Kelso-Crawford-Knoer and Beyond

While the distinction between TU and NTU is sharply present in the initial literature on the topic, more recent theoretical advances have established a bridge between the two strands.[3] The seminal, initial papers in this direction are due to Crawford and Knoer (1981) and Kelso and Crawford (1982); we now refer to these two contributions as CKK. The main idea can be summarized by referring to the cornerstone of the theory of NTU matching, namely, the Gale-Shapley algorithm.

Let me briefly recall the nature of the algorithm. Consider a "pure" NTU framework—i.e., there exists no technology that would allow transferring utility between agents. Assume that the sets X and Y are finite. A simple but powerful algorithm, due to Gale and Shapley (1962), enables us to explicitly construct a stable matching. The algorithm is in several stages. At stage 1, all agents on one side of the market (say, all women) contact their most desired partner and propose. Note that some women may prefer singlehood to any (available) man; then they contact the dummy partner $\emptyset_Y$, which in practice means that they will remain single. Now, some men may receive no offer (then they do nothing), while others receive one offer or more. If all offers received by man i are ranked (by i) below singlehood, they are declined. If some are better than singlehood, then i declines all of them but one (obviously, the one he prefers), which is put on hold. At stage 2, women whose offer has been declined contact their second most desired partner. Again, each man compares all received offers (including singlehood and possibly the offer on hold from the previous stage) and declines all but one (which is put on hold). At stage 3, women whose offer has been declined contact their third most

---

[3] Indeed, part of the literature gathers, under the general term NTU, all models that do not explicitly assume TU; that is, NTU, in this interpretation, encompasses both situations where transfers are not feasible (what I call NTU stricto sensu) and situations where tranfers are freely available, but the Pareto frontier is not a straight line (what I call ITU). See, for instance, Hatfield and Milgrom (2005).

desired partner, and so on. The algorithm stops either when no offer is declined or when women have contacted all their potential mates; in all cases, men match with the last offer they have put on hold (if any) or remain single (if none).

Several remarks can be made regarding this algorithm. One is that if the number of agents is finite, the algorithm must stop in finite time; indeed, the number of stages cannot exceed the number of men in Y, since each woman can contact any given man at most once. Second, whenever the algorithm stops, it must be that a stable matching has been reached. Indeed, it cannot be the case that a woman is matched while she would prefer remaining single (she would not have contacted that partner to start with). Nor can it be that a man is married while he would rather be single (he would have declined that offer when made). And consider any pair (i, j) who are *not* married to each other; then either i has contacted j and her offer was turned down—but then j has a mate he strictly prefers to i—or i has not contacted j—but then i is matched with a man she contacted *before* contacting j; i.e., someone she prefers to j. In all cases, it cannot be the case that *both* i and j would prefer being married to each other rather than their current situation.

Gale and Shapley show several additional properties of this algorithm. One is that the outcome is, among all *stable* matchings, the one that is preferred by *all* women, while it is also the one that *all* men like the least.[4] Moreover, it is incentive-compatible for women, in the sense that their dominant strategy is to follow their actual preferences—there is no possible gain in contacting anybody else than the preferred potential partner among those not yet proposed. Note, however, that the latter property does not hold for men: there may be some gain in strategically discarding an offer while holding on to a less liked one.

At any rate, the logic of the Gale-Shapley algorithm seems highly specific to the NTU framework: the idea of proposing a potential partner, who may turn you down or not, seems quite incompatible with the market logic implicit in the TU model. Not so, remarked CKK. The exact structure of the Gale-Shapley algorithm can be applied, with a minor twist, to TU problems as well—and, in fact, to all bilateral, one-to-one matching models, including the most general versions of ITU. How can one introduce transfers in Gale-Shapley? Well, let's start by discretizing the set of transfers: any possible transfer must involve an *integer* number of some very small unit (say, cents if transfers are in dollars, although a cleaner theoretical version would entail "micro utiles"—since transfers are measured in utility terms). Then let's change the Gale-Shapley algorithm by allowing—this is the twist— that when i contacts j, i's offer entails a proposed distribution of intra-couple

---

[4] Obviously, the symmetric version of the algorithm, in which men make offers and women decline or put on hold, will lead to a stable matching with the opposite properties—preferred by all men and hated by all women. If the two matchings coincide, then there is a unique stable matching. If not, the set of stable matching has a nice, algebraic structure—namely, it is a *lattice*. See, for instance, Roth and Sottomayor (1990).

resources: no longer "would you marry me?", but instead "would you marry me if I am willing to transfer you up to X?". If turned down, i has now two choices: either contact someone else or go back to j with a new offer—say, X plus one micro-unit. Not too romantic, perhaps, but note that the previous argument still applies exactly. The algorithm will still stop in finite time (that's where discretization of transfers is helpful), and it can only stop at a stable matching, for which not only matching patterns but also the corresponding payoffs are determined.

An additional advantage of this formulation is that it emphasizes the auction-like nature of TU models and of matching models with transfers in general. In essence, what women are doing in the CKK version of the algorithm is to *bid* for man j; and man j will "sell" himself to the "highest bidder". The notion of a "high bid" is not as straightforward as it sounds: people are bidding in utiles, not in dollars, so a given transfer of physical resources may translate into vastly different transfers of utility depending on who is offering (presumably, a tiny—or even negative—monetary transfer may be quite appealing when associated with matching with Angelina Jolie). Still, it is the case that even the least attractive woman could in principle match with a very attractive spouse, provided that she is willing to offer him a large enough amount—i.e., to bid enough for him. The problem, however, is that such an offer may just be too costly for her. If the total surplus that their matching generates is very low, offering a lot to a potential partner means keeping very few for oneself—so few, actually, that the offer may not be worth being made.

A large, recent literature has deeply improved our understanding of the theoretical links between matching and auction theory; moreover, the scope of these works goes far beyond one-to-one matching (incidentally, Kelso and Crawford (1982) already considered many-to-one matching). The interested reader is referred to Hatfield and Milgrom (2005) and to Hatfield and Kominers (2011) for a reader-friendly presentation.

Lastly, a recent and interesting literature extends the concept of stability to contexts involving asymmetric information. This is not an easy task—and one can readily see why. Consider the Gale-Shapley algorithm described above, with the additional twist that women have some private information regarding, say, their characteristics. The problem, now, is that whenever an offer is made, the man receiving the offer will systematically try to infer, from the terms of the offer, some information about the woman's private characteristics. Technically speaking, the key conceptual problem is to formulate a notion of a blocking pair that takes account of these inferences. Liu et al. (2014) provide such a definition; and they show that the set of stable outcomes thus defined in incomplete-information environments is nonempty and is a superset of the set of complete-information stable outcomes (that is, any matching that is stable under complete information remains stable when information is incomplete, but in addition some new matchings may be stable only under incomplete information).

To summarize:

- Transferable utility (TU) is an *ordinal* property; it states that, for well-chosen cardinalizations of individual utilities, the Pareto frontier is always a straight line with slope -1 (or, with more than two agents, a hyperplane orthogonal to the unitary vector), *irrespective of the economic environment* (prices, incomes, etc.).
- In a collective model of household behavior, where agents make efficient decisions, TU obtains under specific properties of preferences. Namely, for well-chosen cardinalizations, conditional indirect utilities are affine in the conditional sharing rule, with the same coefficient (which can be a function of public consumptions) for all individuals.
- A TU model is *unitary*; all efficient allocations generate the same demand for public goods and the same *aggregate* demand for private goods.
- Lastly, the Gale-Shapley algorithm, initially developed in an NTU context, can readily be applied to TU or even ITU—a property that will be useful later on.

3.2 Optimal Transportation

3.2.1 *Basic Duality Result*

A crucial property of matching models under TU is their intrinsic relationship with a class of linear maximization problems, called *optimal transportation*. Using the same notations as before, consider the following problem: find a measure h on $X \times Y$, the *marginals* of which are F and G, respectively, that maximizes the integral

$$S = \int_{X \times Y} S(x, y) dh(x, y). \tag{3.2.1}$$

From an economic perspective, this problem has a straightforward interpretation; just think of a dictator who can match people at will, and is trying to maximize total welfare. In a TU framework, there is a natural measure of total welfare, namely, the sum of all surpluses generated; that is exactly the meaning of the right-hand side integral in (3.2.1).

However, this class of problems also has a story (an older one, as a matter of fact) in mathematics. It was initially (as early as 1781!) studied by the French mathematician Gaspard Monge, who was facing a problem of earthwork involving the minimization of transportation cost.[5] Considerable progress was made in the

---

[5] The transportation problem could be intuitively described as follows (although Monge's problem was slightly different, the spirit was exactly identical). Assume you want to extract, from

1940s by the Russian mathematician Leonid Kantorovitch; for that reason, these problems are often referred to as optimal-transportation or Monge-Kantorovitch problems. The crucial point is that the problem is *linear* in its unknown—the measure h—since both the maximand in (3.2.1) and the constraints on the marginals are linear in h.[6] This is a key advantage of the formulation in terms of measure. Indeed, any linear maximization problem admits a dual problem. Duality theory establishes that, under mild conditions, if either the primal or the dual problem has a solution, so does the other; moreover, the two solutions are equal. For the optimal transportation problem just stated, the dual takes the following form: Find two functions u and v, respectively defined on X and Y, that minimize the sum

$$\tilde{S} = \int_X u(x) dF(x) + \int_Y v(y) dG(y) \tag{3.2.2}$$

under the constraints

$$u(x) + v(y) \geq S(x, y) \quad \forall (x, y) \in X \times Y. \tag{3.2.3}$$

Let h be a solution to the primal problem (3.2.1). The basic point is that (h, u, v) define a matching, and that this matching is moreover stable. To see why, note first that the dual constraints (3.2.3) are exactly the inequalities characterizing stability. Moreover, the *value* of the dual program—i.e., the optimal value of $\tilde{S}$—can be written as

$$\tilde{S} = \int_X u(x) dF(x) + \int_Y v(y) dG(y)$$
$$= \int_{X \times Y} (u(x) + v(y)) \, dh(x, y),$$

---

a set of mines, large quantities of coal that have to be allocated between various factories. Then X is the set of mines, and the measure F gives the total potential production of each mine; similarly, Y is the set of factories, and G describes the coal demand of each factory; lastly, $S(x, y)$ equals minus the cost of transporting one ton of coal from mine x to factory y. The "measure conditions" (i.e., the requirement that the marginals of h should be F and G) simply reflect the fact that a mine cannot produce more than its capacity, nor can factories use more than their demands. Then $h(x, y)$ is simply the quantity of coal from mine x to be allocated to factory y, the goal being to minimize overall transportation costs.

[6] Monge's initial formulation involved a transportation *map*, i.e., a map T such that the optimal solution takes the form $y = T(x)$. The formulation in terms of transportation *plans* (i.e., finding a *measure h* on the product set) is due to Kantorovich. My presentation follows the Kantorovich approach, which is both more general (there is no reason to impose that all coal from a given mine should go to the same factory) and more tractable. As often is the case in mathematics, adopting a broader perspective actually simplifies the problem!

reflecting the constraints on the marginals of h. By (3.2.3), we therefore have

$$\tilde{\mathcal{S}} \geq \int_{X \times Y} S(x, y) dh\,(x, y)\,.$$

Note, however, that the right-hand side of this inequality is simply the value of the primal program (i.e., the optimal $\mathcal{S}$ in (3.2.1)). But the duality theorem tells us that $\tilde{\mathcal{S}}$ and $\mathcal{S}$ must be equal. That is not possible unless the inequality in (3.2.3) is in fact an equality h-almost everywhere (i.e., for almost any couple (x, y) matched with positive probability).[7] So (3.2.3) must hold as an inequality everywhere and as an equality on the support of h, as required by the definition of a stable matching, and we can conclude that the matching (h, u, v) is stable.

Now, we have just established the equivalence between stability and surplus maximization. Formally, we have the following result:

Theorem 1 *Consider the matching problem defined by the compact sets X, Y, respectively endowed with the measures F and G, and the continuous surplus function S. If a matching (h, u, v) is stable, then h must solve the associated optimal transportation problem*

$$\max_{h'} \int S(x, y) dh'\,(x, y)\,,$$

where the max is taken over all measures the marginals of which are F and G.

Conversely, if the measure h solves the optimal transportation problem just defined, then there exists two functions u and v such that the matching (h, u, v) is stable; moreover, u and v are the dual variables of the optimal transportation problem.

Proof For a formal proof, the reader is referred to Chiappori, McCann, and Nesheim (2010) or Chiappori, McCann, and Pass (2016). Note that compactness and continuity are assumed here for simplicity, and can be relaxed to some extent. ∎

The equivalence between matching and optimal transportation is an old result; in economics, it dates back to Koopmans and Beckman (1957), Shapley and

---

[7] The intuitive interpretation is easy to get. We know that for any x, one at least of the (3.2.3) constraints involving x (possibly the contraint involving the dummy spouse $\emptyset_Y$) must hold with equality, for otherwise the sum in (3.2.2) would not be minimized (since it could be lowered by reducing $u(x)$). The same is true for y; the support of h is precisely the set of couples (x, y) where the constraints is binding.

Shubik (1972), and Becker (1973). A more detailed presentation can be found
in Gretsky, Ostroy, and Zame (1992); Ekeland (2010); Chiappori, McCann, and
Nesheim (2010); and Galichon (2015).

Theorem 1 is a very important result—actually, arguably the strongest result of
matching theory under TU. It establishes the equivalence between a decentralized,
game-theoretic concept (stability) and a centralized, normative problem (surplus
maximization). In that sense, it is clearly reminiscent of two key results in general
equilibrium theory, namely, the first and second welfare theorems. These state that
any market equilibrium is efficient, and that, conversely, in a convex economy, any
efficient allocation can be decentralized as a market equilibrium. Note, however,
that no additional convexity assumption is needed here; assuming that utility is
perfectly transferable is, if anything, a stronger requirement.

3.2.2   An Intuitive Illustration

To better understand the nature of the duality result, it is useful to consider a
simple example. Assume there are exactly two women (1 and 2) and two men
(1 and 2), and that the surplus is given by

$$S(i, j) = s_{ij}, \quad i = 1, 2, j = 1, 2.$$

Assume first that

$$s_{11} + s_{22} > s_{12} + s_{21}, \tag{3.2.4}$$

which means that the total surplus is maximized for the matching (1 matched with
1, 2 matched with 2). Then the matching (1 matched with 2, 2 matched with 1)
cannot be stable. Indeed, the following equalities and inequalities would have to be
satisfied:

$$u_1 + v_2 = s_{12}$$
$$u_2 + v_1 = s_{21}$$
$$u_1 + v_1 \geq s_{11}$$
$$u_2 + v_2 \geq s_{22}.$$

Here, the first two equalities characterize the surplus allocation between the two
couples (1, 2) and (2, 1), while the last two inequalities impose that neither (1, 1)
nor (2, 2) could profitably deviate. Now, adding up the last two inequalities and
substracting the first two equalities gives

$$0 \geq s_{11} + s_{22} - (s_{12} + s_{21}),$$

which contradicts (3.2.4). Conversely, the matching (1 matched with 1, 2 matched with 2) is stable. Indeed, take any (v_1, v_2) such that

$$s_{21} - s_{22} \le v_1 - v_2 \le s_{11} - s_{12} \tag{3.2.5}$$

and define

$$u_1 = s_{11} - v_1 \quad \text{and} \quad u_2 = s_{22} - v_2.$$

Then we have

$$u_1 + v_2 \ge s_{12} \quad \text{and} \quad u_2 + v_1 \ge s_{21},$$

which are exactly the stability conditions. We conclude that the matching that maximizes total surplus is the only stable matching.

Finally, what happens if we have an equality—i.e., if

$$s_{11} + s_{22} = s_{12} + s_{21}? \tag{3.2.6}$$

First, the maximization of total surplus has now two solutions—the two matchings studied before. Secondly, and by the same argument as above, these two matchings are stable, and so is any randomization between them. In fact, if we define $t = s_{12} - s_{11} = s_{22} - s_{21}$, (3.2.6) implies that

$$s_{12} = s_{11} + t \quad \text{and} \quad s_{22} = s_{21} + t.$$

In words: the change in surplus obtained by replacing man 1 with man 2 is the same (i.e., equal to t) whether the spouse is Mrs. 1 or Mrs. 2; total surplus, therefore, cannot be increased by switching spouses. This directly translates into the surplus distribution: stability requires that

$$v_2 - v_1 = t,$$

meaning that man 2 should receive t more than man 1 in any stable matching.

Note, however, that such a case is "knife-edge," in the sense that if we normalize the set of parameters $(s_{11}, s_{12}, s_{21}, s_{22})$ to be taken in $[0, 1]^4$, the subset for which (3.2.6) holds is of measure zero; nonuniqueness is not robust to (almost all) small perturbations of the parameters. In that sense, the matching that maximizes total surplus is "generically" unique.

3.2.3   Implications of the Basic Result

This equivalence has several interesting implications. One concerns existence. Existence of a stable match requires existence of two functions u and v such that (3.2.3) is always satisfied, and is satisfied as an equality on the support of h. This is, in principle, a difficult problem. However, existence of a solution to the primal problem—the optimal transportation—is much easier to get. The set of measures on $X \times Y$ whose marginals are F and G is obviously nonempty (just take the product of F and G); existence of a measure that maximizes total surplus in that set can therefore be established under mild continuity and compactness conditions.

Secondly, we expect the solution to be unique in general. While I will not try to give a precise definition of this notion in the fully general framework, one can remember the intuition provided by the preceding 2×2 example—namely, that while examples with multiple stable matchings can readily be constructed, they are typically not robust to small perturbations. This is in sharp contrast with the NTU case, in which nonuniqueness is a robust phenomenon.

Note, however, that the uniqueness conclusion only applies to the matching (who marries whom), not to the surplus allocation (the us and vs). In our 2×2 example, for instance, any pair (v_1, v_2) that satisfies (3.2.5) can be used to construct payoffs that are compatible with stability. The intuition for this result is that, in a stable matching, the only constraints on the allocation of the surplus within a matched pair is that none of the parties would be better by pairing with another mate. With a finite number of individuals, these conditions create bounds for the stable allocations; within these bounds, there typically exists a continuum of possible allocations. In economic terms, any woman sees each man as a potential substitute for her (stable) partner; but in a finite setting, such substitutes are typically imperfect, leaving some space for bargaining between matched individuals over the exact allocation of the surplus. Things would be quite different with a continuous distribution of types, because then each individual would have several (actually a continuum) of perfect substitutes. As we shall see, it is then generally the case that allocations are exactly pinned down by the stability conditions, possibly up to one common, additive constant.

Finally, and from a more practical perspective, a matching model under TU can be approached from two different (but dual) perspectives. That is, we may either try to find a measure h and two functions u and v satisfying the set of equalities and inequalities described in the definition, or try to maximize total surplus and derive u and v as the solutions to the dual problem. In many cases, the second approach is more tractable; in a continuous setting, for instance, the maximization of total surplus typically generates an optimal control problem that can be solved using standard methods. If, in particular, we want to simulate a matching problem, we only need to numerically solve a linear maximization problem, and very fast algorithms exist for that purpose. Broadly speaking, the existence of two different approaches to tackle the problem is specific to the TU case, and is often a powerful source of tractability.

To summarize:

- Finding an assignment (i.e., a measure on the product space $X \times Y$ the marginals of which are F and G) that maximizes total surplus is an *optimal transportation* problem.

- There is a deep connection between matching and optimal transportation problems. In particular, if a matching (h, u, v) is stable, then h must solve the corresponding surplus maximization problem; conversely, if h maximizes surplus and (u, v) denotes the corresponding dual functions, then the matching (h, u, v) is stable.
- As a consequence, existence and "generic uniqueness" of the stable matching can readily be established.

3.3 Supermodularity and Assortativeness

Let us now briefly concentrate on the one-dimensional case, by assuming that $\bar{X} \subset \mathbb{R}$ and $\bar{Y} \subset \mathbb{R}$. The surplus function S matches $\mathbb{R}^2$ to $\mathbb{R}$, and the qualitative properties of the stable matching are intrinsically related to the properties of the function S.

3.3.1 Supermodularity

A very important property of S is the notion of supermodularity, defined as follows:

Definition 1 *The function S is* supermodular *if for all x, x', y, y' such that $x \leq x'$ and $y \leq y'$:*

$$S(x, y) + S(x', y') - S(x, y') - S(x', y) \geq 0 \qquad (3.3.1)$$

and S is strictly supermodular if, whenever one of the inequalities $x \leq x'$ and $y \leq y'$ is strict, then the inequality in (3.3.1) is strict. The function S is submodular if the inequality (3.3.1) is reversed for all x, x', y, y' such that $x \leq x'$ and $y \leq y'$.

Some comments are in order regarding this property. Note, first, that it is intrinsically one-dimensional; there is no natural extension to higher dimensions, although we will see later what type of property could play a similar role in a multi-dimensional setting. Second, (3.3.1) can also be written as

$$S(x', y') - S(x, y') \geq S(x', y) - S(x, y). \qquad (3.3.2)$$

This form has a natural, economic interpretation. Assume, just to keep things simple, that S is increasing in both x and y; for instance, x and y denote (wife's and husband's) incomes, and a higher income can only increase the surplus. Then the two differences $S(x', y') - S(x, y')$ and $S(x', y) - S(x, y)$, which represent the increase in surplus obtained by replacing x with $x' \geq x$, are both nonnegative; but their respective magnitudes depend on the income of the male with whom x and x'

are paired. Condition (3.3.2) states that the difference is larger for larger incomes: while all men prefer a wealthier wife, the corresponding gain is especially large for wealthier men. Or, said differently: the maximum, additional amount a man would be willing to sacrifice (to bid) for a wealthier woman increases with the man's income. From a standard, economic perspective, the interpretation is that male and female incomes are *complements*:[8] if, say, both of them increase the surplus, then the marginal increase due to one trait is itself increasing in the second.

A third point is that when S is continuously differentiable, then we can, in (3.3.2), let x tend to x'; then whenever $y \leq y'$ we have

$$\frac{\partial S}{\partial x}(x, y') \geq \frac{\partial S}{\partial x}(x, y), \tag{3.3.3}$$

implying that the partial derivative in x must be increasing in y. If, furthermore, S is twice continuously differentiable, then supermodularity is equivalent to

$$\frac{\partial^2 S}{\partial x \partial y} \geq 0$$

and strict supermodularity obtains whenever the second cross-derivative is strictly positive. This property is often known as the *Spence-Mirrlees* condition. Needless to say, the same argument applies, mutatis mutandis, to submodularity—which is equivalent to the second cross-derivative being always negative.

An important point is that both strict supermodularity and strict submodularity imply that the partial derivative $\partial S / \partial x$ is strictly monotonic in y. As such, it is *injective*, in the sense that, for any x and any y, $\bar{y}$,

$$y \neq \bar{y} \Rightarrow \frac{\partial S}{\partial x}(x, y) \neq \frac{\partial S}{\partial x}(x, \bar{y}).$$

As we shall see later, this property can actually be generalized to higher dimensions.

3.3.2   Assortativeness

Supermodularity is a strong assumption, but it has major implications for matching patterns. Specifically:

Proposition 2 *If the function S is strictly supermodular, then the stable matching is strictly positive assortative in the following sense: if, at the stable matching, men*

---

[8] This is the term used, for instance, by Becker in his seminal contributions (1973, 1974).

x and x', with $x < x'$, are matched with women y and y', with $y < y'$, then it must be the case that x is matched with y and x' is matched with y'.

If the function S is strictly submodular, then the stable matching is strictly negative assortative *in the following sense: if, at the stable matching, men x and x', with $x < x'$, are matched with women y and y', with $y < y'$, then it must be the case that x is matched with y' and x' is matched with y.*

Proof The property directly stems from the equivalence between stability and surplus maximization. In the first case, if x were matched with y' and y were matched with x' at a stable matching, switching spouses would by (3.3.1) strictly increase aggregate surplus, which would contradict stability. The argument is similar in the submodular case. ∎

What about the converse conclusion? That is, is it the case that assortative matching implies supermodularity? On the one hand, it is easy to construct examples in which, although the surplus is not supermodular, the resulting stable matching is positive assortative; essentially, one has to be careful in constructing the measures F and G. However, the following result can be demonstrated: if the surplus function S is such that, *for any measures* F and G, stable matching is positive assortative, then S must be supermodular. Indeed, assume that we can find x, x', y, y' such that (3.3.1) is violated, and consider a measure F (resp. G) that concentrates all the mass on x and x' (y and y'). Then the stable match, which maximizes surplus by Theorem 1, must be negative assortative for these measures, a contradiction.

An important message, therefore, is that among married couples, matching patterns depend on the sign of the *second cross-derivative* of the surplus function. This is in sharp contrast with NTU models, where assortativeness typically follows from monotonicity, i.e., from the sign of the *first* derivatives of the surplus function. It is therefore easy to construct examples in which the stable matching is positive assortative under NTU but negative assortative under TU: just take a surplus function that is both increasing and submodular (for instance, $X = Y = [0, 1]$ and $S(x, y) = x^2 - 2xy + y^2 + 2x + 2y$). The intuition is exactly that given in the introduction (see subsection 1.2.2). In a TU framework, assortative matching implies that wealthier people are willing to *bid more* (than a less-wealthy competitor) for a wealthier spouse. In other words, what matters is not whether people are better off with a wealthier spouse (that would be monotonicity), but whether the gain in surplus generated by a wealthier spouse is larger for wealthier men than for poorer men (implying that wealthier men would be willing to bid more aggressively). This is exactly what the sign of the second cross-derivative indicates.

A second implication of this result is that under supermodularity, matching patterns follow exactly income (or trait) rankings: the wealthiest married woman

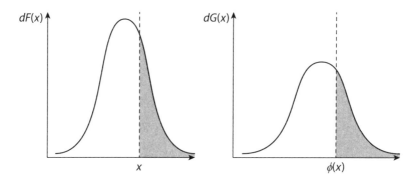

Figure 3.2. Positively assortative matching: the measure conditions.

is matched with the wealthiest married man, the second wealthiest married woman is matched with the second wealthiest married man, and so on. Indeed, assume this regular pattern is broken at some level; say the deviation occurs for the first time at rank n, in the sense that the nth wealthiest married woman x_n is not married to the nth wealthiest married man y_n. If $\phi(x_n)$ and $\psi(y_n)$ respectively denote x_n's husband and y_n's wife, it must be that $\phi(x_n) < y_n$ (since all males above y_n are married to women above x_n), and by the same token $\psi(y_n) < x_n$. But then the two pairs $(x_n, \phi(x_n))$ and $(\psi(y_n), y)$ violate Proposition 2. Note, in particular, that if S is supermodular, the resulting matching pattern *among married couples*, as described above, only depends on the marginal measures F and G—intuitively, x's spouse, say $\phi(x)$, is fully defined by the fact that the measure of the set of men "above" $\phi(x)$ exactly equals the measure of the set of women "above" x. Formally:

$$1 - F(x) = 1 - G(\phi(x)). \tag{3.3.4}$$

Figure 3.2 gives a graphical representation: for any x, $\phi(x)$ must be such that the area shaded on the left-hand side (which represents the density of the female distribution) must equal the area shaded on the right-hand side (which represents the density of the male distribution).

This fact has an immediate implication, which must be stressed: in general, it is *not* possible, from the sole observation of matching patterns, to recover the surplus function S. Indeed, if we observe that marriage is assortative, we may conclude that the surplus is increasing and supermodular. But there is absolutely no way to tell, within the (huge) set of supermodular functions, which one is actually relevant: they would all generate the same patterns. To learn more about the surplus, we need either to observe more (e.g., transfers between mates, or the size of the surplus) or to introduce additional assumptions, possibly on the nature of unobserved heterogeneity (but then whatever we learn on the surplus will be driven by these assumptions, which, moreover, are typically not testable). Both paths will be discussed later on.

Last but not least, we have the following corollary:

Corollary 3 *If S is either strictly supermodular or strictly submodular, the measure associated with a stable matching is unique and pure.*

Proof See Chiappori, McCann, and Pass (2016). ∎

We shall see later how this conclusion generalizes to a multi-dimensional setting.

3.3.3   Two Simple Examples

Let me now show, in two very simple examples, how these tools can be applied to specific economic situations. Start with a two-good model where agents, each characterized by their wage, work a fixed amount of time T and use the income thus generated to buy a private and a public good. Individual utilities are Cobb-Douglas:

$$u_i (C_i, Q) = C_i Q^\alpha,$$

where $\alpha > 0$ is a parameter that characterizes the desirability of the public good. The budget constraint is

$$C_1 + C_2 + P Q = w_1 T + w_2 T,$$

where w_i denotes the wage of agent i and P the price of the public good.

Since labor supply is fixed, agents are de facto matching on income; indeed, the present model is but a particular case of the more general framework discussed below (see subsection 3.4.2). Since preferences are of the GQL type, we are in a TU framework, and the total surplus is given by

$$S (w_1, w_2) = \max \{(C_1 + C_2) Q^\alpha \text{ under } C_1 + C_2 + P Q = w_1 T + w_2 T\}.$$

The solution can readily be computed: it implies

$$C_1 + C_2 = \frac{(w_1 + w_2) T}{1 + \alpha}, \quad P Q = \frac{\alpha (w_1 + w_2) T}{1 + \alpha},$$

generating the surplus:

$$S (w_1, w_2) = \frac{\alpha^\alpha T^{1+\alpha} P^{-\alpha}}{(1 + \alpha)^{1+\alpha}} (w_1 + w_2)^{1+\alpha}.$$

Matching patterns are defined by the sign of the second cross-derivative of the surplus; here,

$$\frac{\partial^2 S\,(w_1, w_2)}{\partial w_1 \partial w_2} = \frac{\alpha^{\alpha+1}\,T^{1+\alpha}\,P^{-\alpha}}{(\alpha+1)^\alpha}\,(w_1 + w_2)^{\alpha-1} > 0,$$

and matching is positive assortative.

Let us now slightly twist the previous model, by assuming that the public good, instead of being purchased on the market, is produced by the agents. Specifically, agent i may devote a fraction t_i of their time to domestic production and the remaining $T - t_i$ to market work (at the same wage w_i, as before). The production function of the public good is Cobb-Douglas:

$$Q = t_1 t_2.$$

The model is still of the TU form; therefore, the household maximizes the sum of utilities

$$\max_{C_1, C_2, t_1, t_2} \ (C_1 + C_2)\,(t_1 t_2)^\alpha$$

under a new budget constraint

$$C_1 + C_2 + w_1 t_1 + w_2 t_2 = (w_1 + w_2)\,T.$$

Again, the solution can readily be derived:

$$C_1 + C_2 = \frac{(w_1 + w_2)\,T}{1 + 2\alpha}, \quad w_1 t_1 = w_2 t_2 = \frac{\alpha\,(w_1 + w_2)\,T}{1 + 2\alpha}.$$

Note, in particular, that the time an individual devotes to domestic production is inversely proportional to the person's wage. The surplus is now

$$S\,(w_1, w_2) = \frac{\alpha^{2\alpha}\,T^{1+2\alpha}}{(1 + 2\alpha)^{1+2\alpha}}\,(w_1 + w_2)^{1+2\alpha}\,w_1^{-\alpha}\,w_2^{-\alpha}.$$

What about matching patterns? Again, we can compute the second cross-derivative; now, however,

$$\frac{\partial^2 S\,(w_1, w_2)}{\partial w_1 \partial w_2} = -\frac{\alpha^{2\alpha+1}\,T^{2\alpha+1}\,(w_1 + w_2)^{2\alpha-1}}{w_1^{\alpha+1}\,w_2^{\alpha+1}\,(2\alpha+1)^{2\alpha+1}}\,\left(w_1^2 + w_2^2 + \alpha\,(w_1 - w_2)^2\right) < 0,$$

and we conclude that matching is *negative assortative*: high-wage men marry low-wage women and conversely.

The intuition for this result relies on the notion of (partial) *specialization*. The optimal allocation of time requires low-wage people to devote much time to domestic production. But then a high-wage spouse can concentrate on market work, generating a large income and a high level of private consumption while benefiting from the large supply of public goods provided by the partner's domestic work. Note that, in this example, specialization is only partial, in the sense that both individuals contribute to domestic production; this is a direct consequence of the Cobb-Douglas form.[9] Still, it is sufficient to trigger negative assortative patterns.

The specialization logic thus described is reminiscent of what has been called "traditional households," where the husband works full time while the wife stays at home. This interpretation, however, is more problematic than it seems, for two reasons. First, the model is symmetric; therefore, it also predicts that educated women, whose potential wage is high, should marry less-educated husbands who would specialize in domestic production—and this is definitely not a commonly observed pattern. Second, a striking feature of historical matching patterns is that even when traditional households are the dominant form of household organization, we do not observe strong negative assortative matching patterns. One possible explanation is that domestic production includes not only simple chores, but also raising children, and the parents' human capital stocks are important inputs in the latter process. Such a feature may actually restore positive assortative matching; I will come back later to this very important issue.

3.3.4   Who Are the Singles?

Coming back to the general framework, a point should be noted: the assortativeness conclusion holds *for married individuals* only—that is, it characterizes matching patterns among the subsample of individuals who are married at the stable matching. However, Proposition 2 is silent about the determination of this subsample; nothing is said about who gets married and who remains single.

As it turns out, the determination of singlehood is not directly related to supermodularity or submodularity (i.e., to the sign of the second cross-derivative of the surplus function). Rather, it depends on the value of the function and of its *first* derivatives—i.e., on whether (and when) the surplus is positive and increasing.

To illustrate this fact, consider the following three examples, in which we concentrate on female singles (similar examples for either males or both genders are easy to construct). In each case, the surplus is supermodular, so there is

---

[9] In a Cobb-Douglas production function, inputs are complements, so domestic work by the high-wage partner improves the productivity of the low-wage spouse. If inputs are instead perfect substitutes, then complete specialization would obtain, with each partner concentrating exclusively on either market or domestic work—a formulation that would be close to Becker's original intuition. See, for instance, Pollak and Wachter (1975) and Pollak (2013).

assortative matching among married individuals; and in each case, some women (and some men, since we assume equal population sizes) remain single. However, in the first case the singles are the poorest women; in the second case they are the wealthiest; in the last case they are women with intermediate income.

To keep things simple, we shall consider the same population distributions in each case. In what follows, thus:

- Women are uniformly distributed on the interval [0, 2] (the density being equal to 1/2).
- Men are uniformly distributed on the interval [0, 1] (the density being equal to 1).

Example 4 *The first surplus is*

$$S(x, y) = (x - 1) y.$$

Note, first, that

$$\frac{\partial S}{\partial x} = y, \quad \frac{\partial S}{\partial y} = x - 1 \quad \text{and} \quad \frac{\partial^2 S}{\partial x \partial y} = 1,$$

so that S is increasing in x, increasing in y for $x \geq 1$, and supermodular.
The stable matching is the following:

- *Any woman $x \geq 1$ is matched with a man $y = \phi(x) = \frac{x}{2}$.*
- *Women with $x < 1$ and men with $y < \frac{1}{2}$ remain single.*

The intuition is clear: women endowed with an x smaller than 1 can only create negative surplus by marrying; therefore they are better off single. Women with $x \geq 1$ marry, and since S is increasing in y for $x \geq 1$, they marry the wealthiest men, i.e., those whose income is at least 1/2 (the total mass of whom is exactly 1/2, that is, exactly the mass of women above 1). Indeed, if an open set of males with income above 1/2 was left single, then necessarily an open set of males with incomes below 1/2 would be married. But S being increasing in y, replacing married men with income less than 1/2 with single men with income more than 1/2 would increase total surplus, which contradicts stability. Lastly, assortative matching between married individuals gives $x = 2y$.

Example 5 *Assume, now, that*

$$S(x, y) = \frac{2}{(x + 1)(y + 1)} - 1.$$

Here,

$$\frac{\partial S}{\partial x} = -\frac{2}{(x+1)^2(y+1)} < 0, \qquad \frac{\partial S}{\partial y} = -\frac{2}{(x+1)(y+1)^2} < 0$$

and $\quad \dfrac{\partial^2 S}{\partial x \partial y} = \dfrac{2}{(x+1)^2(y+1)^2} > 0,$

so now S is decreasing in x and y while still supermodular. The situation is now opposite to the previous example, and the stable matching goes as follows:

- Any woman $x \le \bar{x}$, where $\bar{x} = \frac{1}{2}\sqrt{17} - \frac{3}{2} \cong 0.562$, is matched with a man $y = \phi(x) = x/2$.
- Women with $x > \bar{x}$ and men with $y > \bar{x}/2$ remain single.

The intuition is exactly as before, except for the fact that S is now decreasing—so that only low values of x and y generate a positive surplus. Incidentally, $\bar{x}$ is determined by the fact that the surplus for the couple $(\bar{x}, \bar{x}/2)$ is exactly zero.

Example 6 In the last example, the surplus is

$$S(x, y) = 4x^2y - 4x + 1,$$

so that

$$\frac{\partial S(x, y)}{\partial x} = 8xy - 4, \qquad \frac{\partial S(x, y)}{\partial y} = 4x^2 \ge 0$$

and $\quad \dfrac{\partial^2 S(x, y)}{\partial x \partial y} = 8x > 0.$

The surplus is still supermodular, increasing in y, but nonmonotonic in x; it is decreasing for $x < 1/2y$, minimum for $x = 1/2y$, and increasing after that. The stable matching is now more complex:

- All women with $x \ge \bar{x} \cong 1.267$ are married to a man $y = \phi(x) = x/2$.
- All women with $\bar{x} > x > \bar{x}' \cong 0.311$ are single.
- All women with $x \le \bar{x}'$ are married to a man $y = \phi(x) = x/2 + .478$,

where $\bar{x}$ is the larger solution to $S(\bar{x}, \bar{x}/2) = 0$ and $\bar{x}' \neq \bar{x}$ is such that $S(\bar{x}', \bar{x}/2) = 0$.

Again, the only married couples are those who generate a positive surplus; due to the nonmonotonicity of S in x, these happen to involve only low- or high-income women.

These examples show clearly that the monotonicity of S plays a crucial role in determining who is married and who remains single. This intuition is confirmed by the following result:

Proposition 7 *Assume that S is strictly increasing in x. If x is married at a stable matching and $x' > x$, then x' is married at a stable matching.*

Assume that S is strictly decreasing in x. If x is married at a stable matching and $x' < x$, then x' is married at a stable matching.

Proof I just prove the first statement (the proof of the second is identical). Assume it does not hold; then matching x's husband with x' instead of x (and leaving x single) would strictly increase total surplus, a contradiction since stability requires surplus maximization. ∎

3.3.5   The Twist Condition

Let us now assume that $X \subset \mathbb{R}^m$ and $Y \subset \mathbb{R}^n$, with $m \geq 1$ and $n \geq 1$.[10] As I said above, the notion of assortative matching cannot easily be generalized to such multiple dimensions. A direct (and somewhat minimal) extension would be the following: assume that one cross partial derivative $\partial^2 S / \partial x_k \partial y_l$ is positive; we can, without loss of generality, assume that $k = l = 1$. If, at a stable matching, the two women $x = (x_1, x_2, \ldots, x_m)$ and $x' = (x'_1, x_2, \ldots, x_m)$, with $x'_1 > x_1$, are matched with the two men $y = (y_1, y_2, \ldots, y_n)$ and $y' = (y'_1, y_2, \ldots, y_n)$, with $y'_1 > y_1$, then it must be the case that x is matched with y and x' is matched with y'. In the same vein, if $\partial^2 S / \partial x_k \partial y_l > 0$ for all k, l, and if, at a stable matching, the two women $x = (x_1, x_2, \ldots, x_m)$ and $x' = (x'_1, x'_2, \ldots, x'_m)$, with $x'_k > x_k$ for all k, are matched with the two men $y = (y_1, y_2, \ldots, y_n)$ and $y' = (y'_1, y'_2, \ldots, y_n)$, with $y'_l > y_l$ for all l, then it must be the case that x is matched with y and x' is matched with y'. A more general property is derived by Lindenlaub (2015). She shows that if $m = n$ and the surplus function takes the form

$$S(x, y) = \sum_k f_k (x_k, y_k),$$

with $\partial^2 f_k / \partial x_k \partial y_k \geq 0$ for all x, y, k, then the matching is unique, pure, and generalized assortative in the sense that x is matched with $y = \phi(x)$ such that $\partial \phi_k / \partial x_k \geq 0$ for all k.

These properties, however, only apply to specific cases and only provide partial characterizations. A less immediate but practically more relevant generalization

---

[10] This subsection is largely borrowed from Chiappori, McCann, and Pass (2016).

is provided by the so-called *twist* condition. Assume that S is continuously differentiable; then:

Definition 8 *The function S satisfies the twist condition if, for each fixed $x \in X$ and $y_0 \neq y \in Y$,*

$$D_x S(x, y) \neq D_x S(x, y_0).$$

Here, $D_x S(x, y)$ denotes the vector of partial derivatives of S with respect to the various components of x. The twist condition is therefore equivalent to the *injectivity* of $y \mapsto D_x S(x, y)$ for each fixed x. For instance, in a one-dimensional context ($m = 1 = n$), the classical Spence-Mirrlees condition imposes that either $\frac{\partial^2 S}{\partial x \partial y} > 0$ or $\frac{\partial^2 S}{\partial x \partial y} < 0$ over $X \times Y$, which implies that $y \mapsto \frac{\partial S}{\partial x}(x, y)$ is strictly monotone (and hence injective) for each fixed x. It is in this sense that the twist condition can be viewed as a nonlocal generalization of the Spence-Mirrlees condition.

Now, although assortativeness cannot be generalized to a multidimensional setting, uniqueness and purity can, and the twist condition is sufficient to guarantee both properties, as stated by the following result:

Theorem 9 *Assume that F is absolutely continuous with respect to the Lebesgue measure and the surplus S satisfies the twist condition. Then the stable measure is unique and pure, in the sense that there exists a function ϕ mapping X to Y such that any $x \in X$ is matched with $y = \phi(x)$.*

Proof See Chiappori, McCann, and Pass (2016). ∎

In practice, for any multidimensional matching problem, one can first verify whether the twist condition is satisfied; if it is, then the stable matching is unique and pure, which drastically simplifies the analysis—notably because the stable measure is born by the graph of some function ϕ.

To summarize:

- In a one-dimensional context, if the surplus is supermodular, then the stable matching is unique and positive assortative; conversely, if the stable matching is positive assortative for all measures on X and Y, then the surplus must be supermodular (and similar conclusions obtain for submodularity and negative assortativeness). In other words, *among married couples*, matching patterns exclusively depend on the *second cross-derivative* of the surplus function.

- It follows that marital patterns depend on the specific nature of the marital surplus. For instance, a model where marital gains stem from the joint consumption of a public good purchased on the market typically generates positive assortativeness. However, if the public good is domestically produced, efficiency may require specialization within the household, which may lead to negative assortative matching.
- In any case, the sign of the second cross-derivative is not relevant for the determination of singles; here, it is the value of the function and of its first derivatives that matters.
- A possible generalization of supermodularity to a higher dimension is the *twist* condition, which essentially states that the gradient of the surplus with respect to one set of variables (say, x) is injective in the others (here, y). It guarantees uniqueness and purity of the stable matching.

3.4   Individual Utilities and Intrahousehold Allocation

3.4.1   Recovering Individual Utilities

Coming back to the household model introduced in section 3.1.3, let me now show how the equilibrium conditions can be used to recover intrahousehold allocations. I consider here the case in which individual traits are one-dimensional—i.e., $X \subset \mathbb{R}$ and $Y \subset \mathbb{R}$; multidimensional matching will be studied in chapter 5. More importantly, I assume that the distributions F and G of male and female incomes are absolutely continuous and atomless, with convex support; this means, in practice, that there exists an interval (possibly unbounded) of incomes on which the densities of F and G are always positive and outside of which these densities are zero. As we shall see, this assumption guarantees that individual utilities are exactly determined by the stability constraints (although possibly up to a common, additive constant). I also assume that S is increasing and $S(x, y) > 0$ for all (x, y), meaning that any two individuals are always better off married to each other than single. This assumption will be relaxed in the next section, in which I allow differences in taste—implying in particular that some pairs would rather remain single than married to each other. Lastly, I consider the case in which S is supermodular. In our one-dimensional setting, matching patterns are then fully determined by the two distributions F and G. Specifically, any married x is matched with some $y = \phi(x)$, where ϕ is defined by equation (3.3.4); conversely, any married y is matched with some $x = \psi(y)$, where $\psi = \phi^{-1}$.

Now, let $u(x)$ and $v(y)$ denote the respective utilities of married woman x and married man y. Then,

$$S(x, \phi(x)) = u(x) + v(\phi(x)) \quad \text{and}$$
$$S(\psi(y), y) = u(\psi(y)) + v(y).$$

Moreover, stability requires that

$$u(x) + v(y) \geq S(x, y) \text{ for all } (x, y).$$

Therefore,

$$u(x) = \max_{y} S(x, y) - v(y) \quad \text{and} \tag{3.4.1}$$

$$v(y) = \max_{x} S(x, y) - u(x),$$

where the max in the first (resp. second) equation is reached for $y = \phi(x)$ ($x = \psi(y)$).

The envelope theorem applied to the first equation (or, equivalently, the first-order condition of the second equation) gives

$$u'(x) = \frac{\partial S}{\partial x}(x, \phi(x)).$$

Similarly,

$$v'(y) = \frac{\partial S}{\partial y}(\psi(y), y).$$

These conditions are important: they imply that *both $u(x)$ and $v(y)$ are determined by the stability conditions*, up to an additive (integration) constant each. That is,

$$u(x) = K + \int_{\underline{x}}^{x} \frac{\partial S}{\partial x}(t, \phi(t)) \, dt \quad \text{and}$$

$$v(y) = K' + \int_{\underline{y}}^{y} \frac{\partial S}{\partial y}(\psi(t), t) \, dt$$

where $\underline{x}$ and $\underline{y}$ respectively denote the lower bounds of the support of F and G. Moreover, the sum $K + K'$ is pinned down by the equality

$$u(x) + v(\phi(x)) = S(x, \phi(x)),$$

which implies that

$$K + K' = S(x, \phi(x)) - \int_{\underline{x}}^{x} \frac{\partial S}{\partial x}(t, \phi(t)) \, dt - \int_{\underline{y}}^{\phi(x)} \frac{\partial S}{\partial y}(\psi(t), t) \, dt.$$

In the end, utilities are thus determined up to one common, additive constant K. The determination of K depends on the respective size of the male and female populations. Whenever these sizes differ, then K—therefore the entire set of individual utilities—is exactly determined. To see how, assume for instance that there are more women than men. Then all men are married, but some women remain single; and because S is increasing in x, only the poorest women are single. Now, consider the poorest married woman $\tilde{x}$. She must be indifferent between marriage and singlehood, because she has a perfect substitute (the wealthiest, unmarried woman), who is single. It follows that, in the couple $(\tilde{x}, \phi(\tilde{x}))$, he receives all of the surplus

$$v(\phi(\tilde{x})) = S(\tilde{x}, \phi(\tilde{x})),$$

which immediately gives

$$K' = S(\tilde{x}, \phi(\tilde{x})) - \int_{\underline{y}}^{\phi(\tilde{x})} \frac{\partial S}{\partial y}(\psi(t), t) \, dt.$$

Note that this argument can be reversed in the opposite case in which men outnumber women (then the wife of the last married man gets all the surplus). In both cases, the remaining constant is pinned down.

In the knife-edge case where there are exactly as many men as women, however, the constant is undetermined, although it is bounded by the fact that in the poorest couple both the husband and the wife must be at least as well off as if they were single.

An important consequence is *that frictionless models typically exhibit a discontinuity in intrahousehold allocation when the sex ratio (defined as the ratio of the male to the female population sizes) varies in the neighborhood of 1.* Indeed, when men are on the short side of the market (even by an infinitesimal amount), then in the poorest married couple, the husband gets all the surplus. Slightly change the sex ratio, however, so that men slightly outnumber women, and suddenly, in the same poorest married couple, the women receive the total surplus. And this discontinuous switch at a sex ratio of exactly 1 is not limited to the poorest couples; it propagates along the income distribution, so that each man's and each woman's shares are affected by exactly the same amount (technically, the switch only affects the additive constant K). This discontinuity is a by-product of two specific features of the model: its frictionless nature on the one hand and the one-dimensional, deterministic nature of the matching game on the other hand. In the next chapter, we shall relax the second assumption by allowing for variations in tastes (which will be technically represented by a stochastic component in the surplus); as we shall see, the discontinuity will then disappear.

3.4.2 Particular Case: Matching on Income

The Setting

Let us now see how these tools can be readily used to address some of the issues raised in the introduction. Specifically, we want to model the consequences of an overall increase in female wages on the marriage market equilibrium, and more specifically on the equilibrium allocation of resources and utility within each couple. As argued in the first chapter, we expect a global change of this nature to impact intrahousehold allocations. We shall now see that the model just described can easily provide a first calibration of these effects.

Consider the simple but quite useful model in which agents only differ by their incomes, and preferences satisfy the ACIU condition defined in section 3.1.3 (which guarantees TU). The surplus, thus, is defined by

$$S(p, P, x, y) = V_H(p, P, x + y) - V_1(p, P, x) - V_2(p, P, y),$$

where V_H is the household's indirect utility

$$V_H(p, P, x + y) = \max [u_1(q_1, Q) + u_2(q_2, Q)]$$

under the constraint

$$\sum_{i,n} p^i q_n^i + \sum_I P^I Q^I = x + y,$$

while V_i is i's indirect utility *when single*; for agent 1, for instance,[11]

$$V_1(p, P, x) = \max u_1(q_1, Q)$$

under the constraint

$$\sum_i p^i q_1^i + \sum_I P^I Q^I = x.$$

---

[11] Here, we assume that agents, when single, consume the same commodities as when married; the only difference is that some commodities (the vector Q) are consumed publicly by matched couples but privately by singles. An alternative assumption is that singlehood imposes $Q = 0$; see, for instance, Chiappori et al. (2015).

As noted above, under ACIU we have

$$V_H(p, P, x + y) = \max_{Q,x} a_1(p, Q) + a_2(p, Q) + b(p, Q) \left(x + y - \sum_K P^K Q^K \right),$$

and V_H, being the max of a family of increasing affine function in $(x + y)$, is increasing and convex in $(x + y)$. In particular,

$$\frac{\partial^2 S}{\partial x \partial y} = \frac{\partial^2 V_H}{\partial x \partial y} = \frac{\partial^2 V_H}{\partial (x + y)^2} > 0$$

and S is supermodular. Also, one can readily check that S is increasing and $S(x, y) > 0$ for all $x, y > 0$.

From now on, for notational simplicity, we omit prices and consider utilities as functions of incomes only. Denote, as before, $u(x)$ and $v(y)$ the respective payoffs of Mrs. x and Mr. y. Remember that u and v are the additional utilities generated by marriage over and above the individual's utility as a single; in other words, the total utilities, at the stable match, of Mrs. x and Mr. y are given by

$$\bar{u}(x) = u(x) + V_1(x), \quad \bar{v}(y) = v(y) + V_2(y).$$

Then (3.4.1) can be written as

$$\bar{u}(x) = \max_y V_H(x + y) - \bar{v}(y). \tag{3.4.2}$$

Therefore,

$$\bar{u}'(x) = V_H' (x + \phi(x)), \tag{3.4.3}$$

and similarly

$$\bar{v}'(y) = V_H' (\psi(y) + y). \tag{3.4.4}$$

The Linear Shift Assumption

We now make a simplifying assumption on the form of male and female income distributions:

Definition 10 *The male income distribution is a linear shift of the female income distribution if (i) there are as many men as women, and (ii) there exists $\alpha, \beta > 0$ such that*

$$F(t) = G(\alpha t - \beta) \text{ for all } t \tag{3.4.5}$$

for some $\alpha > 1, \beta < 0$.

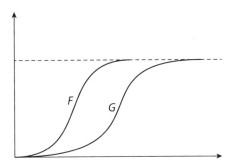

Figure 3.3. A linear upward shift.

An illustration is provided in figure 3.3. For instance, if incomes of both men and women are lognormally distributed with parameters (μ_M, σ_M) for males and (μ_F, σ_F) for females, the linear shift condition is satisfied when $\sigma_M = \sigma_F$—a form that fits existing data pretty well.

The linear shift property implies that, under assortative matching and with populations of equal size, a woman with income x is paired with a man with income $y = \alpha x - \beta$. With the previous notations, therefore, $\phi(x) = \alpha x - \beta$ and $\psi(y) = (y + \beta)/\alpha$. Equations (3.4.3) and (3.4.4) then become

$$\bar{u}'(x) = V_H' \left((\alpha + 1) x - \beta \right), \tag{3.4.6}$$

and similarly

$$\bar{v}'(y) = V_H'(((\alpha + 1)y + \beta)/\alpha), \tag{3.4.7}$$

yielding upon integration:

$$\bar{u}(x) = K' + \frac{1}{1 + \alpha} V_H \left(x + \phi(x) \right) \tag{3.4.8}$$

and

$$\bar{v}(y) = K + \frac{\alpha}{1 + \alpha} V_H \left(\psi(y) + y \right) \tag{3.4.9}$$

with

$$K + K' = 0.$$

As indicated before, utilities are determined up to an additive constant—this is the standard indeterminacy when there are exactly as many women as men. In what follows, we assume $K = K' = 0$. Then the marriage between Mr. x and Mrs. $y = \phi(x)$ generates a marital output $V_H \left(x + \phi(x) \right)$, which is divided between the spouses according to a particularly simple allocation rule: he receives some constant share $\alpha/(1 + \alpha)$ of it, and she gets the remaining $1/(1 + \alpha)$.

Changing Female Incomes

We now turn to examine the impact of changes in the income distributions. Start from a situation in which men have a higher income, in the sense that their distribution dominates in the first degree the income distribution of women. This requires $F(t) > G(t)$ for all t; assume, to keep things simple, that $\beta = 0$ and $\alpha > 1$. In the initial situation, therefore, husbands get a larger share of the marital gain than their wives.

Consider, now, a *first-degree upward shift* in the distribution of female income, holding the male distribution constant. That is, the proportion of females with incomes exceeding y rises for all y, so that women become more similar to men in terms of their income, as we observe in practice. If we assume that all female incomes are shifted up proportionally—so that each woman maintains her relative rank (quantile) in the income distribution—then assortative matching implies that all women are matched with the same husband (or a husband with the same income) as before. Therefore, all couples benefit from an increase in total income; we are interested in *how* the corresponding increase in household utility is allocated between spouses.

In practice, suppose that the income of every woman is inflated by some common factor $\lambda > 1$ and consider a married couple with initial incomes (x, y). After the shift, the partners remain married but the wife's income is boosted to λx while the husband's income remains equal to y. If $\bar{u}^\lambda(x)$ and $\bar{v}^\lambda(y)$ denote the new individual utilities, we have, from (3.4.8) and (3.4.9),

$$\bar{u}^\lambda(x) = \frac{\lambda}{\alpha + \lambda} V_H\left((\alpha + \lambda)\, x\right) \quad \text{and} \quad \text{(3.4.10)}$$

$$\bar{v}^\lambda(y) = \frac{\alpha}{\alpha + \lambda} V_H\left((\alpha + \lambda)\, x\right).$$

Differentiating in λ around $\lambda = 1$ gives

$$\frac{\partial \bar{u}^\lambda(x)}{\partial \lambda} = \frac{1}{\alpha + 1} x V'_H + \frac{\alpha}{(\alpha + 1)^2} V_H \quad \text{and} \quad \text{(3.4.11)}$$

$$\frac{\partial \bar{v}^\lambda(y)}{\partial \lambda} = \frac{\alpha}{\alpha + 1} x V'_H - \frac{\alpha}{(\alpha + 1)^2} V_H. \quad \text{(3.4.12)}$$

One can readily check that both changes are positive (for the second one, it stems from the convexity of V_H).

We see that the upward shift in women's income has two impacts. First, as we said, it increases total income in all households. This generates some additional surplus; in the computations above, the latter is represented by the term $x V_H'$. This supplement is shared between spouses, in proportion to their respective incomes; in the neighborhood of $\lambda = 1$, the shares are $1/(1 + \alpha)$ and $\alpha/(1 + \alpha)$.

The second effect is more interesting. Indeed, the shift triggers a *redistribution* from the husband to the wife. This is summarized by the second terms in (3.4.11) and (3.4.12), which, not surprisingly, are opposite. Since the wife's share of total income is increased, so is her share of the surplus; the husband therefore transfers to his wife an amount equal to a fraction $\alpha/(\alpha + 1)^2$ of total surplus. One can readily check that the transfer is proportionally larger for wealthier couples, since the ratio $V_H(x + y)/(x + y)$ increases with $(x + y)$ due to the convexity of V_H.

Empirical Application

Lastly, how does this redistribution translate into individual behavior? Here, we need to come back to our ACIU preferences. The first effect—an increase in all households' total income—results in a standard income effect. With well-behaved preferences (i.e., in the absence of inferior goods), the household demand for each public good increases as a function of the income elasticity of household demand for that good. Note that the second effect—the redistribution between spouses—has no impact on the demand for public goods: this could be expected in a TU framework. The same holds for the household's *aggregate* demand for privately consumed commodities: since the household behaves as a single individual maximizing the sum of the spouses' utility, the only consequence is the income effect due to the boost in the household's resources.

Regarding individual consumptions, things are more complex, because the redistribution triggered by the change also impacts the allocation of private consumption within the household. Specifically, since the conditional indirect utility of agent i is

$$v_i (Q, p, \rho_i) = a_i(p, Q) + b(p, Q)\rho_i,$$

we know that an increase dv_i in i's utility must be generated by an increase in i's conditional share $d\rho_i = dv_i/b(p, Q)$. With affine conditional demands for private commodities of the type

$$q_i^k (p, Q, \rho_i) = \alpha_i^k(p, Q) + \beta^k(p, Q)\rho_i,$$

this translates into an increase of the private consumption of commodity k by agent i equal to

$$dq_i^k = \beta^k(p, Q)d\rho_i = \frac{\beta^k(p, Q)}{b(p, Q)}dv_i.$$

In particular, let us for a moment assume, as an illustrative example, that the increase in the wife's income is accompanied by a simultaneous reduction in the husband's income that exactly compensates for it—so that the couple's total income remains unchanged. By the previous argument, the household's aggregate behavior remains unchanged. However, the allocation of private consumption does respond to the change; in practice, all female private consumptions increase, while males' decrease, the sum remaining constant. This can be empirically tested as soon as some private commodities are either exclusive (i.e., consumed exclusively by one spouse) or assignable (i.e., male and female consumptions are independently recorded). In many data sets, for instance, clothing is assignable, since both male and female clothing is observed. On the other hand, leisure is a typical exclusive good; so are, in certain socioeconomic contexts (particularly in some developing countries), smoking, jewels, and others.

Lastly, it is important to note that any variable that changes the spouses' respective powers within the couple, without affecting the couple's total resources, has a similar impact. Such variables are usually known as *distribution factors*.[12] For instance, Chiappori et al. (2015) analyze a legal reform that took place in various Canadian provinces. The reform significantly affected the respective bargaining positions within cohabiting couples by allowing, for the first time, a cohabiting partner to petition for alimony upon separation. A theoretical analysis predicts that such changes in alimony laws should affect existing couples and couples-to-be differently. For existing couples, we are exactly in the situation just described: the reform changes the spouses' respective powers without changing the couple's total resources. One would therefore expect that the reform should benefit the poorer spouse (who gains by being allowed to petition for alimony from the partner); over the period considered, this is generally the wife. For couples not yet formed, things are, however, different. Since the reform affects neither the size of the surplus nor the premarriage income distributions, it should not impact the allocation of *lifetime* utility between spouses. However, it does increase the wife's utility in case of divorce; it must therefore be the case that the wife's utility *while married* is decreased in an exactly compensating way. In practice, under the ACIU assumption, these changes should be visible from the variations they induce in the consumption of exclusive, private goods; in the paper, the authors concentrate on leisure.

The empirical analysis exploits the fact that each province extended these rights in different years and required different cohabitation length, which provides a nice second- or third-difference setting. The empirical results confirm the theoretical predictions. Among cohabiting couples united long enough before the reform, obtaining the right to petition for alimony led women to lower their

---

[12] See Browning, Chiappori, and Weiss (2014) for a precise discussion.

labor force participation. These patterns, however, do not hold—and are actually reversed—for newly formed cohabiting couples.

3.4.3 Exogenous versus Endogenous Sharing Rules: A Simple Example

The Setting

A distinctive characteristic of TU (or ITU) models is the endogenous nature of intrahousehold allocations. As we have just seen, stability imposes strict constraints not only on matching patterns, but also on how the surplus generated by any match can be divided between spouses. In the continuous case, on which we mostly concentrate, the intrahousehold allocation of consumption and welfare is actually pinned down (possibly up to one additive constant) by these conditions. In the family economics literature, however, some contributions borrow a different path, and assume that intracouple distribution is exogenously given—by, for example, tradition, social norms, or equity consideration. The model just described allows us to better understand the consequences of such an exogenous rule.

Let us explore these issues on a simple example. Specifically, let us consider the matching-on-income framework presented in subsection 3.4.2, and let us further simplify it by assuming that there is exactly one public and one private good and that preferences have the Cobb-Douglas form

$$u_i (q_i, Q) = q_i Q.$$

It follows that a household solves (normalizing prices to 1)

$$\max (q_1 + q_2) Q \text{ under } (q_1 + q_2) + Q = x + y.$$

One can readily check that the solution is

$$q_1 + q_2 = Q = \frac{x + y}{2},$$

generating a surplus:

$$S(x, y) = H(x + y) = \frac{(x + y)^2}{4}.$$

Again, H is convex, therefore, $\partial^2 S / \partial x \partial y = H'' (x + y) > 0$, implying assortative matching.

Stable Matching under TU

As argued before, in a TU context, intrahousehold allocation is driven by the stability conditions associated with the matching game; in particular, it depends not only on the surplus function but also on the distribution of characteristics in the two populations. Let us assume here that there are slightly more women than men. Specifically, male income is uniformly distributed on the interval $[1, 2]$ (with a density equal to 1, so that the total mass of men is equal to 1), while female income is uniformly distributed on the interval $[1 - \varepsilon, 2]$ (with a density still equal to 1, implying a total mass equal to $(1 + \varepsilon)$). Note, in particular, that this setting satisfies the linear shift assumption described above. Only women with income larger than 1 are married, and assortative matching implies that individuals marry a partner with the same income. Equations (3.4.3) and (3.4.4) then become

$$\bar{u}_1'(x) = H'(2x) = x; \tag{3.4.13}$$

therefore,

$$\bar{u}_1(x) = \frac{1}{2}x^2 + K$$

and similarly

$$\bar{u}_2(y) = \frac{1}{2}y^2 + K'.$$

Total surplus is, therefore,

$$S(x, x) = \bar{u}_1(x) + \bar{u}_2(x) = H(2x),$$

implying that

$$K' = -K.$$

To pin down the constant K, consider a woman with income just equal to 1. The allocation in her couple must leave her just indifferent between marriage and singlehood; otherwise her husband could marry a single women with income just below 1 and receive a larger share. Her utility when married is therefore exactly what she would get if alone. By herself, her income would be 1; she would spend half of it on each good, generating a utility of $1/4$; therefore,

$$\bar{u}_1(1) = \frac{1}{2} + K = \frac{1}{4}$$

$$\Rightarrow K = -\frac{1}{4} \quad \text{and} \quad K' = \frac{1}{4},$$

so that the distribution of surplus is finally

$$\bar{u}_1(x) = \frac{1}{2}x^2 - \frac{1}{4}, \quad \bar{u}_2(y) = \frac{1}{2}y^2 + \frac{1}{4}. \tag{3.4.14}$$

Stable Matching under NTU

Assume, now, that the intrahousehold allocation is *not* determined by the equilibrium conditions; instead, it is *exogenously* given—say, by tradition or social norms. Assume, for instance, that whatever the context, the wife always gets a proportion k of total private consumption, whereas the husband receives $(1 - k)$. For any choice Q of public expenditures, we thus have

$$q_1 = k(x + y - Q), \quad q_2 = (1 - k)(x + y - Q),$$

so that individual utilities are

$$u_1 = k(x + y - Q)Q, \quad u_2 = (1 - k)(x + y - Q)Q.$$

We also need to describe the choice of the level of public expenditures. The simplest (and arguably most natural) solution is to assume efficiency. In our framework, there is (as before) only one efficient amount, equal to $(x + y)/2$; utilities are therefore

$$u_1(x, y) = k\frac{(x + y)^2}{4}, \quad u_2(x, y) = (1 - k)\frac{(x + y)^2}{4}. \quad (3.4.15)$$

A first and crucial remark, at this point, is that both u_1 and u_2 depend on x *and* y: $u_1(x, y)$ describes the utility that Mrs. x would get if married to Mr. y and sharing resources according to the exogenous rule (the interpretation for u_2 is similar). In other words, we are now in an NTU framework, in which an given match provides each agent with some exogenously given utility.

Second, we see that both u_1 and u_2 are increasing in the sum $x + y$. As we have seen before, under NTU such a monotonicity is sufficient to guarantee assortative matching. In other words, matching patterns will be *the same* as before: only women with an income larger than 1 marry, and their spouse has the same income. This situation is by no means exceptional; it is often the case that matching patterns alone do not allow distinguishing between TU and NTU.

The surplus allocation between spouses, however, is drastically different. It was given by (3.4.14) under TU. In the NTU case, however, since matching is assortative, (3.4.15) implies that the utility reached by Mrs. x is

$$u_1(x, x) = kx^2,$$

while for Mr. y,

$$u_2(y, y) = (1 - k)y^2.$$

We can now analyze how these different allocations impact individual welfare. Start with individual rationality. Can it be the case that, with such an exogenous allocation, some married individuals would be better off as singles? The answer, here, is clear: any k between $1/4$ and $3/4$ is such that no individual rationality constraint is violated.

Stability, however, is a different matter. In fact, for any possible k, there will be violations of stability; specifically, there will be pairs of individuals (actually a lot of them) who are not married to each other, but would be better off divorcing their current partner (if any) and remarrying each other. To see why, assume for a start that the social rule is equalitarian, so that $k = 1/2$. Then men at the bottom of the distribution get a utility around 0.5. However, there exist single women with an income close to 1, and whose utility is currently about 0.25. By marrying one of them, the total surplus would again be around 1, of which he could get, say, 0.625 and she would receive 0.375—for each of them, a gain of 0.125 with respect to the initial situation. Of course, such an agreement would violate the social norm: in the new couple, he would receive more than half the surplus. Note, however, that *both* individuals would be willing to depart from the social norm: for her, receiving slightly less than 0.5 is still much better than being single. In other words, the social norm must be imposed against the unanimous agreement of the spouses.

Of course, an equalitarian social norm may not be credible, particularly in a situation where men have the comparative advantage of being on the short side of the market. A more realistic outcome would be a biased allocation; a natural candidate, in fact, would be an allocation that leaves women at the bottom of the distribution, just indifferent between being single or married (which would discard the deviations just described). This happens for $k = 0.25$. The problem, now, will be with other women, particularly those at the top of the income distribution. A woman with an income equal to 2 is married to a husband with the same income; together, they generate a total surplus of 4, of which she only gets a fourth (i.e., 1). On the other hand, the lowest-income husbands generate, with their spouse, a total surplus of 1, of which they receive 0.75. Should they remarry the dissatisfied high-income women, the total surplus would be 2.25—more than enough to give each of them more than what they currently have; for instance, he could receive 1 and she 1.25, a net gain of 0.25 for each of them. Again, the new allocation violates the social norm (now she gets more than one-fourth of the total); but again, *both* spouses agree with the violation.

Obviously, the result is general. It does not depend on the exogenous rule being linear. In fact, any exogenous rule other than (3.4.14) would lead to the same conclusion, since only (3.4.14) is immune to bilateral deviation of this type (that is exactly the definition of stability in the TU sense). Nor does it rely on the Cobb-Douglas utilities or uniform distributions; the conclusion would be the same (although the computations would be more cumbersome) for any preferences satisfying TU. The message is clear: whenever the exogenously given sharing rule differs from that characterizing stable allocations in the TU context, bilateral deviations will be possible. And even if, in some given context, the exogenous rule happens to coincide with the stable one, this coincidence would not be very robust, since any changes in either preferences or income distributions would destroy it.

Lastly, when the exogenous rule differs from the stable one, should we expect the bilateral deviations just described to materialize into a series of divorces? Probably not. If the social norm is strong enough to be enforced for all couples (including the newly formed ones), then divorce has no point: the remarriages require a deviation from the norm to be beneficial. If, on the other hand, enforcement is lax, so that deviations are actually possible, then Pareto-improving changes do not require divorce to be implemented: couples can internally renegotiate their allocation back to stability (after all, the matching *patterns* are always the efficient ones). The conclusion, therefore, is rather that an exogenously imposed rule, unless it constitutes a good approximation of the stable one, will typically create strong incentives to renegotiate new agreements that are violating the rule. In the end, if the conflict between stability and social norms leads to serious discrepancies between the stable allocation and the actual one, one would expect social norms to face major challenges—precisely because they need in many cases to be imposed against the will of both potential deviators.

To summarize:

- With continuous distributions of characteristics, individual utilities are exactly pinned down by the stability conditions, possibly up to a common, additive constant. The latter is moreover determined when population sizes are different. Also, individual utilities can typically be recovered in closed form from the stability conditions.
- When couples match only on income, one can readily predict the impact of an increase of, say, women's incomes on intrahousehold allocation. In practice, it triggers a redistribution from husband to wife that can be quantified. Under assortative matching, the redistribution is typically larger for wealthier couples.
- Whenever intrahousehold allocations are constrained by exogenous social norms that do not satisfy stability conditions, there exist bilateral deviations that would increase both deviators' well-being.

3.5 Link with Hedonic Models

3.5.1 Hedonic Models

Hedonic models consider competitive spot markets in which sellers produce and buyers acquire "objects" (or "contracts"), which may come in a wide range of qualities.[13] What is peculiar to many competitive hedonic markets, including those for housing, workers, automobiles, pensions, insurance contracts, and many others, is that in the market for these contracts, a large number of buyers and sellers trade fixed quantities (actually, often only one unit) of products whose value (to buyers and/or sellers) depend on quantifiable qualities, or characteristics. These hedonic characteristics are known to the buyers and/or sellers at the time of the transaction and, as a result, are reflected in the equilibrium market price. In these markets, the set of "potential" products—i.e., the set of products that could technologically be produced—is very large (or even infinite), but only a small number will actually be produced at equilibrium. Think, for instance, of an automobile being described by its size, power, design, color, and a number of other features, which different people value differently. In principle, the set of feasible combinations of characteristics is very large; in practice, however, only a (relatively) small number of models will actually be offered. For given buyer and seller preferences, the problem posed by such a market is to decide how supply equilibrates with demand to determine the set of commodities actually produced and consumed (or the set of contracts actually exchanged) on the market, and the price $P(z)$ at which each type of product z is traded. Note that such an equilibrium implicitly defines a pairing or matching of buyers with sellers who choose to enter into this market by agreeing to contract or exchange with each other.

Formally, we now consider three compact, separable metric spaces $\bar{X}, \bar{Y}, \bar{Z}$, which we can think of as being respectively the set of customers, producers, and product characteristics. As before, spaces $\bar{X} \subset \mathbb{R}^n$ and $\bar{Y} \subset \mathbb{R}^m$ are endowed with measures F and G, respectively, representing the distribution of buyer and seller types throughout the population; both $F(X)$, and $G(Y)$ are of finite mass. And again, I allow for the possibility that some agents choose not to participate by augmenting the spaces $X := \bar{X} \cup \{\emptyset_X\}$, $Y := \bar{Y} \cup \{\emptyset_Y\}$, and $Z = \bar{Z} \cup \{\emptyset_Z\}$, where, $\emptyset_X, \emptyset_Y$ and $\emptyset_Z$ can be respectively interpreted as a partner for any unmatched sellers, a partner for any unmatched buyers, and an unproduced commodity; the measures F and G are extended accordingly. Preferences are quasilinear: the utility of buyer x purchasing product z at price $P(z)$ is $U(x, z) - P(z)$, where u is continuous, and the profit of producer y selling product z at price $P(z)$ is $P(z) - C(y, z)$, where $C(y, z)$ is a continuous cost function; to translate the notion of nonparticipation, I use the normalization

$$U(x, \emptyset_Z) = C(y, \emptyset_Z) = P(\emptyset_Z) = 0.$$

As previously, we want to allow for randomization. A hedonic equilibrium will therefore be defined as a measure α over the product set $X \times Y \times Z$ and a price

---

[13] The presentation of this section is directly borrowed from Chiappori, McCann, and Nesheim (2010). © Springer-Verlag 2009. With permission of Springer.

function $P(z)$ such that

- the marginals of α over X and Y coincide with F and G, respectively;
- for (α-almost) all points $(\bar{x}, \bar{y}, \bar{z})$ in the support of α, we have

$$\bar{z} \in \arg\max_{z} U(\bar{x}, z) - P(z) \quad \text{and} \tag{3.5.1}$$

$$\bar{z} \in \arg\max_{z} P(z) - C(\bar{y}, z).$$

In such an equilibrium, each triple (x, y, z) in the support of α represents a mutually agreeable exchange of product z between seller y and buyer x, where z is a combination of characteristics most favored by both seller y and buyer x independently, given market prices P.

3.5.2   *Hedonic Equilibrium and Stable Matching*

The class of hedonic models has attracted much attention in economics. Chiappori, McCann, and Nesheim (2010) have shown that there exists a canonical relationship between hedonic models of the type just described and matching equilibria. A precise proof of this statement can be found in the original article; here I shall just give an intuitive argument supporting this result. Consider the hedonic problem described above, and define the surplus function S by

$$S(x, y) = \sup_{z \in Z} U(x, z) - C(y, z), \tag{3.5.2}$$

which is well defined and continuous, since Z is compact and U and C are continuous. Consider the matching model defined by the spaces X and Y, with the respective measures F and G, and the surplus function S.

First, with any hedonic equilibrium, one can associate a stable matching. Let (α, P) be such an equilibrium, and let μ be the projection of α over $X \times Y$. Also, define the functions u and v by

$$u(x) = \sup_{z \in Z} U(x, z) - P(z) \quad \text{and} \tag{3.5.3}$$

$$v(y) = \sup_{z \in Z} P(z) - C(y, z).$$

Note, first, that

$$u(x) + v(y) \geq S(x, y) \quad \text{for all } (x, y).$$

Indeed, the sup in (3.5.2) is reached for some $\bar{z} \in Z$, but then

$$u(x) \geq U(x, \bar{z}) - P(\bar{z}) \quad \text{and} \quad v(y) \geq P(\bar{z}) - C(y, \bar{z})$$

by definition of u and v; therefore,

$$u(x) + v(y) \geq U(x, \bar{z}) - P(\bar{z}) + P(\bar{z}) - C(y, \bar{z}) = S(x, y).$$

Also, if $\mu(x, y) > 0$, then there exists some $\bar{z} \in Z$ such that $\alpha(x, y, z) > 0$. But this implies that

$$u(x) = U(x, \bar{z}) - P(\bar{z}) \text{ and } v(y) = P(\bar{z}) - C(y, \bar{z});$$

therefore,

$$u(x) + v(y) = U(x, \bar{z}) - P(\bar{z}) + P(\bar{z}) - C(y, \bar{z}) \leq S(x, y)$$

and we conclude that $u(x) + v(y) = S(x, y)$; therefore, (μ, u, v) define a stable matching.

Conversely, assume that (μ, u, v) is a stable matching. To prove that there exists an associated, hedonic equilibrium, we need to define (i) a measure α over the product set $X \times Y \times Z$ and (ii) a price function $P(z)$ for each potential product z. Constructing α from the measure μ of the stable matching is easy. For any given (x, y) in the support of μ—in English, for any buyer and seller who match with positive probability—we only need to decide which product they will trade; but it can only be one that maximizes their joint surplus, i.e., that solves (3.5.2). Finding an equilibrium price schedule is slightly more complex. Note first that for any (x, y, z),

$$u(x) + v(y) \geq S(x, y) \geq U(x, z) - C(y, z).$$

Here, the first inequality is the stability condition, while the second stems from the definition of S. It follows that for any (x, y, z),

$$C(y, z) + v(y) \geq U(x, z) - u(x);$$

therefore,

$$\inf_{y \in Y} \{C(y, z) + v(y)\} \geq \sup_{x \in X} \{U(x, z) - u(x)\} \tag{3.5.4}$$

For any given z, choose a price $P(z)$ such that

$$\inf_{y \in Y} \{C(y, z) + v(y)\} \geq P(z) \geq \sup_{x \in X} \{U(x, z) - u(x)\};$$

then one can easily show that $P(z)$ is an equilibrium hedonic price schedule.

This result has important implications. One is that the existence of a hedonic equilibrium is equivalent to that of a stable matching in a TU matching problem, therefore of a solution to a linear maximization problem. This can be guaranteed under weak assumptions regarding continuity and compactness. Second, the problem of uniqueness can also be addressed in a more direct and often much simpler way. In a one-dimensional setting, the standard Spence-Mirrlees condition (see below) is sufficient (although by no means necessary) to warrant uniqueness; it can be extended to a multidimensional framework, generating the so-called twist conditions described above. Last but not least, both Spence-Mirrlees and the twist generalization also imply purity of the equilibrium. A point stressed by Chiappori, McCann, and Pass (2016) is that, in a hedonic context, purity often has a natural interpretation in terms of the qualitative features of the equilibrium (notably, in terms of "bunching").

How general is the equivalence between hedonic and matching models? The interested reader is referred to Chiappori, McCann, and Pass (2016) for a precise discussion. Let me just make a simple but important remark. In the hedonic model just described, the buyer's utility depends, besides the buyer's characteristics, on the product purchased and the price paid for it; however, it does *not* directly depend on the seller's identity. Of course, at the equilibrium, the buyer will buy from a specific seller; but she would just be indifferent with buying the same product, at the same price, from any other seller. Similarly, the seller's profit depends on his cost, on the quality of the product he sells, and on the price at which he sells it—but not directly on the buyer's identity. This property is crucial for the previous argument to work; without it, equation (3.5.4) would not hold, and consequently the existence of an equilibrium price schedule could not be established.[14]

3.5.3   *Example 1: A Competitive IO Model*

Let us now consider two examples that illustrate the previous concepts. One is "well behaved," in the sense that it satisfies a supermodularity property, resulting in assortative matching; we will see, in particular, how the previous arguments

---

[14] This remark is crucial for understanding how the techniques of matching models can be applied to models of perfect competition under adverse selection; see Chiappori, McCann, and Pass (2015) for a detailed analysis.

allow one to compute the equilibrium price schedule. The second is more complex and illustrates the nature of equilibrium in the absence of supermodularity or submodularity.

Thus in the first example, agents are willing to buy a product (say, a computer) that exists in different qualities. We assume here that the quality is one-dimensional: the set of product qualities ranges from "poor" to "excellent," and agents have to trade off quality with price.[15] Regarding this trade-off, agents have heterogeneous tastes. Specifically, each agent is characterized by some parameter x that represents her taste for quality; her utility is $U(x, z) - P$, where $U(x, z) = xz$ denotes the utility that agent x derives from a product of quality z, and P is the price of the product. In words, x measures the amount this particular agent is willing to pay for an additional "unit" of quality. Let us assume that x is uniformly distributed on $[0, 1]$.

Lastly, products are produced by firms with different productivities; namely, the cost for firm y to produce quality z is

$$C(y, z) = \frac{z^2}{2y},$$

where the productivity parameter y is uniformly distributed on $[1, 2]$. To keep things simple, we assume that each firm can only produce a fixed quantity of computers (which can be normalized to 1). The question, therefore, is: at equilibrium, which agent will buy which product quality, produced by which firm, and at what price?

To characterize the equilibrium, let us simply follow the same path as in the formal analysis described above. First, this hedonic model is equivalent to a matching problem where the surplus function is

$$S(x, y) = \max_z xz - \frac{z^2}{2y}.$$

Here, the maximum is obtained when $z = xy$, leading to

$$S(x, y) = \frac{1}{2}x^2 y.$$

Since S is continuous, the existence of a stable matching, therefore of a hedonic equilibrium, is guaranteed. Moreover, the surplus is supermodular, implying

---

[15] An interesting generalization would allow for multidimensional characteristics (i.e., computers differ in speed, memory size, screen resolution, design, etc.). The same techniques would actually apply; the interested reader is referred to Chiappori, McCann, and Pass (2016).

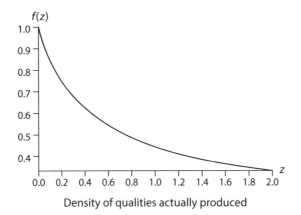

Density of qualities actually produced

Figure 3.4. Density of qualities actually produced.

assortative matching: agents who value quality will buy better products from the more productive firms, which have a comparative advantage producing them. Given the assumptions made on the distributions, this implies that agent x buys from the firm $F(x) = x + 1$; the product, therefore, is $z = xy = x(x + 1)$, implying that the set of qualities actually produced and sold on the market is the interval $[0, 2]$. The density of the corresponding distribution is given by figure 3.4; note, in particular, that more low-quality products are produced than high-quality ones, despite the uniform distribution of x.

Regarding the price schedule, we could just follow the same approach as in subsection 3.5.2. There is, however, an easier way. Let us first compute the utility of agent x and the profit of firm y. As before,

$$u'(x) = \frac{\partial S}{\partial x}(x, F(x)) = x(x + 1);$$

therefore,

$$u(x) = \frac{x^3}{3} + \frac{x^2}{2} + K.$$

Conversely, firm y is matched with agent $G(y) = F^{-1}(y) = y - 1$, and its profit is

$$v(y) = S(G(y), y) - u(G(y))$$
$$= \frac{1}{6}(y - 1)^3 - K.$$

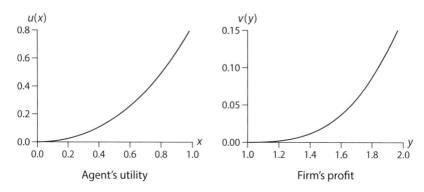

Figure 3.5. An agent's utility and a firm's profit.

As before, utilities and profits are determined up to an additive constant. Here, however, the latter can be pinned down by imposing that the least productive firm (corresponding to $y = 1$) makes zero profit; this gives $K = 0$. We can check that

$$u(x) + v(x+1) = \frac{x^3}{3} + \frac{x^2}{2} + \frac{1}{6}x^3$$
$$= S(x, x+1),$$

so that the agent's utility and the profit of the firm to which she is matched add up to the total surplus they generate. The following figure 3.5 describes an agent's utility and a firm's profit as a function of the relevant characteristic.

Lastly, the hedonic price satisfies

$$u(x) = U(x, z) - P(z)$$

for $z = x(x+1)$. Therefore, product z is purchased by agent

$$x = \frac{1}{2}\sqrt{4z+1} - \frac{1}{2} \tag{3.5.5}$$

and the price is

$$P(z) = U(x, z) - u(x) = xz - \left(\frac{x^3}{3} + \frac{x^2}{2}\right),$$

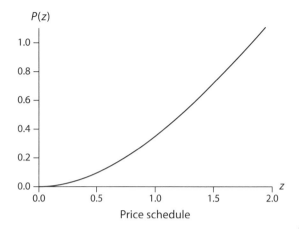

Figure 3.6. The price schedule.

which, using (3.5.5), gives

$$P(z) = \frac{1}{3}z\sqrt{4z+1} + \frac{1}{12}\sqrt{4z+1} - \frac{1}{2}z - \frac{1}{12}$$

This price schedule is plotted below (figure 3.6).

3.5.4   *Example 2: Randomized Matching*

As a second illustration of the relationship between matching and hedonic models, the following simple example is due to Chiappori, McCann, and Nesheim (2010). Consider a circular lake of total perimeter 1, around which are located a large population of students and a large number of schools (or school slots); in practice, we take both distributions (of students and of schools slots) to be continuous and of the same mass—so, potentially, there are exactly enough slots to accommodate all the students. Students (as well as schools) only differ by their location on the lake's shore, respectively indexed by $x \in [0, 1]$ and $y \in [0, 1]$ for the location of student x and of school y. When commuting to their school, students incur a transportation cost that increases with the distance between their and the school's locations; in particular, each student x would, everything equal, prefer to be matched to a school with the same location as hers to minimize transportation expenses. Specifically, we take the commuting cost to be

$$C(x, y) = 1 - \cos(2\pi(x - y)).$$

The cost is maximum (and equal to 2) when $x - y = 1/2$, i.e., when the locations of the student and the school are opposite each other around the lake. Conversely, when $x = y$, the transportation cost is zero—the school is located just next door to the student's home. The same is true, however, for $x - y = 1, 2$ or any integer, because then the student and the school are still at the same location: starting from any point and walking around the full perimeter of the lake (which corresponds to $x - y = 1$) brings you back to your starting point. This is important because, as we shall see, it implies that the surplus can be neither supermodular nor submodular—and in fact cannot satisfy any twist or single crossing condition: the cost and all its derivatives are periodic (that is, $C(x, y) = C(x + 1, y) = C(x, y + 1)$), and no periodic function can be monotonic.

Of course, schooling has a benefit for the student, and we assume this benefit is large enough to compensate for even the largest commuting cost; in practice, let us take it to be 2, so that the total gain of schooling, net of transportation cost, is

$$S(x, y) = 2 - C(x, y) = 1 + \cos(2\pi (x - y)),$$

which is maximum (and equal to 2) when $x = y$, and minimum (and equal to 0) when $x - y = 1/2$.

Lastly, each school y can charge a tuition $t(y)$, which is school-specific (but not student-specific); this tuition is endogenously determined at the equilibrium. When deciding which school to attend, students consider both its location (which defines the transportation cost) and the tuition. We assume that the school's profit Π equals the revenue (i.e., the tuition $t(y)$) minus some fixed cost K common to all schools:

$$\Pi = t(y) - K.$$

Let us, for the sake of notational simplicity, normalize K to be zero. Students' utilities are quasi-linear in the tuition:

$$u = S(x, y) - t(y).$$

Note that agents have identical preferences regarding tuitions—they all want to pay less—but heterogeneous preferences regarding location: each student likes schools located close to her.

We can now consider three equivalent problems.

- The first problem is that of a social planner who wants to allocate students to schools. Given our assumptions (identical students, identical schools), the only criterion the planner considers is total transportation cost over the population, which must be minimized. This is a standard, genuine optimal transportation problem; note that it does not involve tuition at all, at least explicitly.

- Alternatively, consider the same situation from a decentralized perspective. Students are looking for schools; schools are looking for students. At the end, each student will be attending a school (or none). When could such a situation *fail* to be stable? First, if a student ends up in a school so expensive she would rather not go to school at all (taking into account the commuting costs); indeed, she would just quit. Second, if a school is losing money on a student (say, because the tuition does not cover the fixed cost); then it would just decline to accept the student. Third, if a student would prefer attending a school other than the one where she is currently registered (say, because it is closer), and the school is willing to accept her, then she would leave the initial school and move to the better one. Whenever none of these three situations takes place, the allocation of students to schools (technically, the *match*) is stable—according to the technical definition of stability given above. Indeed, what we have here is a matching model in which the two sets X and Y are respectively the sets of students and schools, each endowed with the distribution of locations around the lake; and the pairwise surplus from matching student x to school y is $S(x, y)$. It is, moreover, a TU problem. Transfers are possible (they correspond to the tuitions charged by the schools), and the TU property directly stems from the quasi-linearity of student preferences: if student x is matched with school y, then whatever the tuition $t(y)$, the sum of the school's profit and the student's utility is always $S(x, y)$:

$$\Pi + u = t(y) + S(x, y) - t(y) = S(x, y)$$

- Lastly, we can also see the problem as a hedonic model. Here, the "product" (the education provided by a given school) is fully defined by the school's location y; technically, producer y can only produce the product $z = y$. Then the tuition charged by school y is just the hedonic price of product $z = y$. The question, therefore, is whether there exists a system of tuitions $t(z)$ such that a market equilibrium is reached—the equilibrium being defined in the (usual) sense that for each school, the number of students applying to that school equals the number of slots available (the standard market-clearing condition).

We see, in this simple example, that the situation can be seen as belonging to either the optimal transportation, the matching, or the hedonic family; these are equivalent representations of the same formal structure. In particular, note that while the first formulation—in terms of optimal transportation—does not explicitly involve tuitions, they are implicitly present; they are dual variables of the optimal transportation problem, reflecting the scarcity constraints of the various schools.

Formally, let $X_0 = Y_0 = \mathbf{S}^1$ be the circle of length 1, and

$$S(x, y) = 1 + \cos(2\pi(x - y)).$$

Note that $S(x, y) \geq 0$, so that participation is complete: all students will go to school. As mentioned earlier, the model is neither supermodular nor submodular; indeed,

$$\frac{\partial S}{\partial x} = -2\pi \sin(2\pi x - 2\pi y),$$

which is not monotonic in y.

Now, what does the solution—the optimal transportation plan, the stable matching, or the hedonic equilibrium—look like? Well, the answer depends on the initial distributions of students and schools—technically, the measures on the spaces X and Y. Start with the simplest case in which $F = G$, meaning students and schools have the same distribution on the circle; in practice, at any location there are as many students as slots. Then the solution to the optimal transportation is obvious: just send each student to the school at her location, which leads to a total transportation cost of . . . zero (hard to beat!). For the matching formulation, the measure corresponding to the stable matching has its support on the graph of the function $y = x$ (which, in plain english, means that each agent is matched with probability 1 to the school next door). Remember, though, that a solution also involves two utility functions $u(x)$ and $v(y)$, representing the allocation of surplus between students and schools. It is easy to see that for any pair $(\bar{u}, \bar{v})$ of nonnegative constants such that $\bar{u} + \bar{v} = 2$, $u(x) = \bar{u}$, and $v(y) = \bar{v}$ works; note, in particular, that all schools are equally well-off, implying that they all charge the same tuition. Lastly, the hedonic price schedule is very simple. Take any $\bar{t}$ between 0 and 2; then each school charging a tuition $t(y) = \bar{t}$ is an equilibrium. Note that, in this case, the measure corresponding to the stable matching is unique and pure, despite the fact that the surplus function is neither supermodular nor submodular. However, the price schedule (or equivalently the individual utilities and profits) are determined only up to a common constant; this is a standard outcome because we assumed there were exactly as many students as slots.

However, the model becomes much more interesting when the densities associated with F and G are different. Assume, for instance, that the distribution of students is concentrated around $x = \frac{1}{4}$, while the distribution of schools is concentrated around $y = \frac{3}{4}$; that is, most of the students live on the north side of the lake while most of the schools are located on the south side. In this case, the optimal matching is still unique; but it is very different from the previous case. Indeed, it is

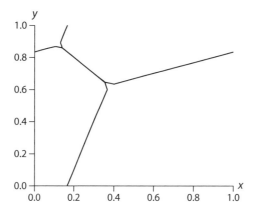

Figure 3.7. Stable matching in the school example.

impossible to match all students to a school near their residence. The support of the unique optimal measure is shown in figure 3.7, where students' locations are on the horizontal axis and schools on the vertical one.[16] All students $x \in \left[0, \frac{1}{8}\right] \cup \left[\frac{3}{8}, 1\right]$ (i.e., all students located where schools are plentiful) are matched to a single school near to their home. For example, $x = 0.1$ is matched to $y = 0.867$, located on the other side of the origin at a distance of 0.233. But students $x \in \left(\frac{1}{8}, \frac{3}{8}\right)$ can be matched to either of two schools, one nearby (at a distance less than or equal to $\frac{1}{4}$) and one farther away (at a distance greater than $\frac{1}{4}$). In equilibrium, these students are indifferent between the two locations, because the difference in tuitions exactly compensates for the variations in transportation costs. The payoff functions u and v of the students and schools can also be computed. The students and schools that are in scarce supply, $x = \frac{3}{4}$ and $y = \frac{1}{4}$, obtain the highest surplus; those who are abundant, $x = \frac{1}{4}$ and $y = \frac{3}{4}$, obtain the lowest.

In this example, the stable matching is not pure; the optimal measure assigns a fraction of each of the abundant students to two possible school locations, one at a distance less than $\frac{1}{4}$, the other farther away. The intuition goes as follows. Because there is such a large number of students near $x = \frac{1}{4}$ and schools near $y = \frac{3}{4}$, not all students near $x = \frac{1}{4}$ can find a place in a school nearby; there is a social benefit from having some students travel a great distance. However, the corresponding cost is compensated for by a lower tuition. The equilibrium is such that schools located near $\frac{1}{4}$, where they are scarce, charge a higher price to their students, whereas in the neighborhood of $\frac{3}{4}$, schools are abundant and cannot charge high fees—but most students must accept high transportation costs to attend them.

---

[16] The reader is referred to Chiappori, McCann, and Nesheim (2010) for technical details.

Lastly, it should be noted that this equilibrium, although it is not pure, is unique. Chiappori, McCann, and Nesheim (2010) provide conditions that are sufficient for uniqueness even in the absence of purity.

To summarize:

- There exists a canonical relationship between hedonic and matching models. In particular, a large family of hedonic models are equivalent to a matching problem under TU.
- Existence and generic uniqueness results follow; moreover, matching techniques allow one to derive the equilibrium price schedule.
- However, this equivalence requires that sellers (resp. buyers) do not directly care about the identity of the buyer (seller).

4

Matching by Categories

4.1   Accounting for Unobservable Heterogeneity

In this section, I describe a specific but empirically very relevant family of models. The main motivation is to provide a richer representation of heterogeneity between individuals that would account not only for such economic aspects as income or education, but also for more subjective (and less easily observable) ones, such as idiosyncratic preferences for marriage in general and for specific types of spouses in particular.

Start with the simple model that describes matching on income or education, as described in subsection 3.4.2. The predictions are quite crude. Given supermodularity of the surplus, we expect strict assortative matching—the wealthiest man marries the wealthiest woman, the second wealthiest man marries the second wealthiest woman, and so on; moreover, we expect all individuals on one side of the market to be married. None of these expectations fit actual data. While we do see assortative matching—for instance, a positive correlation between the husband's and wife's education—it never takes the systematic form just described. Similarly, the probability of singlehood decreases with income, but remains positive at all income levels.

A natural explanation for these discrepancies is that in real life, individuals match on several characteristics; while economic determinants such as income or education do play a significant role, they are by no means exclusive. Moreover, several (and probably most) of these other dimensions—whether they involve tastes, physical attractiveness, or others—are unobserved by the empirical economist. Still, they cannot be neglected, lest one is doomed to the simplistic marital patterns generated by the one-dimensional model.

The problem, however, is to allow for such a rich environment while keeping the model tractable. A standard strategy in microeconomics is to analyze the type of unobserved heterogeneity we have in mind as random individual shocks that can be dealt with through a stochastic framework. For instance, we may think of adding, to the surplus generated by any pair of agents, a stochastic component representing all the other aspects that are relevant for the agents but not observed by us. The very nature of matching models, however, generates specific difficulties with this approach, particularly as we are not only interested in matching patterns (who marries whom) but also in the resulting allocation of the surplus (i.e., in individual payoffs). Indeed, payoffs are, from a mathematical viewpoint, dual variables of the surplus maximization problem. How a given, stochastic structure introduced in the primal problem (the surplus function) would affect dual variables is an extremely difficult problem, about which little is known as of now.

4.1.1   The Separability Assumption

There is, however, one case in which this problem can be solved; this case has been analyzed by Dagsvik (2000), Choo and Siow (2006), Chiappori, Salanié, and Weiss (2017), and others. Let us first introduce some structure. We consider a large number of agents belonging to a small number K of categories. One may think, for instance, of levels of education (from high school dropout to graduate schools), or age, or income classes, or any other trait. These categories are the main reason we are interested in the problem to start with; for instance, we want to understand matching patterns by income or education, as in the motivating puzzles discussed at the beginning of the book. Still, we want to account for the fact that individuals in the same category may have different tastes (or other unobservable characteristics), and that this unobserved heterogeneity explains some observed patterns (for instance, the fact that, although educated women typically marry educated men, we do still observe couples with very different educational attainments—although not many).

As argued above, a standard tool for introducing unobserved heterogeneity is to model it as a random shock. Therefore, take a given woman i, belonging to category I, and a given man j, belonging to category J. We shall assume that the surplus they generate is the sum of a deterministic component $z(I, J)$ that only depends on their categories, and a stochastic term $\varepsilon_{i,j}$ that is pair-specific:

$$S(i, j) = z(I, J) + \varepsilon_{i,j}, \tag{4.1.1}$$

and similarly for singles:

$$S(i, \emptyset) = z(I, \emptyset) + \varepsilon_{i\emptyset} \quad \text{and} \quad S(\emptyset, j) = z(\emptyset, J) + \varepsilon_{\emptyset j},$$

where, as before, both $z(I, \emptyset)$ and $z(\emptyset, J)$ can be normalized to zero, and where $\varepsilon_{i\emptyset}$ and $\varepsilon_{\emptyset j}$ respectively represent i's and j's idiosyncratic preferences for singlehood.

The crucial assumption is the following:

Assumption (Separability) *The random term $\varepsilon_{i,j}$ is of the form*

$$\varepsilon_{i,j} = \alpha_i^J + \beta_j^I, \tag{4.1.2}$$

where the random variables α_i^J, $i \in I$, $J = 1, ..., K$ and β_j^I, $j \in J$, $I = 1, ..., K$ are independent.

The random term $\varepsilon_{i,j}$ is thus additively separable into two terms, α_i^J and β_j^I. The former is woman-specific but only depends on the husband's category; the latter is man-specific but only depends on the wife's category. It may be, for instance, that each woman has idiosyncratic preferences on her husband's education (and conversely): even among high school graduates, some individuals may put more emphasis than others on their spouse having a college degree. But that is by no means the only possible interpretation. Remember, indeed, that the αs and βs contribute to the total surplus, not to any particular preference. Therefore, a large α_i^J may alternatively reflect the fact that Mrs. i has some specific quality that is particularly valued by husbands from category J (say, she is a very good classical pianist, a trait that men with a graduate degree value most).

4.1.2 How Can Separability Be Justified?

The separability assumption is restrictive indeed: essentially, it requires that a given woman i only cares about her spouse's category, not about the particular individual she marries within this category. Still, it can be justified by three arguments. One is parsimony. We all know that, when it comes to real-life mating, noneconomic aspects (tastes, cultural background, common interests, physical attractiveness, and many others) play a significant role. But these are traits that, at least in most data sets, we do not observe. Moreover, little is known regarding their practical implications for matching. For instance, a crucial issue for any matching framework is whether the husband's and wife's corresponding surplus is supermodular or submodular (equivalently, whether male and female traits are substitutes or complements). In plain English: while every woman (presumably) prefers a good-looking man, is the importance of the partner's physical appearance stronger for beautiful women? On this, we are largely ignorant (beyond casual empiricism and anecdotal evidence). And it is typically the type of question an economist should be reluctant to consider: data are scarce,[1] theory of no help, and at the end of the day we are not that much interested in the answer (particularly if our main purpose is to understand matching by education). In such a context, parsimony considerations strongly suggest that we concentrate on the questions of interest—say, matching by education—and neglect side issues such as the exact identity (or the specific unobserved characteristics) of the chosen spouse. This is exactly what separability allows us to do. Note, in particular, that separability

---

[1] However, Chiappori, Oreffice, and Quintana-Domeque (2012), using BMI as an indicator of physical attractiveness, do not reject the null that it is perceived identically by all partners. In the same vein, Dupuy and Galichon (2014), using a detailed Dutch data set that includes data on a large number of characteristics, including physical appearance and personality traits, find empirical evidence that personality traits significantly affect matching, although the specific patterns differ across genders.

implies that the marginal contribution to the surplus of the unobserved trait α_i of Mrs. i does not depend on the unobservable trait of her partner (although, crucially, it does depend on the partner's category). In other words, separability assumes away submodularity or supermodularity in unobservable characteristics.

A second and more technical justification deals with the covariance structure that should be postulated on the pair-specific shocks ε_{ij}, should they be introduced. Independence, which might sound like a natural solution, is actually quite bad. For one thing, if the αs and the βs really capture some unobserved but important trait such as physical attractiveness, it is difficult to believe that the corresponding effect would not be correlated among potential mates. More importantly, a matching model based on the surplus in (4.1.1) with independent shocks will predict very strange matching patterns when population sizes become large, an issue that is analyzed in detail by Chiappori, Nguyen, and Salanié (2015). The key intuition, here, is that what matters for i's choice of a mate is the *largest* realization of the ε_{ij} when j varies—i.e., $\varepsilon_i^M = \max_j \varepsilon_{ij}$. Now, if the support of ε is bounded, then, for a large enough male population, this max is basically equal to the upper bound for most women (and conversely), so that randomness all but disappears. Alternatively, the support may be unbounded (as is the case in most empirical applications, which routinely assume extreme value distributions). But then this max goes to infinity and becomes the dominant factor, with unwelcome consequences. Expected utilities go to infinity, implying that the economic factors we are interested in (which only have a finite impact) become essentially irrelevant. Regarding matching patterns, there would be basically no singles, because $\varepsilon_{i\emptyset}$ is just one of the numerous draws of the ε_{ij}s, and the probability that it happens to be above (one half of) the largest draw becomes very small when the latter goes to infinity. On the other hand, assuming a specific covariance structure would be too demanding, especially in the context of this simplified model: there is basically no hope that such a structure could be identified from matching patterns.[2]

Lastly, the separability assumption should be seen in the broad context of a frictionless matching model. As discussed above, the absence of frictions greatly

---

[2] Chiappori, Nguyen, and Salanié (2015) investigate a more general version of (4.1.2); specifically, they consider the form

$$\varepsilon_{i,j} = \sqrt{1 - \frac{\sigma^2}{2} \left(\alpha_i^J + \beta_j^I \right)} + \sigma \eta_{ij}, \tag{4.1.3}$$

where $\sigma \in [0, \sqrt{2}]$ and the α_i^J, β_j^I and η_{ij} are independent type 1 extreme value. For $\sigma = 0$, this boils down to the separable form (4.1.2), while for $\sigma = \sqrt{2}$, one gets independent, pair-specific shocks only. In particular, they estimate data generated by (4.1.3) using the (in that case misspecified) form (4.1.2) for average-size samples (i.e., a few hundred individuals). They find that the resulting bias in the estimation of the deterministic part is small and often negligible for reasonably low values of σ.

simplifies the analysis; it also allows us to concentrate on some basic stylized patterns without needing ad hoc assumptions on the nature of frictions, the search technology, or others. Still, its realism depends on how it is used. In the logic of matching by categories, the absence of frictions essentially means that any man, including high school dropouts, may be able to *meet* a college graduate woman. Whether these women would be interested in matching is another issue altogether: it may well be the case that for most college graduate women, male high school dropouts are of little appeal. Such a situation is fully compatible with our setting: it simply means that the distribution of $\alpha_i^{J_0}$, if J_0 denotes the category "high school dropout," has a very negative mean, at least when i belongs to the "graduate" category. Then the number of unbalanced couples will probably be very low, but this is due to preferences, not frictions—and we remain within the logic of our model. What a frictionless setting would be incompatible with is a situation where, on the marriage markets, the various categories are so strictly isolated from each other that matching across categories would be impossible to even consider. Such situations did certainly exist in some places and times (think of race in the US during the first half of the twentieth century, or in South Africa under the apartheid regime); but insofar as we are not in an extreme context of that type, neglecting frictions may well be acceptable.

The story is quite different, however, if we allow for pair-specific preferences; then assuming away frictions amounts to postulating that any man may be able to meet *all* women—and that he will select the one in several millions with whom the "fit," as summarized by the ε_{ij}, is the highest. With large populations, this assumption becomes increasingly hard to swallow; and, not surprisingly, it tends to generate the kind of pathological matching patterns described above. A possible conclusion is that, if one is really willing to introduce pair-specific shocks, then a search model, in which frictions are explicitly allowed and modeled, may be a better choice. Then again, in most cases there is no compelling argument for introducing such shocks.

4.1.3 Dual Structure under Separability

We now state the main result of this section.

Proposition 1 (Choo and Siow 2006; Chiappori, Salanié, and Weiss 2017)
Assume the surplus has the form (4.1.1), where the εs satisfy the separability property (4.1.2). Then there exists $2 \times K^2$ numbers, U^{IJ} and V^{IJ}, $i, J = 1, ..., K$, such that

- *For all I, J,*

$$U^{IJ} + V^{IJ} = z(I, J).$$ (4.1.4)

- *If $i \in I$ is married to $j \in J$ at the stable matching, then the payoffs are:*

$$u_i = U^{IJ} + \alpha_i^J \quad and \quad v_j = V^{IJ} + \beta_j^I.$$

In other words, the payoff of Mrs. i is the sum of two components: a deterministic effect U^{IJ}, which only depends on the categories of i and i's spouse, and the stochastic, i-specific term α_i^J. In particular, we have exactly characterized the stochastic structure of the dual variables of the surplus maximization program: it is precisely that of the stochastic terms in the separable structure, up to a shift in mean. Also, Proposition 1 also applies to singles under the normalization $U^{I\emptyset} = V^{\emptyset J} = 0$ for all I, J; then $u_i = \alpha_i^{\emptyset}$ and $v_j = \beta_j^{\emptyset}$.

A precise proof of Proposition 1 is in Chiappori, Salanié, and Weiss (2017). Here, we just provide the economic intuition for that result. The basic insight is that i receives her entire specific contribution α_i^J to the surplus—she does not share it with her spouse. This is the natural outcome of competition between husbands. Should j require even a small fraction of α_i^J, another man j' from J would be willing to undercut j and accept an even smaller fraction; and remember that, from i's perspective, all men from J are perfect substitutes, so she would not mind matching with j' instead of j. The same argument, of course, is valid for men. So if α_i^J reflects i's physical attractiveness, which is equally valued by all men in J, she will receive the full price of it; and if α_i^J represents i's intrinsic pleasure of marrying a spouse in J, she will be entitled to the full amount of this pleasure.

From an empirical perspective, Proposition 1 has a very important consequence: the matching problem can be decomposed into a series of individual maximization problems, as stated by the following result:

Corollary 2 *Under the assumptions of Proposition 1, individual i is matched with a spouse in J if and only if*

$$U^{IJ} + \alpha_i^J \geq U^{IL} + \alpha_i^L \quad for\ L = \emptyset, 1, ..., K \qquad (4.1.5)$$

and i remains single if and only if

$$\alpha_i^{\emptyset} \geq U^{IL} + \alpha_i^L \quad for\ L = 1, ..., K, \qquad (4.1.6)$$

A similar conclusion holds for men.

In other words, u_i can be seen as the price i will receive on the matching market. It consists of a deterministic component that only depends on the categories of i and i's spouse and on i's idiosyncratic contribution α_i. And i's choice can simply be modeled as selecting the spousal category for which the corresponding sum is highest (remember that under separability, i only cares about her spouse's category, not his precise identity). This turns out to be extremely useful for empirical applications, because it allows us to directly transpose the whole machinery of discrete choice models to the (a priori more complex since two-sided) matching problem.

As we shall see below, the thresholds U^{IL} and V^{LJ} can be econometrically identified from a discrete choice model of marital patterns for each male and female category (remember that $U^{I\emptyset}$ and $V^{\emptyset J}$ have been normalized to zero). For instance, an educated woman will choose to remain single if condition (4.1.6) holds. Importantly, this choice depends on the values V^{IJ}, which are endogenous and therefore reflect the situation on the marriage market: in such a model, any change in either the deterministic component of the surplus or the distribution of male and female by category will change the matching patterns of *everyone*. Last but not least, once we have estimated the thresholds U^{IJ} and V^{IJ}, we can compute their sum $z(I, J)$, which is just the deterministic component of the surplus generated by the matching of a woman from category I with a man from category J. In particular, we can evaluate the respective importance of economic and noneconomic factors (as respectively summarized by the deterministic and stochastic components).

4.1.4 A Comparative Static Result

The structure just described is much more flexible than the basic model of deterministic matching on income and education; it allows a richer set of behavioral patterns, including idiosyncratic preferences for singlehood or nonassortative matching. Still, it retains the main properties of the bare-bone, deterministic framework. In particular, the notion of assortative matching, which has so far been developed in a purely deterministic context, has an interesting implication for the stochastic model, which has been put forth by Graham (2011). Take any two categories K and L and consider the subsample of couples in which both spouses belong to either of these categories. We have therefore four possible types of match, two of which are assortative (in the sense that both the wife and the husband belong to the same category, either K or L) while the other two are not.

Now, let λ^K (resp. μ^K) denote the proportion of women (resp. men) in the subsample who belong to category K (so that the remaining $1 - \lambda^K$ and $1 - \mu^K$ belong to L). Under random matching, the proportion of couples for each of the four categories (KK, KL, LK, and LL) would respectively be equal to $\lambda^K \mu^K$, $\lambda^K(1 - \mu^K)$, $(1 - \lambda^K)\mu^K$, and $(1 - \lambda^K)(1 - \mu^K)$. We shall take these values as a benchmark and compare them with the actual proportions of the various couples in the subsample—which we denote $\sigma_{KK}, \sigma_{KL}, \sigma_{LK},$ and σ_{LL}. Then we have the following result:

Proposition 3 *(Graham 2011) Assume the surplus has the form (4.1.1), where the εs satisfy the separability property (4.1.2) and the αs and βs are independent and identically distributed. Then at the stable matching, the subsample exhibits assortative matching patterns, in the sense that*

$$\sigma_{KK} + \sigma_{LL} \geq \lambda^K \mu^K + (1 - \lambda^K)(1 - \mu^K) \tag{4.1.7}$$

if and only if the deterministic component is supermodular:

$$z(K, K) + z(L, L) \geq z(K, L) + z(L, K). \tag{4.1.8}$$

Proof See Graham (2011). ∎

Some comments are in order. Start with condition (4.1.7). The expression on the left-hand side represents the fraction of the subsample located "on the diagonal," i.e. couples who are matched assortatively; on the right-hand side, we have what this proportion would be if matching was random. The assortative matching pattern, here, is simply that more couples are assortatively matched (and less nonassortatively) than one would expect under random matching. Condition (4.1.8), on the other hand, is the standard, supermodularity assumption, expressed for the deterministic component. In a pure, deterministic setting, such a condition would imply perfect assortative matching in the usual sense. In particular, one (at least) of the two "off-diagonal" cells would be empty.[3] Because of the unobserved heterogeneity component, all cells are typically nonempty: some women in L will marry a husband in K because their draw of α_i^K (and the husband's draw of β_j^L) are particularly high. Then assortative matching has a more realistic empirical translation: many individuals are married with their own—the exact meaning of "many" being defined vis-à-vis the benchmark of random matching. Note that this property—which is immediately testable—holds irrespective of the exact distribution of the random shocks.

Actually, we can prove a slightly more general property. Consider *two* models, both of the form (4.1.1):

$$S(i, j) = z(I, J) + \alpha_i^J + \beta_j^I \text{ and}$$
$$\tilde{S}(i, j) = \tilde{z}(I, J) + \tilde{\alpha}_i^J + \tilde{\beta}_j^I$$

---

[3] If the respective proportion of individuals belonging to category K were identical across genders, supermodularity would imply, in a deterministic model, that all men in K marry a woman in K. With different proportions (say, more women than men in K and the opposite in L), some women belonging to K would marry men in L; but the opposite could not happen.

Assume that the marginal distributions are the same in the two models, and that the random terms α_i^J and $\tilde{\alpha}_i^J$ (resp. β_j^I and $\tilde{\beta}_j^I$) are drawn from the *same* stochastic distribution for all I, J; the only difference between the two models, therefore, must lie in the deterministic components z and $\tilde{z}$.

Next, take as before any two categories K and L and consider the subsample of couples in which both spouses belong to either of these categories. Assume that the deterministic component of the second model is *less supermodular* than that of the second, in the sense that

$$z(K, K) + z(L, L) - z(K, L) - z(L, K)$$
$$\geq \tilde{z}(K, K) + \tilde{z}(L, L) - \tilde{z}(K, L) - \tilde{z}(L, K).$$

Then, at the stable matching, the first model is more assortative (over these two categories) than the second, in the sense that

$$\sigma_{KK} + \sigma_{LL} \geq \tilde{\sigma}_{KK} + \tilde{\sigma}_{LL}$$

In words: for the two categories K and L, if the first deterministic component is more supermodular than the second, then there will be more couples on the diagonal (i.e., matched assortatively) in the first model than in the second; equivalently, more individuals are married with their own in the first population than in the second. Again, this property is immediately testable and holds irrespective of the exact distribution of the random shocks. It can be shown that it generalizes Graham, in the sense that if the second model is such that, for any I, J, K, L,

$$\tilde{z}(I, K) + \tilde{z}(J, L) - \tilde{z}(I, L) - \tilde{z}(J, K) = 0,$$

then the corresponding stable matching is precisely the random matching.

To summarize:

- Introducing a random component in the surplus function (reflecting, for instance, unobserved characteristics) generates a difficult, stochastic optimal tranportation problem of which not much is known in general. However, under a separability condition initially introduced by Dagsvik (2000) and Choo and Siow (2006), the stochastic structure of the dual variables (i.e., the distributions of individual utilities) can be fully characterized.
- In particular, under the separability conditions, the matching problem can be reduced to a series of individual, discrete choice models of a standard nature, which greatly facilitates empirical applications.
- In such a separable, stochastic setting, supermodularity of the deterministic component of the surplus function has a simple translation; namely, more couples are observed to match assortatively than would be expected under random matching.

4.2   The Choo-Siow Model

4.2.1   The Basic Structure

We now investigate more precisely the econometric structure induced by the separability assumption. First, note that condition (4.1.5) can also be written as

$$\alpha_i^J - \alpha_i^L \geq U^{IL} - U^{IJ} \quad \text{for } L = \emptyset, 1, ..., K \tag{4.2.1}$$

Assume, following Dagsvik (2000) and Choo and Siow (2006), that the distribution of the αs and βs is type 1 extreme value; in particular, the α_i^J and β_j^I have mean zero and variance $\frac{\pi^2}{6}$. Then we have a standard logistic model; in particular, for any I and any $i \in I$:

$$\gamma^{IJ} \equiv \Pr(i \text{ matched with a woman in } J)$$

$$= \frac{\exp(U^{IJ})}{\sum_H \exp(U^{IH}) + 1} \tag{4.2.2}$$

and

$$\gamma^{I0} \equiv \Pr(i \text{ single}) = \frac{1}{\sum_H \exp(U^{IH}) + 1}, \tag{4.2.3}$$

where, as before, U^{I0} has been normalized to 0. Similarly, for any J and any woman $j \in J$:

$$\delta^{IJ} \equiv P(j \text{ matched with a man in } I)$$

$$= \frac{\exp(V^{IJ})}{\sum_H \exp(V^{HJ}) + 1} \quad \text{and} \tag{4.2.4}$$

$$\delta^{0J} \equiv P(j \text{ single}) = \frac{1}{\sum_H \exp(V^{HJ}) + 1}, \tag{4.2.5}$$

with the normalization $V^{0J} = 0$.

These formulas can be inverted to give

$$\exp(U^{IJ}) = \frac{\gamma^{IJ}}{1 - \sum_H \gamma^{IH}} \tag{4.2.6}$$

and

$$\exp(V^{IJ}) = \frac{\delta^{IJ}}{1 - \sum \delta^{HJ}};$$ (4.2.7)

therefore,

$$U^{IJ} = \ln\left(\frac{\gamma^{IJ}}{1 - \sum_H \gamma^{IH}}\right)$$ (4.2.8)

$$V^{IJ} = \ln\left(\frac{\delta^{IJ}}{1 - \sum \delta^{HJ}}\right),$$ (4.2.9)

where we assume that there are singles in each class ($\gamma_{I0} > 0$ and $\delta_{0J} > 0$ for each I, J, implying that $\sum_H \gamma^{IH} < 1$ and $\sum_H \delta^{HJ} < 1$ for all I, J). Note that a direct consequence of these results is that it is possible, from the sole observation of marital patterns, to exactly identify the utilities U^{IJ} and V^{IJ} for all (I, J).

Finally, we can readily compute the class-specific expected utilities described above:

$$\tilde{u}^I = E\left[\max_J(U^{IJ} + \tilde{\alpha}_i^{IJ})\right].$$

In words, $\tilde{u}^I$ is the expected utility of an agent in class I, given that this agent will chose a spouse in his preferred class. From the properties of Gumbel distributions, we have

$$\tilde{u}^I = E\left[\max_J(U^{IJ} + \alpha_i^J)\right]$$

$$= \ln\left(\sum_J \exp(U^{IJ}) + 1\right) = -\ln(\gamma^{I0}).$$ (4.2.10)

and similarly

$$\tilde{v}^J = \ln\left(\sum_I \exp(V^{IJ}) + 1\right) = -\ln(\delta^{0J}).$$ (4.2.11)

Again, these expected values can be directly computed from the data. In many applications, they play a key role because they provide an empirical estimate of the payoff received on the marriage market from having a given level of education. In particular, for any two levels I and $I' > I$, the difference $\tilde{u}^I - \tilde{u}^{I'}$ is the *marital premium* resulting from an investment in education from level I to level I'; this premium, as we shall see, may play a key role in individual decisions to invest in human capital.

4.2.2   The Matching Function

A related concept, which is often used by demographers, is that of a *matching function*. Think of the model as a black box in which the inputs would be the marginal distributions of the male and female populations—i.e., in our case, the number of individuals in each category. What a matching function does is generate from these inputs a matching matrix, which gives the proportion of couples in each possible pair (husband's category, wife's category) plus the number of male and female singles in each category. Formally, if m^I (resp. n^J) denotes the number of women (men) in category I (J), then a matching function is any set of formulas that determines the γ^{IJ} and δ^{IJ} from the vectors $(m^I, I = 1, ..., K)$ and $(n^J, J = 1, ..., K)$.

It should be clear, from the previous discussion, that any well-specified matching models generate a specific matching function, which typically depends on a few structural parameters; in turn, these parameters may in general be estimated from observed matching patterns (more on this below). For instance, in the Choo-Siow model, the relevant parameters are the $z(I, J)$ for $I, J = 1, ..., K$; indeed, for a given value of these parameters, one can compute the stable match (or equivalently the surplus-maximizing measure), therefore the various matching probabilities. Conversely, however, several matching functions that are commonly used in the literature (particularly in sociology or demography) are not explicitly based on a matching model. For instance, the following matching function has been widely used (often under slightly generalized versions) :

$$\ln \gamma^{IJ} = a \ln m^I + b \ln n^J + c, \qquad (4.2.12)$$

where a, b, and c are structural parameters. The main advantage of this function is its simplicity; in particular, estimating the parameters can be done by simple regressions. However, whether it can be derived from an explicit model of matching is dubious. A first problem is that a structural model would generate patterns that satisfy a basic property—namely, that the probabilities add up to one:

$$\sum_{J=1}^{K} \gamma^{IJ} + \gamma^{I0} = 1 \quad \text{for all } I, \quad \text{and} \quad \sum_{I=1}^{K} \delta^{IJ} + \delta^{0J} = 1 \quad \text{for all } J.$$

For the form (4.2.12), however, no restriction on the structural parameters can guarantee that adding up will obtain for all distributions m and n.

Secondly, (4.2.12) excludes the existence of "spillovers": since γ^{IJ} only depends on m^I and n^J, changes in the numbers of males and females in *other* categories cannot affect the proportion of (I, J) marriages. In a matching model, on the contrary, spillover effects are paramount: increasing the proportion of men in any category $L \neq J$ changes the global nature of the matching game, and all resulting probabilities are impacted. We will describe later on the specific aspects that these spillover effects take in the Choo-Siow model. For the time being, let us simply keep in mind that a matching game is, by nature, global, and that a "reduced-form" matching function that has not been derived from a structural model may fail to capture these global interactions in a consistent way.

4.2.3   Heteroskedasticity: A Short Discussion

An important property of the model just presented is homoskedasticity: the variance of the unobserved heterogeneity parameters is the same for all education classes.[4] This can be an extremely strong assumption, particularly because it severely restricts the respective importance of the observed and unobserved components in the matching framework (as summarized by the ratio of the unobserved variance to the total variance). We may want to extend the framework to allow this crucial parameter to vary freely between education classes. Such an extension would be especially welcome in a model in which agents' investment in human capital is endogenously determined as part of the equilibrium (a case that will be discussed in section 5.1). Indeed, human capital investment typically depends, among other things, on the agents' marital preferences—agents who want to marry "up" are more likely to invest. It follows that even if the distribution of preferences ex ante (i.e., before the agent chooses an education level) is iid, the conditional distribution given the chosen level of education will depend on this level, because of the selection operated on these preferences.

Luckily, the previous framework can readily be extended to allow for heterogeneity. First, allowing for different means can readily be done. Assume for instance that

$$\alpha_i^J = a_I^J + \tilde{\alpha}_i^J \quad \text{and} \quad \beta_j^I = b_J^I + \tilde{\beta}_j^I,$$

where $\tilde{\alpha}_i^J$ and $\tilde{\beta}_j^I$ are standard, type 1 extreme value with zero mean. Here, the mean a_I^J of α_i^J is class-specific (hence the subindex I), reflecting the fact that the mean of the conditional distribution depends on the education level. Then (4.1.1)

---

[4] This subsection is directly borrowed from Chiappori, Salanié, and Weiss (2012).

and (4.1.2) become

$$S(i, j) = z(I, J) + a_I^J + \tilde{\alpha}_i^I + b_j^I + \tilde{\beta}_j^I$$
$$= \tilde{z}(I, J) + \tilde{\alpha}_i^J + \tilde{\beta}_j^I,$$

where $\tilde{z}(I, J) = z(I, J) + a_I^J + b_j^I$; and the model applies up to a reinterpretation of the deterministic component z, which now also encompasses class-specific preference means.

The case of heteroskedasticity is slightly more complex. Assume that the random terms α and β are such that

$$\alpha_i^{IJ} = \sigma^I \tilde{\alpha}_i^{IJ}$$
$$\beta_i^{IJ} = \mu^J \tilde{\beta}_i^{IJ},$$

where the $\tilde{\alpha}_i^{IJ}$ and $\tilde{\beta}_j^{IJ}$ follow independent Gumbel distributions. Then the previous computations can be generalized as follows. For any I and any $i \in I$, we now have

$$\gamma^{IJ} = \frac{\exp(U^{IJ}/\sigma^I)}{\sum_H \exp(U^{IH}/\sigma^I) + 1}, \quad \gamma^{I0} = \frac{1}{\sum_H \exp(U^{IH}/\sigma^I) + 1}$$

and similarly, for any J and any woman $j \in J$,

$$\delta^{IJ} = \frac{\exp(V^{IJ}/\mu^J)}{\sum_H \exp(V^{HJ}/\mu^J) + 1}, \quad \delta^{0J} = \frac{1}{\sum_H \exp(V^{HJ}/\mu^J) + 1}. \tag{4.2.13}$$

As above, these formulas can be inverted to give

$$\exp(U^{IJ}/\sigma^I) = \frac{\gamma^{IJ}}{1 - \sum_H \gamma^{IH}}; \tag{4.2.14}$$

and

$$\exp(V^{IJ}/\mu^J) = \frac{\delta^{IJ}}{1 - \sum \delta^{HJ}}; \tag{4.2.15}$$

therefore,

$$U^{IJ} = \sigma^I \ln \left(\frac{\gamma^{IJ}}{1 - \sum_H \gamma^{IH}} \right)$$

$$V^{IJ} = \mu^J \ln \left(\frac{\delta^{IJ}}{1 - \sum \delta^{HJ}} \right)$$

and the class-specific expected utilities become

$$\bar{u}^I = E \left[\max_J (U^{IJ} + \sigma^I \tilde{\alpha}_i^{IJ}) \right] = -\sigma^I \ln (\gamma^{I0}) \text{ and}$$

$$\bar{v}^J = -\mu^J \ln (\delta^{0J})$$

In words, $\bar{u}^I$ is the expected utility of an agent in class I, given that this agent will chose a spouse in his preferred class. From the properties of Gumbel distributions, we have

$$\bar{u}^I = \sigma^I E \left[\max_J (U^{IJ}/\sigma^I + \tilde{\alpha}_i^{IJ}) \right]$$

$$= \sigma^I \ln \left(\sum_J \exp (U^{IJ}/\sigma^I) + 1 \right) \tag{4.2.16}$$

and similarly

$$\bar{v}^J = \mu^J \ln \left(\sum_I \exp (V^{IJ}/\mu^J) + 1 \right). \tag{4.2.17}$$

Heteroskedasticity has several implications. First, the expected utility of an arbitrary agent in class I, as given by (4.2.10), is directly proportional to the standard deviation of the random shock. Indeed, remember that the agent chooses the class of his spouses so as to maximize his utility; and the expectation of the maximum increases with the variance. It follows that the utility generated by the access to the marriage market cannot be exclusively measured by the probability of remaining single (reflected in the $-\ln (\gamma^{I0})$ term).

This remark, in turn, has important consequences for measuring the marital college premium. To see that, start from a model in which the random component of the marital gain is homoskedastically distributed (i.e., the variance is the same across categories: $\sigma^I = \mu^J = 1$ for all I, J). The marital college premium is measured by the difference $\bar{u}^I - \bar{u}^K$, where I is the college education class

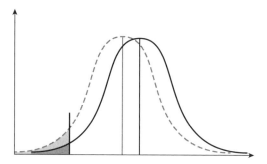

Figure 4.1. Homoskedastic.

whereas K is the high school graduate one. Condition (4.2.10) then implies that

$$\bar{u}^I - \bar{u}^K = \ln\left(\frac{\gamma^{K0}}{\gamma^{I0}}\right).$$

In words, the gain can directly be measured by the (log) ratio of singlehood probabilities in the two classes. The intuition is that people marry if and only if their (idiosyncratic) gain is larger than some threshold. If these random gains are homoskedastically distributed, then there is a one-to-one correspondence between the mean of the distribution for a particular class and the percentage of that class that is below the threshold and remains single: the higher the mean, the smaller the proportion (see figure 4.1, where the blue distribution has both a higher mean and a smaller proportion below the threshold). For instance, if we see that college graduates are more likely to remain single than high school graduates ($\gamma^{I0} > \gamma^{K0}$, implying that $\ln(\gamma^{K0}/\gamma^{I0}) < 0$), we would then conclude that the expected marital gain is smaller for college graduates ($\bar{u}^I < \bar{u}^K$), and therefore that the marital college premium is negative.

Consider, now, the heteroskedastic version. Things are different here, because the percentage of singles depends on both the mean and the variance. If educated women are more likely to remain single, it may be because the gain is on average smaller, but it may also be that the variance is larger (even with a higher mean), as illustrated in Figure 4.2. The one-to-one relationship no longer holds and a higher percentage does not necessarily imply a smaller mean; here, for instance, the blue distribution still has a smaller proportion below the threshold, but its mean is smaller—and so is its variance. One has to compute the respective variances—which, in turn, may affect the computation of the marital college premium. Specifically, we now have

$$\bar{u}^I - \bar{u}^K = \sigma^K \ln(\gamma^{K0}) - \sigma^I \ln(\gamma^{I0}). \qquad (4.2.18)$$

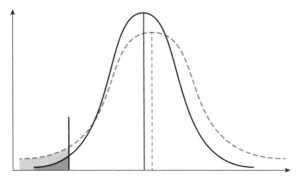

Figure 4.2. Homoskedastic.

If $\gamma^{I0} > \gamma^{K0}$ and $\sigma^I \leq \sigma^K$, one can conclude that $\bar{u}^I - \bar{u}^K < 0$; but whenever $\sigma^I > \sigma^K$, the conclusion is not granted and depends on the precise estimates.

Generally, education influences marital prospects through four different channels: it increases marriage probabilities, it changes the potential "quality" (here education) of the future spouses, and it affects both the size of surplus and its allocation within the household. In the special homoskedastic version of the model, these four channels are intrinsically mixed, and the expected utility of each spouse is fully determined by the percentage of persons in the same education class that remains single. The heteroskedastic version is much richer; welfare impacts go beyond the sole probability of marriage, and involve other considerations. Consequently, the conclusions drawn from the model significantly depend on the assumptions made regarding its homoskedasticity properties. It is therefore important that these assumptions be testable rather than ad hoc—i.e., that homoskedasticity be imposed by the data (or at least compatible with them) rather than assumed a priori. In that sense, the estimation of the variances is a crucial part of the identification process.[5]

4.2.4 Covariates

The basic framework just described can be extended to the presence of covariates; i.e., we may specify the α's and β's as functions of observed individual

---

[5] Note, however, from equations (4.2.10) and (4.2.11) that if the variances are assumed to be constant across time, then the *variations* in singlehood probability must still reflect similar changes in the expected gains from marriage. In other words, if we find that the percentage of, say, unskilled women remaining single has increased between two cohorts c and c', we can unambiguously conclude that the gains from marriage have diminished for these women over the period.

characteristics (other than their class). Let X_i be a vector of such characteristics of man i, and Y_j of woman j. We may use the following stochastic structure (where, for simplicity, we disregard heteroskedasticity):

$$\alpha_i^{IJ} = X_i.\zeta_m^{IJ} + \tilde{\alpha}_i^{IJ}$$

$$\alpha_i^{I0} = X_i.\zeta_m^{I0} + \tilde{\alpha}_i^{I0}$$

$$\beta_j^{IJ} = Y_j.\zeta_f^{IJ} + \tilde{\beta}_j^{IJ}$$

$$\beta_j^{0J} = Y_j.\zeta_f^{0J} + \tilde{\beta}_j^{0J},$$

where $\zeta_m^{IJ}, \zeta_f^{IJ}$ are vector parameters, with the normalization $U^{I0} = \zeta_m^{I0} = 0$ and $V^{0J} = \zeta_f^{0J} = 0$, and where, as above, the $\tilde{\alpha}_i^{IJ}$ (resp. $\tilde{\beta}_j^{IJ}$) follow independent, type 1 extreme value distributions $G(-k, 1)$. Then the computations are as above, and we can estimate for $i \in I$:

$$\gamma^{IJ} = \Pr(i \text{ matched with a woman in } J)$$

$$= \frac{\exp(U^{IJ} + X_i.\zeta_m^{IJ})}{\sum_H \exp(U^{IH} + X_i.\zeta_m^{IH}) + \exp(X_i.\zeta_m^{I0})}$$

$$\gamma^{I0} = \Pr(i \text{ single}) = \frac{\exp(X_i.\zeta_m^{I0})}{\sum_H \exp(U^{IH} + X_i.\zeta_m^{IH}) + \exp(X_i.\zeta_m^{I0})}$$

and the conclusions follow. In particular, these models can be estimated running standard (multinomial) logits.

4.2.5   Comparative Statics in the Choo-Siow Model

Basic Properties

In a sense, the Choo-Siow framework is the simplest version of a matching model under TU that allows for unobserved heterogeneity. Still, it is quite complex—and this complexity simply reflects the richness of optimal transportation models. To illustrate this point, let me consider a very special case in which agents belong to only two classes—say E (for educated) and N (for noneducated). Let us consider a female and a male population of respective mass m and n; let m^E and $m^N = m - m^E$ denote the number of educated and noneducated women, and define n^E and $n^N = n - n^E$ similarly for men. The surplus generated by matching woman i

in class I with man j in class J is, as above,

$$S(i, j) = z(I, J) + \alpha_i^J + \beta_j^I,$$

where the αs and βs are type 1 extreme value random variables. In other words:

- The matching model is fully defined by its fundamentals, i.e., the parameters m_E, m_N, n_E, n_N and $z(N, N), z(N, E), z(E, N), z(E, E)$.
- The solution (i.e., the stable matching) will consist of probabilities γ^{IJ} and δ^{IJ}, where $I, J \in \{\emptyset, E, N\}$; remember that γ^{IJ} is the probability that a woman in class I either marries a man in class J (if $J = N, E$) or remains single (if $J = \emptyset$), and similarly for the δs; these probabilities, in turn, can directly be derived from the numbers U^{IJ} and V^{IJ} through equations (4.2.2), (4.2.3) and (4.2.4), (4.2.5).

What the Choo-Siow model does, in practice, is to provide a system of equations allowing one to compute γs and δs from the fundamentals. A recent paper by Decker et al. (2011) analyzes these equations from an algebraic perspective and provides interesting comparative statics results. Rewrite equations (4.2.2), (4.2.3) and (4.2.4), (4.2.5) as

$$\gamma^{IJ} = \exp(U^{IJ})\gamma^{I0} \quad \text{and} \quad \delta^{IJ} = \exp(V^{IJ})\delta^{0J}. \tag{4.2.19}$$

Now, let m^{IJ} denote the total *number* of couples, where the woman is in class I and the man is in class J. This number can be computed in two ways: it equals the number of women in I multiplied by the probability that a woman in I marries a man in J, but also the number of men in J times the probability that a man in J marries a woman in I. Formally:

$$m^{IJ} = m^I \gamma^{IJ} = n^J \delta^{IJ}.$$

Moreover, the number of single women with education I is simply

$$m^{I0} = m^I \gamma^{I0},$$

and by the same token,

$$m^{0J} = n^J \delta^{0J}.$$

In the end, we have

$$m^{IJ} = \exp{(U^{IJ})}m^{I0} = \exp{(V^{IJ})}m^{0J}$$
$$= \exp{\left(\frac{U^{IJ} + V^{IJ}}{2}\right)}\sqrt{m^{I0}m^{0J}}$$
$$= \exp{\left(\frac{z(I,J)}{2}\right)}\sqrt{m^{I0}m^{0J}}$$

since $U^{IJ} + V^{IJ} = z(I,J)$ by (4.1.4). Defining $\Pi^{IJ} = \exp{(\frac{z(I,J)}{2})}$, we get

$$\frac{m^{IJ}}{\sqrt{m^{I0}m^{0J}}} = \Pi^{IJ}, \quad I = N, E \quad \text{and} \quad J = N, E. \tag{4.2.20}$$

These conditions provide four equations. Moreover, we must have

$$m^{I0} + m^{IN} + m^{IE} = m^I, \quad I = N, E \text{ and} \tag{4.2.21}$$
$$m^{0J} + m^{NJ} + m^{EJ} = n^J, \quad J = N, E;$$

hence four additional equations for a total of eight unknowns—namely, the m^{I0}, m^{0J} and m^{IJ} for $I = N, E$ and $J = N, E$.

Decker et al. (2011) remark that one can reduce it to a system of four quadratic equations in four unknowns. Indeed, define $\upsilon^I = \sqrt{m^{I0}}$ and $\tau^J = \sqrt{m^{0J}}$ for $I = N, E$ and $J = N, E$. Then

$$m^{IJ} = \upsilon^I \tau^J \Pi^{IJ}$$

and (4.2.21) becomes

$$(\upsilon^I)^2 + \upsilon^I \tau^N \Pi^{IN} + \upsilon^I \tau^E \Pi^{IE} = m^I, \quad I = N, E \quad \text{and} \tag{4.2.22}$$
$$(\tau^J)^2 + \upsilon^N \tau^J \Pi^{NJ} + \upsilon^E \tau^J \Pi^{EJ} = n^J, \quad J = N, E$$

They then show that for all nonnegative sets of fundamentals $(m^I, n^J, \Pi^{IJ};$ $I = N, E$ and $J = N, E)$, these equations have exactly one nonnegative solution—confirming the generic uniqueness result that I mentioned earlier. More interesting is the comparative statics. They prove that the following matrix is symmetric and positive:

$$D = \begin{pmatrix} \frac{1}{(\upsilon)^2}D_m(\upsilon)^2 & \frac{1}{(\tau)^2}D_m(\tau)^2 \\ \frac{1}{(\upsilon)^2}D_n(\upsilon)^2 & \frac{1}{(\tau)^2}D_n(\tau)^2 \end{pmatrix},$$

where $\frac{1}{(v)^2} D_m (v)^2$ is the submatrix

$$\frac{1}{(v)^2} D_m (v)^2 = \begin{pmatrix} \frac{1}{(v^N)^2} D_{m_N} \left(v^N\right)^2 & \frac{1}{(v^E)^2} D_{m_N} \left(v^E\right)^2 \\ \frac{1}{(v^N)^2} D_{m_E} \left(v^N\right)^2 & \frac{1}{(v^E)^2} D_{m_E} \left(v^E\right)^2 \end{pmatrix}$$

and the other submatrices are defined in the same way. Moreover, the terms in the off-diagonal submatrices $\frac{1}{(v)^2} D_n (v)^2$ and $\frac{1}{(\tau)^2} D_m (\tau)^2$ are negative. In words: if we increase the supply of, say, educated women, this attracts more men into marriage but reduces the number of women who wish to marry; some educated women who would have chosen marriage before the increase prefer to remain single after the shock. The mechanism operates through transfers: increased competition among women leads to larger equilibrium transfers to their male spouses, which reduces the gain from marriage for women but increases it for men.

Spillover Effects and the Choo-Siow Matching Function

A related point is that while the Choo-Siow model implies the presence of spillover effects, as previously discussed, their nature is strongly restricted by the form adopted. For instance, a consequence of (4.2.20) is that for any female category I:

$$\frac{m^{IN}}{m^{IE}} = \frac{\Pi^{IN}}{\Pi^{IE}} \sqrt{\frac{m^{0N}}{m^{0E}}}. \tag{4.2.23}$$

Remember that the Πs are structural parameters that do not depend on the distribution of the male and female populations. Now, assume that these populations are affected by some exogenous shock—say, a large influx of uneducated immigrants. Typically, the shock will affect differentially the distribution of singles among educated and uneducated males, i.e., the ratio m^{0N}/m^{0E}. In turn, this change will affect *all* marital patterns, particularly all ratios m^{IN}/m^{IE}; these are simply the expected spillover effects. But (4.2.23) implies a very specific impact: all such ratios should be multiplied by the same number. That is, if the ratio m^{0N}/m^{0E} doubles, then the proportion m^{EN}/m^{EE}—the ratio of *educated* women marrying uneducated versus educated men—is multiplied by a factor $\sqrt{2} = 1.41$, and the ratio m^{NN}/m^{NE} (i.e., the same ratio for *uneducated* women) increases by exactly the same proportion. These strong restrictions are imposed by the structure of the model.

Finally, these computations are directly related to the previous discussion on matching functions. What is the exact form of the matching function resulting from the Choo-Siow model? Well, it is quite complex: even in our simple 2×2 setting, the relationship between the marginal distributions m, n and the marital matrix require the resolution of a set of nonlinear equations. However, it is important to note the following property. Equation (4.2.20) can be written as

$$\ln m^{IJ} = \frac{1}{2} \ln m^{I0} + \frac{1}{2} \ln m^{0J} + c^{IJ}. \tag{4.2.24}$$

This is not exactly a matching function, because the right-hand-side variables m^{I0} and m^{0J} are not the total number of individuals in each category, but instead the number of singles; in particular, these variables are *endogenous* and depend on the total population distribution in a complex way. Still, from an empirical perspective, and provided that the endogeneity issue is taken into account adequately, this form seems quite tractable, if only because all variables are directly observed.

A recent contribution by Mourifié and Siow (2014) introduces an interesting extension of this form. In their model, the surplus generated by marriage is affected by "peer effects"; in practice, it depends on the proportion of couples with the same structure in the population. For instance, the choice between marriage and cohabitation may be influenced by social norms and stigmas; the larger the number of cohabiting couples, the smaller the stigma attached to cohabitation and the less costly it is for any couple to adopt this particular form of relationship. This extension leads to a direct generalization of (4.2.24), of the form

$$\ln m^{IJ} = a \ln m^{I0} + b \ln m^{0J} + \frac{z(I, J)}{2}. \tag{4.2.25}$$

Mourifié and Siow refer to this form as the "Cobb-Douglas matching function." The Choo and Siow model corresponds to $a = b = 1/2$; Mourifié and Siow show that the heteroskedastic form introduced by Chiappori, Salanié, and Weiss (see subsection 4.2.3) is compatible with any nonnegative (a, b) such that $a + b = 1$. In contrast, peer effects typically result in $a + b > 1$—a property commonly referred to as *increasing returns to scale* in the matching function.

4.2.6   Testability and Identifiability of the Choo-Siow Model

From an empirical perspective, a model like the one we just described raises two questions. One is testability: are there empirically falsifiable restrictions that stem from the model and can therefore be used to assess its empirical relevance? The second relates to identification: is it possible, from available data, to recover the underlying, structural determinant of the patterns under consideration?

Let me start with two remarks. First, we must be precise about what is meant by "available data": what are the empirical patterns that can be used to test the theory and identify the underlying, structural components? It is safe to assume we can observe matching patterns—i.e., who marries whom. In some cases, however, additional information is available, leading to stronger results; I will come back to this question later on. Second, note that the Choo-Siow model already contains very strong empirical assumptions. The stochastic term is supposed to enter the surplus additively, as in (4.1.1); it is assumed separable; and the stochastic distribution of each term is taken to be exactly known as a homoskedastic type 1 extreme value (which does not depend on any unknown parameter). In a standard, econometric sense, the model is highly parametric.

The Choo-Siow Model Is Exactly Identified

The first conclusion, now, is that the Choo-Siow model, even under its simplest (and most constrained) form, is exactly identified. To see why, remember that the model boils down to a series of logistic regressions defined by equations (4.1.5) and (4.1.6). Thus, in practice and assuming, for instance, that the various categories are education levels, we have one logistic regression by gender and education level; for instance, we consider the subpopulation of high school dropout males and run a multilogit on the education of their partners—and then repeat the process for other levels, as well as for women. Now, the multilogit regression for women with education I exactly identifies the parameters U^{IJ} for all J (with the normalization $U^{I\emptyset} = 0$). Similarly, multilogit regressions for males gives the V^{IJ} for all I, J; in turn, the deterministic components obtain from

$$U^{IJ} + V^{IJ} = z(I, J). \tag{4.2.26}$$

The key remark, here, is that no overidentifying restrictions are generated; whatever the marital patterns we observe, we can run these regressions and ultimately compute the $z(I, J)$ (that is what is meant by "exactly identified").

This exact identifiability result is problematic for two reasons. First, even in its highly parametric version, the Choo-Siow model is not testable. *Any* observed empirical pattern is compatible with the theory for (exactly one) well-chosen set of values of the structural parameters $z(I, J)$. In particular, the model, in its simplest form, predicts exactly nothing about the type of matching patterns that should emerge; equivalently, there is no hope to assess the validity of the model by checking how well it fits the data, since the fit will always be perfect by construction. One can say, in reference to Karl Popper, that the model does not "take risks" with reality, since it is not falsifiable—a major sin in epistemology. An additional concern is that the robustness of the identification is doubtful, precisely because of the exact identification result.

Second, exact identification of the homoskedastic version implies that any (slightly) more general version of the model would be underidentified. In particular, there is no hope of estimating a heteroskedastic version. Now, homoskedasticity is a standard assumption in any logit model, precisely because it is not possible from a discrete choice to estimate the variance of the random component—one can always rescale all other coefficients to normalize the variance to be one. However, what we have here is a *series* of logit regressions, and we are imposing the variance of the random component to be the same *across* them (i.e., for men and women and for all categories). It may well be the case, in reality, that the respective importances of the deterministic and stochastic components vary with gender and education levels (e.g., the unobserved characteristics that are summarized by the random terms are crucially important for uneducated people but of little or no importance for highly educated ones). But the basic version of the Choo-Siow model is simply unable to detect such variations, since there always exists an alternative, homoskedastic structural version that fits the data equally well (i.e., perfectly).

Distributional Assumptions

Can this situation be improved? Note that the problem is *not* with the distributional assumption (i.e., the type 1 extreme value). The latter can be relaxed (see next subsection); but, clearly, any alternative model will have to assume that the random distributions are exactly known, and even then will be exactly identified. I have already mentioned that, in some deep sense, matching models are not identified from the sole observation of matching patterns. No surprise, then, that any attempt at identifying them must involve strong and nontestable restrictions.

Independent Information

A first solution, therefore, is to use additional information to estimate the model. Assume for a moment that the deterministic components of the surplus (the $z(I, J)$ in the equations above) could be observed independently. This would introduce much more structure into the identification process; one way of thinking of it is that while we would still be faced with a series of logistic regressions, conditions (4.2.26) would impose additional (overidentifying) restrictions *across* regressions. Now, is there any hope of independently recovering the surplus? Surprisingly enough, the answer is yes: we just need to observe enough about the individuals' behavior after marriage. Remember that in a TU framework, the surplus is derived from the sum of individual utilities, which couples maximize under a budget constraint. Now, if we observe household behavior (say, consumption and labor supply), we can, by standard consumer theory, recover the maximand, i.e., the surplus. This path is followed by Chiappori, Costa Dias, and Meghir (2017), who consider a multistage model of household behavior. A careful econometric analysis of labor supply behavior after marriage allows one to recover the surplus as a function of the spouses' human capital; then the matching process is analyzed using both matching patterns and surplus estimates.

In the same spirit, there are cases in which transfers between parties are observable. This is typically the case for hedonic models, since prices are observed in general. The literature on nonparametric identification of hedonic models exploits these ideas; the interested reader is referred to Ekeland, Heckman, and Nesheim (2004) and Heckman, Matzkin, and Nesheim (2010), as well as the survey by Chiappori and Salanié (2016).

The Multimarket Framework

Alternatively, one can borrow a standard method from the literature on Industrial Organization and consider a "multimarket" framework. Assume, thus, that one can observe different marriage markets, each characterized by specific distributions of education by gender. Assume, moreover, that the deterministic components (the $z(I, J)$s) are the same in these markets. Then the model becomes highly testable: while matching patterns on each market exactly identify the corresponding deterministic component, there is no reason to expect that these estimates will coincide across markets.

The most interesting aspect of this approach is that it provides structural foundations to notions that are intuitively appealing but hard to formally define. Consider, for instance, the question raised by the first introductory example (see chapter 1) regarding the increase in assortative matching: should the observed evolutions be seen as mechanical consequences of the surge in the number of educated women, or is there also a change in preferences for assortativeness? The model offers an operative translation of these notions, as demonstrated in a recent paper by Chiappori, Salanié, and Weiss (2017, from now on CSW). They consider a multimarket model in which the various markets correspond to different cohorts of the same population (in their case the US); that is, for any cohort t individuals are assumed to enter a matching game defined by the distributions of male and female education at date t and some matching framework à la Choo-Siow defined by a deterministic component $\{z_t(I, J), I, J = 1, ..., M\}$ and stochastic "taste" shocks $\alpha_{i,t}^J$ and $\beta_{j,t}^I$. Assuming that the distributions of tastes does not change over the period, observed changes in matching patterns are due to either changes in the distributions of education or changes in the deterministic components $z_t(I, J)$—and in general to both.

Next, they consider the so-called *supermodular core* of the deterministic components $z(I, J)$; this is defined as the matrix of differences:

$$D_t^{IJKL} = z_t(I, J) + z_t(K, L) - z_t(I, L) - z_t(K, J)$$

for all $I < K$ and $J < L$. Remember that the deterministic component is supermodular (resp. submodular) if and only if all these differences are positive (negative). Now, we can say that *preferences for assortative matching remain constant over a given period if and only if the supermodular core* (i.e., each of the

D_t^{IJKL}) *does not change over the period.* One can readily see that, equivalently, constant preferences for assortative matching implies that the deterministic component $z_t(I, J)$ follows the dynamics

$$z_t(I, J) = z_0(I, J) + \xi_t(I) + \zeta_t(J),$$

where $\xi_t(I)$ and $\zeta_t(J)$ are a category-specific time trend that affect the value of the deterministic surplus, but not its supermodularity. The key point is that, by the results in subsection 4.1.4, if the marginal distributions were kept constant, this dynamic would result in matching patterns the assortativeness of which do not change over time; conversely, therefore, any change in matching patterns under this dynamic would reflect the mechanical effects of changes in marginal distributions. In other words, what we have here is a structural way to disentangle the respective effects of changes in distributions on the one hand, and changes in preferences for assortativeness on the other hand.

Two last remarks about this approach. First, the multimarket Choo-Siow model, *jointly with the assumption of constant preferences for assortative matching,* is highly testable; intuitively, the initial Choo-Siow model enables one to compute the supermodular core for each period, and we are requiring that the latter does not change over time. CSW perform that test for the US over three decades and find that the joint model is strongly rejected for the white population, although not for African Americans. Second, one can slightly relax the assumption by introducing a linear trend in the supermodular core—i.e., by considering a dynamic of the type

$$z_t(I, J) = z_0(I, J) + \xi_t(I) + \zeta_t(J) + \delta^{IJ} t.$$

This model is still vastly overidentified, and one can in addition compute the sign of changes in preferences for assortativeness. CSW find a strong increase in preferences for assortativeness at the top of the distribution (i.e., for individuals with some college and above), but no significant change at the bottom.

4.2.7   Extension: Galichon and Salanié's Cupid Framework

As I said before, one way to go beyond the original model of Choo and Siow (2006) is a relaxation of the distributional assumptions. The framework of Galichon and Salanié (forthcoming) shows how such models can be analyzed and estimated, provided that the data is rich enough and/or enough identifying assumptions are imposed to recover the primitives of the model.

Here is an intuitive presentation of their framework.[6] Start from a model satisfying assumptions (4.1.1) and (4.1.2); the surplus generated by the matching

---

[6] The reader is referred to Galichon (2015) and Galichon and Salanié (forthcoming) for a more detailed presentation.

of $i \in I$ and $j \in J$ is thus

$$S(i, j) = z(I, J) + \alpha_i^J + \beta_j^I, \qquad (4.2.27)$$

and by Proposition 1, individual (realized) utilities are

$$u_i = U^{IJ} + \alpha_i^J \quad \text{and} \quad v_j = V^{IJ} + \beta_j^I,$$

so that the expected payoff of a woman with education I (resp. a man with education J) is

$$\bar{u}_I = E\left[\max_{J=\emptyset,1,\dots,K} (U^{IJ} + \alpha_i^J)\right] \quad \text{and} \quad \bar{v}_J = E\left[\max_{I=\emptyset,1,\dots,K} (V^{IJ} + \beta_j^I)\right].$$

Now, define

$$G_I(U^{I\emptyset}, \dots, U^{IK}) = E\left[\max_{J=\emptyset,1,\dots,K} (U^{IJ} + \alpha_i^J)\right].$$

Note that G_I, being the max of a family of linear functions, is convex. Also, by the envelope theorem,

$$\frac{\partial G_I}{\partial U^{IJ}} = \Pr(U^{IJ} + \alpha_i^J \geq U^{IL} + \alpha_i^L, L = \emptyset, 1, \dots, K).$$

The right-hand side probability is simply the probability that a woman in I is matched with a man in J:

$$\frac{\partial G_I}{\partial U^{IJ}} = \gamma^{IJ}.$$

Consider, now, the *conjugate* or *Legendre-Fenchel transform* of G_I:

$$G_I^*(\gamma^0, \dots, \gamma^L) = \max_{U^0, \dots, U^K} \left(\sum \gamma^L U^L - G_I(U^0, \dots, U^K)\right).$$

By the same token as before, G_I^* is convex and

$$\frac{\partial G_I^*}{\partial \gamma^J} = U^{IJ}. \qquad (4.2.28)$$

This implies that, *if the distribution of the αs and the βs is known*—so that the functions G and G^* can be computed—then the U^{IJ} can readily be recovered from the γ^{IJ}. If we take the distributions of α and β to be type 1 extreme value then the previous computations boil down to (4.2.8) and (4.2.9), just as in the

Choo-Siow model. But formula (4.2.28) is fully general and does not require the distribution to be type 1 extreme value. $G^*\left(\gamma^I\right)$ is called the *generalized entropy* of the corresponding discrete choice problem; it is interpreted as the expected amount of heterogeneity needed to rationalize the choice probabilities of an agent of type I.

To summarize:

- If, to the separable stochastic structure previously described, we add the assumption that distribution of the stochastic terms is type 1 extreme value, we can recover a closed-form relationship between the dual variables U^{IJ}, V^{IJ} and the observed matching probabilities. This is the basic Choo-Siow model, which can be extended in different directions: covariates, heteroskedasticity, and different distributions.
- The basic version of the Choo-Siow model is exactly identified. In particular, if we only observe matching patterns on a single marriage market, the model is not testable and the heteroskedastic generalization would be underidentified.
- Two solutions can be considered for the nontestability issues; one can either use richer data—exploiting, for instance, the fact that household behavior provides independent information about the surplus—or consider a multimarket context.
- In addition, when considering the evolution of the matching patterns in a given population where the marginal distributions are changing over time, the separable framework allows one to formally disentangle the mechanical effects of the marginal changes from possible variations in the structure and, more precisely, in the supermodularity of its deterministic components (the supermodular core)—the latter being interpreted as changes in preferences for assortative matching.

5

Matching under Transferable Utility: Some Extensions

5.1   Preinvestment

5.1.1   The Issue

So far, I have implicitly considered the traits on which agents match as exogenously given. In many cases, however, this assumption is not appropriate. Take human capital: agents deliberately invest in education, and the stock of human capital that characterizes them when entering the marriage market is therefore (at least partly) endogenous. More importantly, it is safe to assume that agents, when deciding their investment, take into account, among other things, its impact on the marriage market. Nineteenth century novels are full of women acquiring an education without any intention of ever entering the labor market—their primary motivation being enhancing their attractiveness on the marriage market and the social life that will follow.

From an economist's perspective, therefore, the joint dynamics of matching and human capital investment is quite complex. The outcomes of the matching process depend on the human capital accumulated by agents; but the accumulation process itself depends on the (expected) returns to education, including those perceived on the marriage market. In other words, what we have is a rational expectations (RE) equilibrium, in which (1) agents have expectations regarding the distribution of education by gender that will prevail on the marriage market, (2) they infer the return on education that will result, and (3) they invest accordingly. The RE equilibrium conditions simply require that the gender distribution of education that results from this process is consistent with the one initially anticipated. Needless to say, we are not assuming that all agents explicitly go through this mental process; simply, they behave as if they did, in the sense that their (aggregate) expectations are not inconsistent with their (aggregate) behavior.

This setting, in turn, raises a host of issues. One is existence. Technically, we have a two-stage game, in which agents first decide on their education, then match based on their previous decisions. A key aspect is that the first stage decisions are made in a *noncooperative* way: agents each decide independently, without coordinating with their future mate (whom they often don't know at the time of the decision). In particular, the relevant equilibrium concept is noncooperative Nash. In principle, this two-stage games might fail to have an equilibrium. Uniqueness is another concern. As we have seen before, matching games under TU generically have a unique stable match. But this simply means that, for each set of first-stage strategies, the second stage equilibrium can be expected to be unique (obviously under some conditions). It may still be the case that different first-stage strategy profiles, each implying a specific second-stage stable match, can all provide an equilibrium of the game.

A last and major concern is efficiency. Since the investment decisions are made in a fully noncooperative way, whether the investment level can be expected to be efficient is not clear. Actually, one may think of several arguments suggesting that some inefficiency should obtain. One argument is a variant of the standard notion that privately funded public goods tend to be underprovided. Remember that the surplus generated by marriage typically stems, at least in part, from the presence of goods that are publicly consumed within the household. Ultimately, investments in human capital boost the income of the investor; when married, the investor will spend part of the additional income on public goods, from which the spouse will also benefit. Because of the noncooperative nature of the investment, the argument goes, this impact on the future spouse's welfare will not be taken into account, resulting in an investment smaller than would be socially optimum.

Interestingly, an alternative argument suggests the opposite conclusion— namely, that agents are likely to invest too much. The story, here, is a "rat race" one. On the marriage market, men compete with other men, and a large stock of human capital may constitute a crucial comparative advantage. This creates an extra incentive to invest, which is not socially optimal: just as in a prisoner's dilemma, all agents overinvest.

5.1.2   *A Simple Example*

Even more interesting is the fact that whenever transfers are feasible between agents, both arguments are typically wrong. In fact, the investments noncooperatively chosen by the agents tend to be efficient, at least for one Nash equilibrium. To see why, let us first consider a very simple model capturing the main features of the situation under consideration. Again, the game is in two stages. At stage one, each agent i chooses a level of human capital σ_i, at a cost $\gamma_i C(\sigma_i)$, where $\gamma_i \in \Gamma$ is an agent-specific cost parameter. In stage two, agents match on their human capital in a TU framework where the surplus generated by a couple (σ_i, σ_j) is some function $S(\sigma_i, \sigma_j)$. We assume, to keep things simple, that all variables are continuous, that C is strictly increasing and convex, and that all solutions are interior.

As usual, the two-stage model is solved backward. Consider first the second-stage matching game, and let $U(\sigma)$ (resp. $V(\sigma)$) be the utility, at a stable match, of a woman (man) entering the game with a human capital σ. These utilities can be recovered using the method described in section 3.5. Stability implies that

$$U(\sigma_i) + V(\sigma_j) \geq S(\sigma_i, \sigma_j)$$

for all (σ_i, σ_j), an equality being reached for couples that match with positive probability. It follows that

$$U(\sigma_i) = \max_{\sigma_j} S(\sigma_i, \sigma_j) - V(\sigma_j), \qquad (5.1.1)$$

and by the envelope theorem:

$$U'(\sigma_i) = \frac{\partial S(\sigma_i, \sigma_j)}{\partial \sigma_i}. \qquad (5.1.2)$$

Similarly (or by writing the first-order conditions of (5.1.2)), we have

$$V'(\sigma_j) = \frac{\partial S(\sigma_i, \sigma_j)}{\partial \sigma_j}$$

Consider now the first-period decision of agent i; it solves

$$\max_{\sigma} U(\sigma) - \gamma_i C(\sigma).$$

Assuming an interior solution, the latter is characterized by its first-order conditions:

$$U'(\sigma_i) = \gamma_i C'(\sigma_i). \qquad (5.1.3)$$

Putting together (5.1.2) and (5.1.3), we see that

$$\frac{\partial S(\sigma_i, \sigma_j)}{\partial \sigma_i} = \gamma_i C'(\sigma_i). \qquad (5.1.4)$$

The right-hand side of this equation is the marginal cost of an additional investment in human capital by agent i, while the left-hand side represents the resulting increase in aggregate surplus. In other words, (5.1.4) states that the marginal social benefit of an additional investment equals its marginal cost—which is a standard condition for efficiency.

5.1.3   *What Was Wrong with the Previous Arguments?*

It is interesting, at this point, to come back to the two previous arguments, both of which predicted some level of inefficiency—although in opposite directions. Start with the rat race story. Should transfers be impossible, this argument would be totally correct: in an NTU context, where agents cannot bid for their preferred mate, the best strategy is to boost one's attractiveness, and this leads to overinvestment. In a TU framework, however, the logic is quite different. Being attractive is not important per se. As I mentioned in section 3.1.9, even the least attractive man could in principle match with a very attractive spouse, provided that he is willing to offer her a large enough share of the surplus (to bid enough for her). The problem, however, is that such an offer may just be too costly for him. In our simple example, where attractiveness is fully defined by the person's stock of human capital, an agent with a low σ could in principle make an attractive offer to an educated potential spouse. However, the total surplus that their matching would generate remains low, because of the small σ; offering a lot to a potential partner means keeping very little for oneself—so little, actually, that the offer is not worth being made.

With that logic, the goal of the initial investment is not to become more attractive; in a more subtle way, it is to boost the potential surplus generated by a match, which increases the person's ability to make strong offers, therefore to attract a more educated partner—which in turn implies an even higher surplus to share. Now, the equilibrium condition (5.1.2) precisely states that the marginal return a person gets from his/her own investment equals the increase in total surplus it generates; and that is what drives efficiency. The logic, here, is similar to the standard argument for efficiency in competitive markets; just think of the share of surplus needed to attract a given mate as the "market price" of that person, as suggested in chapter 2—and remember that agents are "price takers," just as in a standard market equilibrium.

Consider, now, the first story, based on the inefficient private provision of a public good. What that story is missing is that the benefits of the investment are twofold—and the story only considers one. For one thing, more investment by a given person means a higher income for the couple, therefore more expenditions on the public good, part of which will benefit the spouse—and it is correct that this gain is not *directly* taken into account by the investor. There is, however, a second benefit, which consists in being able to attract a wealthier partner, who will also devote part of his/her income to public consumption—from which the agent will benefit without *directly* paying for it. It is not obvious that these two effects should exactly compensate for each other (or that the two benefits should add up to exactly the efficient amount); in fact, they would not if people, for instance, were matched randomly. But the frictionless, competitive nature of the matching game implies that the compensation is exact—again, because the equilibrium price to be paid for a wealthier spouse is exactly the efficient one.[1]

---

[1] For a detailed analysis of the notion of price, see, for instance, Acemoglu (1996).

5.1.4   The Main Result

Let me now be a bit more specific about what the main result exactly is. Forget for a moment the two-stage game just described, and consider an alternative, fictitious model in which the timing has been reversed: agents first meet and match (based on their costs γ), then (jointly) decide on both spouses' human capital investment. The fictitious model should again be solved backwards. Any two agents γ_i and γ_j, if matched, should choose the investment levels so as to maximize total surplus, net of the investment cost:

$$\max_{\sigma_i, \sigma_j} S(\sigma_i, \sigma_j) - \gamma_i C(\sigma_i) - \gamma_j C(\sigma_j). \qquad (5.1.5)$$

Let (σ_i^*, σ_j^*) denote the solution to this maximization program, and $\Sigma(\gamma_i, \gamma_j)$ denote its value. Note that the first-order conditions of program (5.1.5) are exactly (5.1.4)—not a surprise, since by assumption their investment is efficient.

Then we have a standard matching game, in which the two populations are defined by the respective distributions of the cost parameters γ, and the surplus is given by Σ. The outcome, therefore, maximizes total surplus; i.e., the optimal measure μ, defined on the product space $\Gamma \times \Gamma$ (and whose marginals coincide with the measures of female and male cost, respectively), solves

$$\max \int \Sigma(\gamma_i, \gamma_j) d\mu(\gamma_i, \gamma_j),$$

which can also be written as

$$\max \int \left(\max_{\sigma_i, \sigma_j} S(\sigma_i, \sigma_j) - \gamma_i C(\sigma_i) - \gamma_j C(\sigma_j) \right) d\mu(\gamma_i, \gamma_j)$$

Obviously, the total surplus obtained in the fictitious game is the best that can obtain given the structure of the game. Then the main result is the following:

Proposition 1 *There exists a Nash equilibrium of the initial two-stage game that is equivalent to that of the fictitious game, in the sense that (i) the investment level of agent i is exactly σ_i^*, and (ii) i is matched with positive probability with j in the second stage if and only if i is matched with positive probability with j in the fictitious game.*

This result was derived in an early paper by Cole, Mailath, and Postlewaite (2001, from now on CMP); in their paper, they use the notions of ex ante equilibria (corresponding, up to some technical details, to the stable matching of our fictitious game) and ex post equilibria (which considers matching when education is taken as given, pretty much as in the second stage of our initial game).

The result was then extended by Nöldeke and Samuelson (2015), who consider a general framework including TU as well as ITU models.[2]

5.1.5   Coordination Failures and Inefficient Equilibria

The CMP result simply states that the (generically unique) stable matching of the fictitious game always constitutes *one* equilibrium of the two-stage game. But there may be other, inefficient equilibria. The intuition, already described by CMP, relies on the notion of *coordination failure*. Proposition 15 essentially says that if all agents invest efficiently, none has an incentive to deviate. This, however, does not preclude a situation in which all agents invest inefficiently at equilibrium—simply because a deviation towards an efficient investment is not worth the cost as long as other agents invest inefficiently. For instance, if the function S is supermodular, the return agent i gets for an additional investment is the partial $\partial S / \partial \sigma_i$, which is increasing in the partner's investment σ_j; therefore, if j underinvests, i has weaker incentives to invest and will typically underinvest as well. As an extreme case, it may be that agents choose such a low investment level that the gains from marriage simply disappear—in which case they remain single. Indeed, one possible form of inefficiency is insufficient participation in the marriage market. Lastly, if individual investments are not at the efficient level, there is little reason to expect that people will match in an optimal way: some inefficient equilibria may entail mismatch with respect to the (efficient) matching of the fictitious game. All these phenomena are analyzed in detail by Nöldeke and Samuelson (2015), who provide sufficient conditions to guarantee efficiency (therefore generic uniqueness) of the equilibrium in the two-stage game.

To summarize:

- In situations where agents invest in their traits before the matching game, there exists, under mild assumptions, an equilibrium in which investment decisions are made at the efficient level.
- However, other equilibria may exist, reflecting "coordination failures."

---

[2] While technically sophisticated, the Nöldeke-Samuelson result stems from an intuitively simple argument, which could be summarized as follows. In the fictitious game, agents simultaneously maximize in two directions: the choice of the partner *and* the investment level. In the initial game, however, maximization is in two steps: agents first maximize over their investment and then over the choice of a partner. The backward resolution logic, then, implies that agents choose an investment that maximizes their share, which itself obtains from the maximization over partner choice. A general mathematical result tells us that "the max of the max is the max"; i.e., maximizing a function $f(x, y)$ over the two variables x and y is equivalent to maximizing, with respect to x, the function $\phi(x) = \max_y f(x, y)$. That is exactly what is happening here.

5.2   Risk Sharing

A second extension relates to risk sharing. That families are (among many other things) risk-sharing institutions has been abundantly documented. In fact, it may well be the case that among the various mechanisms that individuals use to cope with (noninsurable) risk, intrafamily risk sharing plays a crucial role. For instance, Shore (2010) provides an interesting analysis of household income dynamics over the business cycle. Analyzing variations in the cross-sectional covariance of husbands' and wives' incomes, he shows that the mechanism acts in a countercyclical manner; that is, husbands' and wives' income changes are less positively correlated during a recession. This finding has important macroeconomic implications—after all, policymakers are interested in income shocks affecting households. For instance, while idiosyncratic income risk is larger during downturns *at the individual level*, the pattern does *not* hold for households, precisely because of the countervailing effect of intrahousehold risk diversification.

Now, consider an abstract (and obviously grossly simplified) model, in which the main benefit derived from matching is risk sharing. What type of matching patterns should we observe? And can the matching models described above provide useful tools for analyzing this issue? Actually, although a general analysis would require an ITU setting—more on this in chapter 7—quite a lot can be said even in a TU context.

5.2.1   When Is TU Relevant? A Simple Example

We first show, in a simple example, how TU models can address issues related to risk sharing. Consider an economy with one good only (income), and assume that each woman i and each man j is endowed with some idiosyncratic risk; namely, her (his) income is some random variable $\tilde{x}_i$ ($\tilde{y}_j$). Assume, furthermore, that individuals maximize expected utility, with a Von Neumann Morgenstern (VNM) utility in log; that is, the (expected) utility of a person facing a random income $\tilde{Y}$ is equal to $\mathbb{E}\left[\ln(\tilde{Y})\right]$. Therefore:

- Singles simply receive their expected utility—i.e., $\mathbb{E}\left[\ln(\tilde{x}_i)\right]$ for Mrs. i and $\mathbb{E}\left[\ln(\tilde{y}_j)\right]$ for Mr. j:
- Couples pool their income—so they use the sum $\tilde{Y}_{ij} = \tilde{x}_i + \tilde{y}_j$—and share it according to some sharing rule ρ so that i receives $\rho(\tilde{x}_i, \tilde{y}_j)$ and j gets $\tilde{x}_i + \tilde{y}_j - \rho(\tilde{x}_i, \tilde{y}_j)$; therefore, their respective expected utilities are

$$U_i = \mathbb{E}\left[\ln\rho(\tilde{x}_i, \tilde{y}_j)\right] \quad \text{and} \quad V_j = \mathbb{E}\left[\ln(\tilde{x}_i + \tilde{y}_j - \rho(\tilde{x}_i, \tilde{y}_j))\right].$$

Let me make a few remarks at this point. First, two individuals are always better off married to each other than single. Indeed, they could easily, when married, reach the same utilities as when single—they just need to use a sharing rule that gives $\tilde{x}_i$ to i and $\tilde{y}_j$ to j, an arrangement that could be called autarky, since agents simply mimic what would happen if they were single. However, this rule is not efficient, meaning that there exist alternative sharing rules that give more (expected) utility to both. In particular, this is a model in which there are either no single males or no single females (a single male would always marry a single female); there will actually be no singles at all if the two populations have the same size.

How do we know that autarky is not efficient? Well, this is the second remark: a fundamental result of the theory of collective decision under risk, often referred to as the Mutuality Principle,[3] states that any efficient risk-sharing rule can only depend on the sum $\tilde{x}_i + \tilde{y}_j$ (instead of varying with $\tilde{x}_i$ and $\tilde{y}_j$ independently)—a criteria that autarky obviously violates.

Actually, we can say more about the shape of the (efficient) sharing rule, just because of the logarithmic form of VNM utilities. Indeed, efficiency means that the couple chooses ρ to maximize some weighted sum of individual expected utilities:

$$\max_{\rho} \mathbb{E}\left[\ln \rho\right] + \mu \mathbb{E}\left[\ln(\tilde{x}_i + \tilde{y}_j - \rho)\right] \tag{5.2.1}$$

for some positive μ. First-order conditions give that, for any realization of $\tilde{x}_i$ and $\tilde{y}_j$:

$$\frac{1}{\rho(\tilde{x}_i, \tilde{y}_j)} = \frac{\mu}{\tilde{x}_i + \tilde{y}_j - \rho(\tilde{x}_i, \tilde{y}_j)}$$

or equivalently:

$$\rho(\tilde{x}_i, \tilde{y}_j) = \frac{1}{1 + \mu}(\tilde{x}_i + \tilde{y}_j).$$

So there is a continuum of efficient sharing rules, indexed by μ; they all satisfy the Mutuality Principle since they only depend on total income $(\tilde{x}_i + \tilde{y}_j)$. In addition, we see that all these sharing rules must be *linear* functions of total income, the coefficient being related to the Pareto weight μ. Finally, individual utilities are given by

$$U_i = \ln\left(\frac{1}{1 + \mu}\right) + \mathbb{E}\left[\ln(\tilde{x}_i + \tilde{y}_j)\right] \quad \text{and}$$

$$V_j = \ln\left(\frac{\mu}{1 + \mu}\right) + \mathbb{E}\left[\ln(\tilde{x}_i + \tilde{y}_j)\right].$$

---

[3] The reader is referred to Browning, Chiappori, and Weiss (2014) for a precise discussion.

Now, what is the relationship with TU? Well, here we must remember that TU is an *ordinal* property: it requires that *some increasing transforms* of U_i and V_j add up to some surplus. Here, let us use exponential mapping; i.e., we now cardinalize i's utility as $\exp(U_i)$ and j's utility as $\exp(V_j)$. Note that this by no means contradicts expected utility maximization, an assumption that we maintain all along; what I am saying, here, is just that maximizing i's expected utility U_i is equivalent to maximizing its exponential $\exp(U_i)$—not a controversial statement.

With the new cardinalization, utilities are now

$$\bar{U}_i = \exp U_i = \frac{1}{1+\mu} \exp\left(\mathbb{E}\left[\ln(\tilde{x}_i + \tilde{y}_j)\right]\right) \text{ and}$$

$$\bar{V}_j = \exp V_j = \frac{\mu}{1+\mu} \exp\left(\mathbb{E}\left[\ln(\tilde{x}_i + \tilde{y}_j)\right]\right)$$

and we see that the set of Pareto-efficient allocations satisfies

$$\bar{U}_i + \bar{V}_j = \exp\left(\mathbb{E}\left[\ln(\tilde{x}_i + \tilde{y}_j)\right]\right).$$

This is a clean TU formula, in which the surplus is defined by

$$S(\tilde{x}_i, \tilde{y}_j) = \exp\left(\mathbb{E}\left[\ln(\tilde{x}_i + \tilde{y}_j)\right]\right).$$

The last remark is the following. Assume that agents i and j, when matched, are asked to choose the income distributions $\tilde{x}_i$ and $\tilde{y}_j$. Well, their choice is independent of the Pareto weight μ: they simply opt for the distributions that maximize the surplus $S(\tilde{x}_i, \tilde{y}_j) = \exp(\mathbb{E}[\ln(\tilde{x}_i + \tilde{y}_j)])$. This is quite a surprising property; indeed, it states that when the group maximizes a weighted sum of individual expected utilities, the solution will be the same whatever the weights. Now, remember that the Pareto weight μ can be interpreted as an index of j's power in the decision process (in the sense that the larger the μ, the more utility j will receive). So what we see is that the choice of the income processes does not depend on the spouses' respective powers in the decision process: whatever the powers, they are unanimous in preferring the processes that maximize the surplus. In other words, the couple behaves as a single decision maker whose VNM is logarithmic—just as each of the two spouses.

5.2.2   When Is TU Relevant? A General Result

The previous example establishes several facts. First, it may be the case that a model describing matching to share risk is compatible with TU. Second, it is also the case, at least in our example, that such couples behave as a single decision maker—what is often called the *representative consumer* property.

How general are these conclusions? Are they specific to the logarithmic VNM utilities? Or could they hold for other utilities as well? The answer, surprisingly, happens to be the same for both for the TU and the representative consumer properties. For the moment, let us maintain the assumption of a single consumption good—it will be relaxed in the next subsection.

Let us first define a particular class of VNM utilities, the ISHARA family:

Definition 1 *A set of VNM utilities* $u_1, ..., u_n$ *are ISHARA if and only if*

- *each utility is of the harmonic absolute risk aversion (HARA) form, meaning that*

$$-\frac{u_i''(x)}{u_i'(x)} = \frac{1}{\alpha_i + \beta_i x}$$

for all i and x; and
- *the coefficients* β_i, *often called the shape coefficients, are identical across individuals:*

$$\beta_i = \beta \quad \text{for} \quad i = 1, ..., n.$$

The second property is usually called *identical shape* (IS), which explains the ISHARA acronym. Not surprisingly, the log example we considered was in the ISHARA family (with $\alpha_i = 0$ and $\beta_i = 1$ for all i). But the class is much larger. For instance, constant absolute risk aversion (CARA) utilities, defined by

$$u_i(x) = -\exp(-\alpha_i x),$$

are ISHARA for all values of the parameters α_i (they correspond to $\beta_i = 0$ for all i); this is exploited, for instance, in Townsend's (1994) seminal paper on risk sharing in Indian villages. Similarly, constant relative risk aversion (CRRA) utilities, defined by

$$u_i(x) = \frac{x^{1-\beta_i}}{1 - \beta_i} \quad \text{for} \quad \beta_i \neq 1 \quad \text{and}$$
$$u_i(x) = \ln x \text{ (corresponding to } \beta_i = 1) ,$$

are ISHARA if and only if all coefficients β are equal (they were all equal to 1 in our example).

Now, an important result by Mazzocco states the following:

Proposition 2 (Mazzocco 2004) *A set of agents satisfies the representative consumer property if and only if individual VNM utilities are ISHARA*

Proof See Mazzocco (2004). ∎

It is quite easy to see that for ISHARA preferences, the representative consumer property is satisfied; the crucial point is that, whenever preferences are ISHARA, then efficient sharing rules must be affine in income (i.e., such that $\rho(x) = ax + b$), and the conclusion follows easily. What is more difficult to establish is the converse property: if we consider a set of VNM utilities that are not ISHARA, then one can find choice situations in which the same group, when maximizing a weighted sum of their expected utilities, will opt for different outcomes depending on the weights; that is precisely what Mazzocco does.

Let us now consider the TU property. Again, the ISHARA property turns out to be crucial. Indeed, a result by Schulhofer-Wohl (2006) states the following:

Proposition 3 (Schulhofer-Wohl 2006) *Consider a matching model of the type described above, in which individual VNM utilities are ISHARA. Then the matching model belongs to the TU class: there exists a specific cardinalization of individual expected utilities such that the Pareto frontier is a straight line of slope −1 (or, with more than two agents, a hyperplane orthogonal to the unit vector) for all possible income distributions.*

Conversely, assume that a set of VNM utilities is such that there exists a specific cardinalization of individual expected utilities such that the Pareto frontier is a straight line of slope −1 (or, with more than two agents, a hyperplane orthogonal to the unit vector) for all possible income distributions. Then the VNM utilities are ISHARA.

Proof See Schulhofer-Wohl (2006). The basic intuition is easy to grasp. First, one can readily check that ISHARA preferences generate a TU model; again, it is a direct consequence of the fact that the sharing rule is affine in total income. Conversely, if preferences satisfy the TU property, then it must be the case that the group's decisions do not depend on the Pareto weights (since, for the relevant cardinalization, agents unanimously want to maximize the intercept of the Pareto frontier); by Mazzocco's result, this requires ISHARA. ∎

5.2.3 *An Integrated Example*

Preferences

As an illustration, let us consider a simple model encompassing both an explicit model of household behavior and a risk-sharing component. Assume, as before, that each woman i (each man j) is endowed with some random income $\tilde{x}_i$ ($\tilde{y}_j$). However, we now have several goods; for the sake of simplicity, let us assume that when married, individuals consume a private good q and a public good Q, although the generalization to any number of goods is easy. Agents maximize expected utility, and the VNM utility of person k is Cobb-Douglas:

$$u_k(q_k, Q) = (q_k Q)^{\frac{1-\gamma}{2}}, \quad k = i, j,$$

where $\gamma > 0$ is a parameter.

Ex Post Optimal Consumption

Note first that the model belongs in fact to the TU family. To see why, let us first consider the situation ex post, i.e., once incomes have been realized. Suppose that i and j are married to each other; their budget constraint is

$$p(q_i + q_j) + P Q = x_i + y_j,$$

where p and P denote the prices of the private and public goods, respectively, and x_i and y_j denote realized incomes. Now, preferences are GQL (see section 3.1), so any Pareto-efficient allocation maximizes the sum

$$\Sigma = (u_i)^{\frac{2}{1-\gamma}} + (u_j)^{\frac{2}{1-\gamma}} = (q_i + q_j)Q$$

under the budget constraint. Therefore:

$$q_i + q_j = \frac{x_i + y_j}{2p}, \quad Q = \frac{x_i + y_j}{2P},$$

implying that the Pareto-efficient allocation such that i consumes exactly q of the private good generates (ex post) utilities:

$$u_i = \left(q \frac{x_i + y_j}{2P}\right)^{\frac{1-\gamma}{2}}, \quad u_j = \left(\left(\frac{x_i + y_j}{2p} - q\right)\frac{x_i + y_j}{2P}\right)^{\frac{1-\gamma}{2}}.$$

Ex Ante Efficient Behavior

Let us now adopt an ex ante perspective—that is, let us talk about risk sharing. The question, here, is: How should q be determined, as a function of income realization, so that risk is shared efficiently within the couple? Here, "efficiently" refers to standard Pareto efficiency; i.e., the function $q(x, y)$, which determines q for each possible pair of income realizations, must maximize some weighted sum of utilities:

$$\max_q \mathbb{E}\left[\left(q(x, y)\frac{x+y}{2P}\right)^{\frac{1-\gamma}{2}}\right] + \mu\mathbb{E}\left[\left(\left(\frac{x+y}{2p} - q(x, y)\right)\frac{x+y}{2P}\right)^{\frac{1-\gamma}{2}}\right],$$

the expectation being taken over incomes; here, μ is the Pareto weight of Mr. j.

First-order conditions give

$$q(x_i, y_j)^{-\frac{1+\gamma}{2}}\left(\frac{x_i+y_j}{2P}\right)^{\frac{1-\gamma}{2}} = \mu\left(\frac{x_i+y_j}{2p} - q(x_i, y_j)\right)^{-\frac{1+\gamma}{2}}\left(\frac{x_i+y_j}{2P}\right)^{\frac{1-\gamma}{2}}$$

or, simplifying and taking both sides to the $\left(-\frac{2}{1+\gamma}\right)$ power,

$$q(x_i, y_j) = \mu^{-\frac{2}{1+\gamma}}\left(\frac{x_i+y_j}{2p} - q(x_i, y_j)\right),$$

which finally gives

$$q(x_i, y_j) = \frac{\mu^{-\frac{2}{1+\gamma}}}{1 + \mu^{-\frac{2}{1+\gamma}}}\frac{x_i+y_j}{2p}.$$

Note that the Mutuality Principle is again satisfied: q—therefore individual utilities—only depends on the realization of total income.

Responses to Income Shocks

As a first application, let us consider the consequences of a shock affecting the income of one of the spouses. First of all, which income is affected is irrelevant: only the impact on total income matters. Second, the previous results, expressed in logs, tells us that:

$$\ln q_i = \ln\left(\frac{\mu^{-\frac{2}{1+\gamma}}}{1 + \mu^{-\frac{2}{1+\gamma}}}\right) - \ln(2p) + \ln(x_i + y_j)$$

$$\ln q_j = \ln\left(\frac{1}{1 + \mu^{-\frac{2}{1+\gamma}}}\right) - \ln(2p) + \ln(x_i + y_j) \text{ and}$$

$$\ln Q = -\ln(2P) + \ln(x_i + y_j);$$

therefore:

$$\frac{dq_i}{q_i} = \frac{dq_j}{q_j} = \frac{dQ}{Q} = \frac{d(x_i + y_j)}{x_i + y_j}.$$

In words: the shock affecting total income impacts all consumptions, which are reduced by the same percentage. Of course, this particular conclusion is specific to the Cobb-Douglas form. But it illustrates one mechanism through which risk is dampened at the household level: what matters is the income loss *as a proportion of total income*—and that is always less (and sometimes much less) than the variation as a proportion of the individual's income.

Matching

Next, let me get back to matching. First, the previous analysis shows that the respective expected utilities of i and j are uniquely determined by the parameter μ. Specifically (and with the same notations as above):

$$U_i = \left(\frac{\mu^{-\frac{2}{1+\gamma}}}{1 + \mu^{-\frac{2}{1+\gamma}}}\right)^{\frac{1-\gamma}{2}} \left(\frac{1}{4pP}\right)^{\frac{1-\gamma}{2}} \mathbb{E}\left[(x + y)^{1-\gamma}\right]$$

$$V_j = \left(\frac{1}{1 + \mu^{-\frac{2}{1+\gamma}}}\right)^{\frac{1-\gamma}{2}} \left(\frac{1}{4pP}\right)^{\frac{1-\gamma}{2}} \mathbb{E}\left[(x + y)^{1-\gamma}\right].$$

A first conclusion is that, once an efficient risk-sharing mechanism exists, individuals have CRRA preferences vis-à-vis (aggregate) income risk. In other words, in a household where individuals have the same, constant index of relative risk aversion, the group can be represented by a single consumer, whose preferences are also CRRA with the same index. Note, incidentally, that this conclusion was expected: CRRA preferences with identical relative risk aversion are ISHARA, so that Mazzocco's result applies.

In particular, we see that

$$U_i^{\frac{2}{1-\gamma}} + V_j^{\frac{2}{1-\gamma}} = \frac{1}{4pP} \left(\mathbb{E}\left[(x + y)^{1-\gamma}\right]\right)^{\frac{2}{1-\gamma}},$$

implying that, for the cardinalization $\bar{U}_i = U_i^{\frac{2}{1-\gamma}}$, the TU property is satisfied, and total surplus is

$$S(\tilde{x}_i, \tilde{y}_j) = \frac{1}{4pP} \left(\mathbb{E}\left[(\tilde{x}_i + \tilde{y}_j)^{1-\gamma}\right]\right)^{\frac{2}{1-\gamma}}.$$

Now, what do we learn from this example? Essentially, that it is relatively easy to construct a reasonable model entailing TU, even for dealing with issues with risk sharing. The recipe is quite simple. First, from an ordinal viewpoint, preferences must be of Chiappori and Gugl's ACIU form (of which GQL is a particular case). This implies, in particular, that the demand for public goods is the same for all Pareto-efficient outcomes; the latter only differ by their allocation of private goods, which is driven by the conditional indirect utilities—which, by ACIU, are affine in the sharing rules. Therefore, efficient risk sharing amounts to efficiently choosing the sharing rule—and we are back to a one-commodity problem. Second, from a cardinal perspective, preferences must satisfy the ISHARA property; indeed, in a one-commodity world, this is equivalent to TU.[4]

These conditions are necessary and sufficient. If they are satisfied, then the whole machinery of TU matching—the link with optimal transportation, the dual definition of utilities, etc—can readily be applied to the problem at stake.

To summarize:

- Matching models involving risk sharing may in some cases be compatible with the TU framework.
- This is the case, in an expected utility framework, if

  - ex post utilities satisfy TU, i.e., the ACIU condition of Chiappori and Gugl (2015);
  - ex ante utilities belong to the ISHARA family.

5.3 Multidimensional Matching

In my presentation of the general theory (in chapter 3), I made no assumption about the dimension of the characteristics spaces X and Y. Indeed, a useful feature of matching theory under TU is precisely that its main properties do not require one-dimensional sets (or any specific assumptions of that type). The analysis of multidimensional matching problems actually generates interesting insights that I will now briefly summarize.

In what follows, I therefore assume that $X \subset \mathbb{R}^n$ and $Y \subset \mathbb{R}^m$, with $n \geq m \geq 1$. The surplus is therefore a function $S\left(x^1, ..., x^n, y^1, ..., y^m\right)$. As before, I will assume that S is smooth (say, twice continuously differentiable), and the the measures F and G (on spaces X and Y, respectively) are absolutely continuous and atomless; these assumptions, while not absolutely necessary, greatly simplify the exposition.

---

[4] In our example, ordinal preferences were GQL (a particular case of ACIU), whereas the cardinalization was CRRA with identical coefficients, which satisfies ISHARA.

5.3.1   Index Models

Definition

I start with the specific but empirically important case of index models. The idea, here, is that the multiple characteristics of agent i, $x_i = (x_i^1, ..., x_i^n)$, matter for the surplus (therefore for the matching game) only through some one-dimensional index $I_i = I(x_i^1, ..., x_i^n)$, where I is a smooth function mapping $\mathbb{R}^n$ to $\mathbb{R}$; that is, the surplus function can be written as

$$S(x^1, ..., x^n, y^1, ..., y^m) = s(I(x^1, ..., x^n), y^1, ..., y^m)$$

for some function s. The economic interpretation is clear: although Mrs. i is characterized by the entire vector $(x_i^1, ..., x_i^n)$, in practice only the corresponding index I_i matters. In particular, if two women i and k have different characteristics $(x_i \neq x_k)$ but the same index $(I(x_i) = I(x_k))$, then they are perfect substitutes on the marriage market.

An even more specific case obtains when *both* sides of the market exhibit an index structure; that will be the case if there exists two index functions, I and J, such that

$$S(x^1, ..., x^n, y^1, ..., y^m) = s(I(x^1, ..., x^n), J(y^1, ..., y^m)).$$

Note that, in that case, the matching game is de facto unidimensional. Let Φ and Γ respectively denote the *push-forward* measure of F and G through I and J; these are the measures induced on $\mathbb{R}$ by the relationship:

$$\Phi(A) = F(I^{-1}(A)) \quad \text{and} \quad \Gamma(B) = G(J^{-1}(B)), \ \forall A, B.$$

In words, the probability of any set A of possible values for index I is the probability (under measure F) of the set $I^{-1}(A)$ of agents whose index belongs to A. Now, Chiappori, Oreffice, and Quintana-Domeque (2012, from now on COQ) have shown that there is an equivalence between the set of stable matches in the initial, multidimensional matching game and that of the "reduced" game defined by the surplus s and the sets $I(X)$ and $J(Y)$, endowed with the measures Φ and Γ. In particular, the dual utilities u and v of the multidimensional model, which summarize the division of the surplus between matched partners, only depend on the partners' indices:

$$u(x^1, ..., x^n) = \bar{u}(I(x^1, ..., x^n)) \quad \text{and} \quad v(y^1, ..., y^m) = \bar{v}(J(y^1, ..., y^m)).$$

Finally, it is important to understand the full economic meaning of the index assumption. For that purpose, it is useful to relax the assumption and consider, for a particular vector of male characteristics $\bar{y}$, the set of female characteristics x

defined by the equation

$$S(x, \bar{y}) = \bar{s}. \tag{5.3.1}$$

From the perspective of Mr. $\bar{y}$, all such women are perfect substitutes: they all generate the same surplus. In the matching game, they will typically come with different prices (i.e., equilibrium utilities $u(x)$), and if he chooses one of them as his spouse it will be the least expensive one. The crucial point, however, is that although these women are perfect substitutes from his perspective (marrying any of them does not change the surplus generated by the couple), this equivalence is valid only for him. Another male, endowed with different characteristics (say y'), would have a totally different ranking of potential spouses. Technically, the new set would be defined by the equation

$$S(x, y') = \bar{s}',$$

which does not coincide with (5.3.1). In particular, consider the trade-offs between the various characteristics which describe the compensations needed to maintain the surplus: if I marginally decrease one characteristic, say x^1, by how much should I increase another characteristic, say x^2, for the surplus *generated with* $\bar{y}$ to remain unchanged? The answer is given by the ratio

$$r_{12} = \frac{\partial S(x, \bar{y})/\partial x_1}{\partial S(x, \bar{y})/\partial x_2},$$

which is formally equivalent to a marginal rate of substitution in standard consumer theory. Note that this ratio depends on $\bar{y}$: considering the same trade-off from the perspective of y' would typically change the ratio.

What happens, now, if we add the index assumption? Then the set of women who are perfect substitutes for each other is characterized by the equation $I(x) = \bar{\imath}$ for some $\bar{\imath}$, and that equation does *not* depend on male characteristics. In other words, under the index assumption, if two women are perfect substitutes for one man, they are perfect substitutes for all of them. The trade-offs between the various characteristics are given by the ratios

$$r_{12} = \frac{\partial S(x, \bar{y})/\partial x_1}{\partial S(x, \bar{y})/\partial x_2} = \frac{\partial I(x)/\partial x_1}{\partial I(x)/\partial x_2}.$$

These do not depend on y and are therefore identically perceived by all potential partners. This property plays a crucial role in the empirical implementation of the concept.

Empirical Implementation

In practice, even when individual characteristics x_i are fully observed, the index function I is not; it must be empirically recovered. Moreover, it is typically the case that only some characteristics are observed, whereas others must be treated as unobserved heterogeneity (see chapter 3, section 6). But a simple empirical strategy allows one to recover the index function. The key insight is to exploit the property that two agents with the same index are perfect substitutes. Technically, let us posit that the k first components of x_i are observable, while the remaining $n - k$ are not. COQ make two assumptions at that point. First, the index property is satisfied for the *observable characteristics* $(x^1, ..., x^k)$:

$$S(x^1, ..., x^n, y^1, ..., y^m) = s(I(x^1, ..., x^k), x^{k+1}, ..., x^n, y^1, ..., y^m).$$

Second, the conditional distribution of the unobservable characteristics $(x^{k+1}, ..., x^n)$, given the observable ones $(x^1, ..., x^k)$, only depends on the index $I(x^1, ..., x^k)$.

If these assumptions are satisfied, stable matching patterns exhibit a strong property; namely,

Proposition 1 (COQ 2012) *Take any two vectors* $x_i = (x_i^1, ..., x_i^k)$ *and* $x_{i'} = (x_{i'}^1, ..., x_{i'}^k)$ *of female observable characteristics, such that* $I(x_i^1, ..., x_i^k) = I(x_{i'}^1, ..., x_{i'}^k)$. *Then for any vector* y_j *of male observable characteristics, the probability that* x_i *is matched with* y_j *at a stable matching is equal to the probability that* $x_{i'}$ *is matched with* y_j *at a stable matching.*

In practice, take all women whose vector of observable characteristics generate the same index value—i.e., all i such that $I(x_i) = \bar{i}$ for some $\bar{i}$. The observable characteristics of their husbands may differ, essentially because they differ in their unobservable characteristics $(x_i^{k+1}, ..., x_i^m)$. But if we only condition on observable characteristics, these women are all equally likely to be matched with any of these husbands. In order to empirically exploit this fact, let us compute any moment of the conditional distribution of the husband's observable characteristics given the wife's—say, the conditional mean $E[y^s \mid x^1, ..., x^k]$; note that such moments can be econometrically estimated (even nonparametrically). By the previous proposition, this conditional mean only depends on the index $I(x^1, ..., x^k)$. It follows that

$$\frac{\partial E[y^s \mid x^1, ..., x^k]}{\partial x^t} = \frac{\partial E[y^s \mid x^1, ..., x^k]}{\partial I} \frac{\partial I}{\partial x^t} s$$

for all s and all t. If we take two different female characteristics t and t', we therefore have

$$\frac{\partial E\left[y^s \mid x^1, ..., x^k\right] / \partial x^t}{\partial E\left[y^s \mid x^1, ..., x^k\right] / \partial x^{t'}} = \frac{\partial I / \partial x^t}{\partial I / \partial x^{t'}}.$$

These equations allow one to exactly identify the "level curves" of index I, i.e., the shape of the sets defined by $I(x) = \bar{\imath}$ for some $\bar{\imath}$; the index, therefore, is identified up to an increasing transform. Moreover, in the previous relationship, the right-hand side does not depend on s—and more generally on the particular moment of the distribution that we are considering. This provides a set of overidentifying restrictions, that can be used to test the adequacy of the index assumptions.

In practice, COQ consider two characteristics, social status (as proxied by income or education) and physical attractiveness (as proxied by the person's body mass index, or BMI). Using data from the Panel Study of Income Dynamics (PSID), they show that the overidentifying restrictions are indeed satisfied, and they compute the "rates of substitutions" between the various characteristics (e.g., how much higher must income be to compensate for a larger BMI—compensation meaning here that the index is unchanged).

Still, the index assumption is strong and cannot be expected to work in all circumstances; most of the time, the trade-off between various male characteristics is seen differently by different women, and conversely. A possible generalization, provided in a recent article by Dupuy and Galichon (2014), is to introduce several indices. Assume that agents are characterized by a large number n of attributes; then it may be useful to "summarize" them into a smaller number k of aggregate indices. The basic index approach corresponds to the case $k = 1$; in general, however, k, although much smaller than n, must be chosen larger than 1—and then the model is explicitly k-dimensional. Dupuy and Galichon (2014) show how to statiscally estimate the smallest k compatible with the data, and illustrate their methodology on a unique Dutch household survey containing information about education, height, BMI, health, attitude toward risk, and personality traits of spouses.

5.3.2 The General Case: Equal Dimensions

The general theory of multidimensional matching is beyond the scope of the present book; the interested reader may refer to Chiappori, McCann, and Pass (2016) for a detailed analysis. Here, I will simply illustrate some main ideas on two simple examples. I will start with the case of equal dimensions: men and women are characterized by the same number of traits.

Assume, thus, that $m = n = 2$ and that the surplus function has the simple form

$$S(x^1, x^2, y^1, y^2) = x^1 y^1 + x^2 y^2.$$

Note, in particular, that this form does *not* satisfy the index property; indeed, the ratio

$$\frac{\partial S(x, \bar{y})/\partial x^1}{\partial S(x, \bar{y})/\partial x^2} = \frac{y^1}{y^2}$$

does depend on y. However, this surplus satisfies the twist condition (see subsection 4.6 of chapter 3); indeed,

$$D_x S(x, y) = (y^1, y^2),$$

which is certainly injective in y. Therefore, the stable match is unique and pure; i.e., there exists two functions ϕ^1, ϕ^2 such that, at the stable match, $x = (x^1, x^2)$ is matched with $y = (y^1, y^2)$, with

$$y^1 = \phi^1(x^1, x^2) \quad \text{and} \quad y^2 = \phi^2(x^1, x^2). \tag{5.3.2}$$

Moreover, the surplus also satisfies the Lindenlaub condition; we therefore know that ϕ_i^i is increasing in x_i^i for $i = 1, 2$.

Lastly, I need to define the measures F and G. Let me take the simplest case, in which the two components are independent and uniformly distributed over some interval, which we can without loss of generality normalize to be $[0, 1]$.

How can we solve for the stable matching? A solution that works in many cases is to "guess" the shape of the stable match, then check that the guess is correct by verifying the stability properties. Here, for instance, given the positive assortative matching property à la Lindenlaub and the symmetry of the model, it is natural to expect that each agent is matched with a partner with the same characteristics—i.e.,

$$\phi^1(x^1, x^2) = x^1, \quad \phi^2(x^1, x^2) = x^2.$$

How can we check that this assignment is stable? The first step is to compute individual utilities. For that, we simply need to remember that $u(x^1, x^2)$ must satisfy

$$\frac{\partial u(x^1, x^2)}{\partial x^i} = \frac{\partial S(x^1, x^2, \phi^1(x^1, x^2), \phi^2(x^1, x^2))}{\partial x^i}.$$

Here, we have

$$\frac{\partial u(x^1, x^2)}{\partial x^i} = \frac{\partial S}{\partial x^i} = \phi^i(x^1, x^2) = x^i,$$

which gives

$$u(x^1, x^2) = \frac{(x^1)^2 + (x^2)^2}{2} + K,$$

where K is a constant. Similarly,

$$v(y^1, y^2) = \frac{(y^1)^2 + (y^2)^2}{2} + K',$$

and for any matched couple—i.e., any couple (x^1, x^2, y^1, y^2) such that $x^i = y^i, i = 1, 2$,

$$u(x^1, x^2) + v(y^1, y^2) = \frac{(x^1)^2 + (x^2)^2}{2} + K + \frac{(y^1)^2 + (y^2)^2}{2} + K'$$

$$= (x^1)^2 + (x^2)^2 + K + K'$$

$$= S(x^1, x^2, x^1, x^2) + K + K',$$

implying that $K' = -K$. In particular, for the couple located at the lower bound of the distribution, $x^i = y^i = 0, i = 1, 2$; therefore,

$$u(0, 0) = K, \quad v(0, 0) = -K.$$

Since the utility of a single has been normalized to 0, the utility of a married person cannot be negative (otherwise he/she would not marry), and finally $K = K' = 0$.

Lastly, we need to check the stability conditions. Take any two individuals (x^1, x^2) and (y^1, y^2) who are *not* matched together. Then it must be the case that

$$u(x^1, x^2) + v(y^1, y^2) = \frac{(x^1)^2 + (x^2)^2}{2} + \frac{(y^1)^2 + (y^2)^2}{2}$$

$$\geq S(x^1, x^2, y^1, y^2) = x^1 y^1 + x^2 y^2.$$

This is equivalent to

$$\frac{(x^1)^2 + (x^2)^2}{2} + \frac{(y^1)^2 + (y^2)^2}{2} - (x^1 y^1 + x^2 y^2) \geq 0$$

or

$$\frac{(x^1 - y^1)^2}{2} + \frac{(x^2 - y^2)^2}{2} \geq 0,$$

which is always satisfied. We conclude that the matching is indeed stable.

Of course, guessing the form of the solution is not always easy. Can we think of a more systematic way of deriving the stable match? Well, all we need to do is to consider the alternative characterization of stable matchings—namely, that they maximize total surplus. In our case, this leads to an optimal control problem that can be solved using standard techniques. Specifically, we know from the twist condition that the stable measure is born by the graph of some function ϕ; equivalently, it is characterized by the relationships (5.3.2). The total surplus is thus

$$S = \int_0^1 \int_0^1 (x^1 \phi^1(x^1, x^2) + x^2 \phi^2(x^1, x^2)) dF(x^1, x^2)$$

$$= \int_0^1 \int_0^1 (x^1 \phi^1(x^1, x^2) + x^2 \phi^2(x^1, x^2)) dx^1 dx^2 \qquad (5.3.3)$$

and this must be maximized under the measure conditions.

What do the latter look like? Well, what we already know in terms of positive assortative matching of the solution can help us to write them in a very tractable way. Take any woman $\bar{x} = (\bar{x}^1, \bar{x}^2)$, and let $(\bar{y}^1, \bar{y}^2) = (\phi^1(\bar{x}^1, \bar{x}^2), \phi^2(\bar{x}^1, \bar{x}^2))$ denote her partner in the stable matching. We know that any woman (x^1, x^2) with $x^1 \geq \bar{x}^1$ and $x^2 \geq \bar{x}^2$ will be matched with a partner (y^1, y^2) such that $y^1 \geq \bar{y}^1$ and $y^2 \geq \bar{y}^2$, and conversely. Therefore, it must be the case, in figure 5.1, that the number of agents located "northeast" of $(\bar{x}^1, \bar{x}^2)$ (dark-shaded area) equals the number of agents located "northeast" of $(\bar{y}^1, \bar{y}^2)$ (light-shaded area). This implies that

$$(1 - \bar{x}_1)(1 - \bar{x}_2) = (1 - \bar{y}_1)(1 - \bar{y}_2).$$

In other words, the measure conditions simply require that the functions ϕ^1 and ϕ^2 satisfy the conditions

$$0 \leq \phi^1(x^1, x^2) \leq 1,$$

$$0 \leq \phi^2(x^1, x^2) \leq 1 \text{ and}$$

$$1 - \phi^1(x^1, x^2) = \frac{(1 - x^1)(1 - x^2)}{1 - \phi^2(x^1, x^2)}.$$

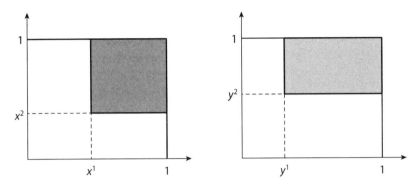

Figure 5.1. Multidimensional measure condition

Note that these conditions do not *require* that $\phi^1(x^1, x^2) = x^1$ and $\phi^2(x^1, x^2) = x^2$ (although these functions obviously satisfy the conditions). For instance, the functions

$$\phi^1\left(x^1, x^2\right) = \frac{x^1 + x^2}{2}, \quad \phi^2\left(x^1, x^2\right) = \frac{x^1 + x^2 - 2x^1 x^2}{2 - x^1 - x^2}$$

also satisfy the conditions; but they generate a value of the surplus (5.3.3) that is smaller than for the optimal ones (0.63 versus 0.67). In fact, one must then solve the optimal control problem consisting of maximizing (5.3.3) under these constraint; the reader can check that the solution is precisely the stable matching $\phi^i\left(x^1, x^2\right) = x^i, i = 1, 2$.

The example just studied is "well-behaved," in the sense that it satisfies the twist condition. However, other cases studied in the literature are more complex. Chiappori, Oreffice, and Quintana-Domeque (2017) analyze a two-dimensional matching model in which one characteristic is continuously distributed while the other is discrete. In their framework, the surplus function does not satisfy the twist conditions. Indeed, they find that for the relevant range of parameters, the matching is typically not pure: it requires that an open set of agents randomize between two different potential spouses. However, even in their example, the dual approach can be used; i.e., the stable matching can be found either by trying to solve the stability conditions or by solving the optimal control problem defined by surplus maximization.

5.3.3   The General Case: Many-to-One Matching

In the second example, one side of the market (say men) is characterized by one trait (say income), whereas women differ in several dimensions.[5] A general analysis of such models is provided by Chiappori, McCann, and Pass (2016); here, I will simply provide a quick illustration of the main notions involved. Thus, assume that $n = 2, m = 1$, and the surplus function is given by

$$S(x^1, x^2, y) = yx^1 + (y)^2 x^2.$$

A first remark is that this case does not belong to the family of index models; indeed,

$$\frac{\partial S/\partial x^1}{\partial S/\partial x^2} = \frac{1}{y},$$

which depends on y. Intuitively, an index model requires that the respective weights, in the surplus function, of the two female characteristics be the same for all potential husbands; here, on the contrary, high-income men put more weight on the second female characteristic (with respect to the first) than low-income men do.

Still, theory allows one to derive predictions that are empirically testable. The crucial remark, here, is that, at a stable match, we expect men with some given income $\bar{y}$ to be matched with a (one-dimensional) *continuum* of women; this is simply a consequence of the difference in dimensions between male and female characteristics. Under mild assumptions, this continuum is a smooth manifold (in our case, a curve), which is called the *iso-husband curve* associated to $\bar{y}$. The equation of such a curve is easy to derive. Indeed, remember that, at a stable match, the utility reached by men with income $\bar{y}$ is given by

$$v(\bar{y}) = \max_{x^1, x^2} S(x^1, x^2, \bar{y}) - u(x^1, x^2).$$

As before, the envelope theorem implies that

$$v'(\bar{y}) = \frac{\partial S(x^1, x^2, \bar{y})}{\partial y}.$$

---

[5] A typical example is a model by Low (2014), in which men only differ by their income, while women differ by income and fertility. An alternative but ultimately equivalent situation arises when, although men are characterized by several traits, the latter can be combined into a single index; as discussed above, the male side is then de facto one-dimensional.

Now, stability requires that all men with the same income have the same utility; it follows that the equation of the iso-husband curve associated with $\bar{y}$ is simply

$$\frac{\partial S(x^1, x^2, \bar{y})}{\partial y} = k(\bar{y})$$

for some $k(\bar{y})$ (the determination of which is discussed later on). Thus, in our case, the equation is

$$x^1 + 2\bar{y}x^2 = k(\bar{y}).$$

We see that (i) the iso-husband curves are straight lines (this is due to the very simple surplus function I started with); (ii) these lines are decreasing in the (x^1, x^2) plane (not surprisingly, since there must be a trade-off between the two female traits); and (iii) the slope is proportional to the husband's income, reflecting the fact, already mentioned, that high-income men put more weight on the second female characteristic than low-income men do.

The intercept $k(\bar{y})$, on the other hand, depends on the measures on the X and Y spaces. Intuitively, given the form of the surplus, the model leads to a type of assortative matching, in the sense that high-income men will match with women with high characteristics. Therefore, we could expect that the set X of female characteristics will be partitioned into a set of curves, each indexed by a male income y, with the property that for any $\bar{y}$, the mass of women *above* the curve corresponding to $\bar{y}$ (who, intuitively, will get a husband richer than $\bar{y}$) equals the mass of men richer than $\bar{y}$.

Will such a construct always work? Unfortunately, not always; the problem is that, depending on the measures, two curves corresponding to two different male incomes may intersect, which seriously complicate the problem.[6] But if we are lucky enough to be in what is called the "nested" case, where the curves never intersect, then we have a straightforward characterization of the optimal matching patterns. The interesting point, here, is that the iso-husband curves are in principle empirically observable, so that predictions of this type can in principle be taken to data—although in practice much remains to be done on that front.

To summarize:

- Under an index assumption, multidimensional models are equivalent to one-dimensional matching models; moreover, these index assumptions are typically testable from matching patterns data.

---

[6] In fact, a result by Chiappori, McCann, and Pass (2016) shows that, as soon as the model is not "quasi-index" (a generalization of index models), there always exist measures such that some curves intersect.

- In general, multidimensional models can be translated into optimal control problems, which can often be more tractable.
- In many-to-one matching problems, one can derive "iso-husband" curves, and under additional conditions, these curves fully characterize the matching patterns.

5.4   Roommate Matching

Another extension is the so-called roommate matching problem. Here, instead of considering the matching of individuals belonging to two different sets X and Y, we assume that people still match by pairs, but both partners belong to the *same* population X. One can think of many examples: same-sex couples of course, but also lawyers teaming up to build a law firm, tennis players playing a double, or even politicians choosing a running mate.

5.4.1   Existence of a Stable Matching: A Counterexample

Strangely enough, this apparently minor variation has significant consequences for the properties of the model. For instance, a stable match may fail to exist, as showed by the following example, borrowed from Chiappori, Galichon, and Salanié (2016, from now on CGS). The population has three individuals. Any unmatched individual has zero utility. The joint surplus created by the matching of any two of them is given by the off-diagonal terms of the matrix

$$\Phi = \begin{pmatrix} - & 6 & 8 \\ 6 & - & 5 \\ 8 & 5 & - \end{pmatrix} \tag{5.4.1}$$

so that individuals 1 and 2 create, if they match, a surplus of 6; 1 and 3 create a surplus of 8, etc.

Assume that there exists a stable matching. A matching in which all individuals remain single is obviously not stable; any stable matching must be such that one person remains single and the other two are matched together. Let (u_x) be the utility that individual of type $x = 1, 2, 3$ gets out of this game; stability imposes $u_x + u_y \geq \Phi_{xy}$ for all potential matches, with equality if x and y are actually matched, and $u_x \geq 0$ with equality if x is single. One can readily check, however, that no set of numbers (u_1, u_2, u_3) satisfying these relationships for all x and y exists: whichever the married pair is, one of the matched partners would increase her utility by matching with the single person. Indeed, if the matched pair is $\{1, 2\}$, then

$$u_1 + u_2 = 6, \quad u_3 = 0, u_2 \geq 0$$

contradicts $u_1 + u_3 \geq 8$: agent 3, being single, is willing to give up any amount smaller than 8 to be matched with 1, while the match between 1 and 2 cannot provide 1 with more than 6. Similarly, if the married pair is $\{2, 3\}$, then

$$u_2 + u_3 = 5, \quad u_1 = 0, \quad u_2 \geq 0, \quad u_3 \geq 0$$

contradicts both $u_1 + u_2 \geq 6$ and $u_1 + u_3 \geq 8$ (so that 1 is willing to give more than 5 and less than 6 to agent 2 to match with her, and more than 5 and less than 8 to 3.) Finally, if the married pair is $\{1, 3\}$, then

$$u_1 + u_3 = 8, \quad u_2 = 0, \quad u_1 \geq 0, \quad u_3 \geq 0$$

is incompatible with $u_1 + u_3 \geq 11$, which follows from combining $u_1 + u_2 \geq 6$ and $u_2 + u_3 \geq 5$ with $u_2 = 0$. Intuitively, since agent 2 is single, 1 could match with her and capture almost 6, while 3 could match with her and capture almost 5; therefore, stability would require that, in the $(1, 3)$ match, 1 gets at least 6 and 3 gets at least 5—which is impossible, since the total surplus they generate is 8. It follows that no stable matching exists.

5.4.2   The Cloned Bipartite Problem

A natural idea, at this point, is to consider surplus maximization. After all, the key argument for existence of a stable matching in the bilateral case is that any matching that maximizes total surplus must be stable—and there always exists a maximizing matching. What happens here? A useful trick introduced by CGS is to "clone" our set of agents; i.e., we now have two sets of agents, $(1, 2, 3)$ and $(1', 2', 3')$, where a' is a clone of a ($a = 1, 2, 3$). Let us consider the *bipartite* matching game between these set $X = (1, 2, 3)$ and $Y = (1', 2', 3')$, where the surplus is still given by matrix Φ (i.e., matching 1 to $1'$ generates a zero surplus, matching 1 to $2'$ generates a surplus of 6, etc.). One can readily see that this problem has two stable matchings, given by the following two matching matrices:

$$m = \begin{pmatrix} 0 & 0 & 1 \\ 1 & 0 & 0 \\ 0 & 1 & 0 \end{pmatrix} \quad \text{and} \quad m' = \begin{pmatrix} 0 & 1 & 0 \\ 0 & 0 & 1 \\ 1 & 0 & 0 \end{pmatrix}.$$

Under m, 1 is matched with $3'$, 2 is matched with $1'$ and 3 is matched with $2'$; under m', 1 is matched with $2'$, 2 is matched with $3'$ and 3 is matched with $1'$. In both cases, total surplus is 19, which is the maximum for this game.

The question, now, is whether it possible to derive, from the stable matching of the cloned bipartite model, a stable matching for our initial roommate matching game. The answer is ambiguous: sometimes it is possible, but not always—and specifically not in this example. The key insight, here, is that a roommate problem comes with an additional set of restrictions that can be expressed in terms of *symmetry*. In the cloned, bipartite problem, no symmetry is required: 1 being matched with $3'$ does not imply that 3 must be matched with $1'$. Indeed, the two solutions just described are asymmetric in that sense. In the roommate case, however, symmetry is inescapable; if 1 is matched with 3, then it must be the case that 3 is matched with 1. An asymmetric solution to the cloned problem cannot be translated into a stable matching of the initial matching game.

This intuition is in fact general: CGS show that a matching in the cloned bipartite model can be associated with a matching in the roommate problem if and only if it is symmetric. As a consequence, they show that a stable matching exists in the roommate problem if and only if the associated cloned bipartite problem admits a stable matching that is symmetric. In our example, no stable matching of the cloned bipartite model is symmetric, therefore can be translated into a stable matching of the roommate problem. The nonexistence result directly follows.

An important consequence of the CGS result is the following. Assume that agents belong to categories, with the property that two agents belonging to the same category are perfect substitutes. Then a stable matching exists in the roommate problem if and only if each category has an even number of members; indeed, in that case the associated bipartite problem always admits a symmetric, stable matching. Moreover, if the number of agents *in each category* is "large," then a limit result obtains: even when there is no stable matching, one may remove a subpopulation of asymptotically negligible size in order to restore the existence of stable matchings (the idea being that the remaining players can always "buy" the subpopulation out of the roommate game by offering them a compensation at a per capita cost that goes to zero when the size of the population goes to infinity).

To summarize:

- In the roommate problem under TU, a stable matching may fail to exist.
- However, if agents belong to categories such that two agents belonging to the same category are perfect substitutes, then:

  – An equilibrium always exists if the number of agents by category is even.
  – If the number of agents per category is large, then stability may be restored by buying out some agents at an infinitesimal cost.

5.5   Divorce and Remarriage

While I have said a lot so far about couple formation, I have been quite silent on the opposite aspect of the relationship—namely, couple dissolution. Yet, divorce is a phenomenon that can hardly be neglected—if only because, in several countries, more than one in three marriages end up in divorce. Such a large probability is likely to be taken into account in the agents' decision process, including in the initial, matching phase: the correct definition of the surplus should include agents' expected utility conditional on divorce. I will now discuss how such issues can be added to the basic framework.

5.5.1   The Basic Model

Preferences

The simplest way of introducing divorce (and more generally match dissolution) into the framework is to consider a two-period model in which agents match during the first period and may, during the second, choose either to continue the relationship or to dissolve it.[7] In the latter case, let us for the moment assume that they remain single. Also, and to keep things simple, we assume that agents maximize expected utility and that preferences are additively separable across periods; and we extend the matching-on-income framework described in section 3.5.2.

It is important to recognize that some factors that influence the second-period decision may not have been known at the matching stage. The standard way of capturing this idea in a parsimonious manner, following Weiss (1977), is to assume that each match generates, over and above the economic gains we have discussed so far, an idiosyncratic, nonmonetary benefit that can be called "match quality." In the simplest version, this nonmonetary component enters utilities additively;[8] then husbands' and wives' individual utilities take the form

$$U_i = u_i(q_i, Q) + \theta_i, \quad i = 1, 2, \tag{5.5.1}$$

where q_i is the vector of $i's$ private consumption, Q is consumption of the public good, and θ_i is the quality of the match. I will assume that θ_i is not observed at the date of marriage; agents decide to match based on the expected value of the

---

[7] The presentation, here, directly follows Chiappori, Iyigun, and Weiss (2016).

[8] Although this assumption is generally made for the sake of tractability, it is testable if we observe both monetary and nonmonetary shocks affecting households. Chiappori, Radchenko, and Salanié (2016), using a rich Russian database, find that it fits actual behavior pretty well.

nonmonetary components.[9] At the end of the first period, the realizations of these components are publicly observed; then agents may decide to remain married (in which case they enjoy the same non monetary benefits during the second period) or to divorce (then they remain single during period 2).

Regarding the economic component of marital gain, I assume as before that u_i satisfies the ACIU property of Chiappori and Gugl (2015, chapter 3). In particular, any efficient allocation maximizes the sum of individual utilities. As before, the economic marital gain per period is then defined as

$$G(t) = \max \sum_i u_i(q_i, Q) \text{ s.t. } p' \sum_i q_i + P'Q = t$$

and the total marital gain is $G(t) + \sum_i \theta_i$, where t denotes total income.

A specific feature of divorce models is that one must, in addition, define each agent's utility if single (which I shall denote $u_i^s(q_i, Q)$). Such a definition is far from obvious, and several thorny issues need to be addressed. For instance, some commodities that used to be publicly consumed by the couple may become private (housing is a typical example). On the other hand, it sounds safe to assume that expenditures on children remain public even after divorce, in the sense that children's welfare still enters both parents' utilities; but the form of individual preferences may be affected (for instance, a noncustodial parent may derive less utility from the child's welfare or consumption). The interested reader is referred to Chiappori, Iyigun, and Weiss (2016) for a precise discussion.

If agents choose to divorce, then they each choose their consumption bundle so as to maximize their utility (as single) under their respective budget constraints. Therefore, the division of income between divorced spouses may play a role (although, as we shall see, in a pure TU framework this role is minimal). Various assumptions can be made at this stage. For instance, we may assume that the actual division is fully determined by legislation; then we can study the impact of legal changes on behavior. Alternatively, we may assume that agents have preemptively decided on an allocation in case of divorce, for instance, in a prenuptial agreement. More complex situations may arise; for instance, courts may decide not to enforce some specific prenuptial agreements (e.g., those deemed "unfair").

Anyhow, in what follows x and y denote the agents' respective period incomes at each period (so that household income is $t = x + y$). In case of divorce, she gets $d_1(x, y) = d(x, y)$ and he gets $d_2(x, y) = x + y - d(x, y)$; then agents each choose their consumption bundle so as to maximize their utility, and I let v_i^S denote

---

[9] In addition, we need to assume that even when it is revealed, θ is not verifiable by a third party, so that agents cannot use marriage contracts contingent on the realization of θ.

the corresponding indirect utility

$$v_i^S(d_i) = \max \left\{ u_i^s \left(q_i, Q \right) \text{ s.t. } p'q_i + P'Q = d_i \right\}.$$

We now introduce the following, simplifying assumption:

Assumption QLUS (Quasilinear Utility if Single) *Utilities when single are quasilinear. In particular, the indirect utility of agent i, when facing prices (p, P) and endowed with income d_i, is proportional to d_i:*

$$v_i^S(p, P, d_i) = \alpha_i(p, P)d_i.$$

In addition, the functions α_i are identical for all agents:

$$\alpha_i(p, P) = \alpha(p, P) \ \forall i.$$

Note in particular that, under QLUS, utility is transferable even when agents are single. In fact, the QLUS assumption is slightly too strong for our purpose. Most results below would still hold if utilities when single were only assumed to be compatible with transferable utility, which is more general than quasilinearity. However, a precise statement would require some complex discussion (in particular regarding which goods remain public and which become private after divorce) that is not necessary at this point; the interested reader is referred to Chiappori, Iyigun, and Weiss (2016).

The Divorce Decision

In order to solve the model, we must, as is usual, proceed backwards: start with the second stage, then analyze the implications for the first-stage decision process.

Let me thus consider the divorce decision. Under the two assumptions I made (TU when married and QLUS), the divorce decision is actually easy to model: agents divorce if and only if the *total* surplus is larger when agents are both single than when they are married to each other. Formally, they divorce if

$$\sum_i v_i^s(d_i(x, y)) > G(x + y) + \sum_i \theta_i,$$

where the sum on the left-hand side stems from the TU property when single. Using QLUS, this becomes

$$\alpha(p, P) \sum_i d_i(x, y) > G(x + y) + \sum_i \theta_i,$$

and since $\sum_i d_i = x + y$,

$$\alpha(p, P)(x + y) > G(x + y) + \sum_i \theta_i,$$

or equivalently,

$$\sum_i \theta_i < \alpha(p, P)(x + y) - G(x + y). \tag{5.5.2}$$

This condition essentially reflects a trade-off between economic and nonmonetary aspects. Indeed, the right-hand side of this inequality equals the opposite of the marital surplus (since it is the difference between the sum of utilities when single and married), while the left-hand side represents the sum of nonmonetary benefits. Note that only that sum matters. In a TU framework, a situation were one agent is very satisfied and the other much less (translating into one very large and one very small θ) does not necessarily lead to divorce, because the better-off partner may be able to compensate the unsatisfied spouse (through economic transfers). Only a small enough *sum* can trigger dissolution.

By the same token, only total income matters. In particular, the function d, which governs the postdivorce allocation of income, does not affect divorce decisions. Nor do various forms of divorce legislation: whether a divorce decision is unilateral or requires mutual consent does not change the outcome, which only depends on the realizations of the monetary and nonmonetary components. This is, in essence, the celebrated Becker-Coase theorem: in our setting, condition (5.5.2) determines whether divorce is efficient or not, irrespective of the various factors influencing resource allocation before or after divorce. It is important to stress, however, that *this property is clearly linked to the specific assumptions (TU and QLUS) that I have made*. In particular, it is *not* a direct consequence of efficiency (as is sometimes claimed in the applied literature). Actually, we shall see later on that the Becker-Coase theorem is not robust to a relaxation of either TU or QLUS, even if we maintain the efficiency requirement.

Moreover, (5.5.2) allows one to explicitly compute the ex ante divorce probability of a couple, conditional on their income:

$$\Pr(\text{divorce}) = \Pi(x + y) = F[\alpha(p, P)(x + y) - G(x + y)], \tag{5.5.3}$$

where F is the cumulative distribution function of $\theta = \sum_i \theta_i$; note that, for simplicity, I assume this distribution to be independent from income, although this assumption could readily be relaxed. Similarly, I will assume that the distribution of θ is absolutely continuous and atomless.

We can see from (5.5.3) that the divorce probability is decreasing in $(x + y)$; remember, indeed, that when agents match on income, the TU assumption requires marital gain G to be convex in total income, whereas QLUS implies that utilities when single are linear. Therefore, if we assume that the distribution of match quality is independent of income, one can expect divorce rates to *decrease* with income—a prediction that is pretty well supported by the data.

First-Period Matching

We can now come back to the first-period matching game. The surplus, now, takes into account both periods, including the risk of divorce. Assume, for the sake of simplicity, that neither incomes nor match qualities change across periods. Then the *realized* sum of utilities over the two periods is

$$\tilde{G}(x+y) = (G(x+y)+\theta) + \delta(1-\Pi(x+y))(G(x+y)+\theta)$$
$$+\delta\Pi(x+y)\alpha(p,P)(x+y)$$

Here, δ is the spouses' common discount factor. In the right-hand side expression, the first term denotes the realization of first-period gain, the second represents the second-period gain conditional on remaining married, and the third takes divorce into account.

When agents meet on the marriage market, what they consider is the *expected* value of this gain; that is

$$\tilde{G}(x+y) = [1+\delta(1-\Pi(x+y))]G(x+y)$$
$$+\bar{\theta} + \delta\Pi(x+y)\alpha(p,P)(x+y)$$
$$+\delta(1-\Pi(x+y))$$
$$\times E[\theta \mid \theta \geq \alpha(p,P)(x+y) - G(x+y)], \qquad (5.5.4)$$

where $\bar{\theta}$ denotes the ex ante expected value of θ. Note that the second term of the right-hand-side expression captures the expected, nonmonetary utility *conditional on remaining married*; in particular, it is higher than the (unconditional) mean $\bar{\theta}$, and its value depends on total income.

Equivalently, (5.5.4) can be written as

$$\tilde{G}(x+y) = [1+\delta(1-F[A(x+y)])]G(x+y)+\bar{\theta} \qquad (5.5.5)$$
$$+\delta\int_{A(x+y)}^{+\infty} tf(t)dt + \delta\alpha(p,P)(x+y)F[A(x+y)],$$

where

$$f(t) = F'(t) \quad \text{and} \quad A(t) = \alpha(p,P)t - G(t).$$

In particular:

$$\bar{G}'(x+y) = [1 + \delta(1 - F[A(x+y)])]G'(x+y) + \delta\alpha(p, P)F[A(x+y)]$$
$$(5.5.6)$$

and

$$\bar{G}''(x+y) = [1 + \delta(1 - F[A(x+y)])]G''(x+y)$$
$$+\delta(A'(x+y))^2 f[A(x+y)] \qquad (5.5.7)$$

and we see that

$$G''(x+y) \geq 0 arrow \bar{G}''(x+y) > 0,$$

implying that the first-period surplus is supermodular. In particular, the model still involves assortative matching on income.

In summary, if we assume (i) TU when married, (ii) quasilinear (or transferable) utilities after divorce, and (iii) independence between income and marriage quality, the model generates a set of testable restrictions. Specifically, we expect assortative matching on income; moreover, divorce rates should not depend on divorce laws and should decrease with income.

Compensations in the Becker-Coase Theorem

As I said earlier, the Becker-Coase theorem requires transferable utility not only during marriage, but also after divorce. The basic argument can easily be summarized in a graph. In figure 5.2, the solid line represents the Pareto frontier when married, whereas the dashed line is the Pareto frontier after divorce. Note that the exact location of the frontier under marriage depends not only on the economic gain, but also on the *total* match quality: a larger realization of θ inflates the Pareto set, whereas it shrinks if θ is negative. In addition, the location of realized utilities over the frontier also depends on each θ_i; keeping the sum θ constant, a larger θ_1 (which necessarily implies a smaller θ_2) moves that location downwards and to the right (to the "southeast").

The crucial point, which reflects the TU assumptions, is that both frontiers are straight lines with the same slope (equal to -1). In particular, these two frontiers cannot intersect; one Pareto set must be included within the other. The Becker-Coase theorem states that, in such a situation, spouses will always adopt the solution that generates the largest Pareto set. In figure 5.2, for instance, they will remain married.

Now, it may well be the case that the *initial* agreement, given the realizations of the nonmonetary components, involves transfers such that one of the spouses

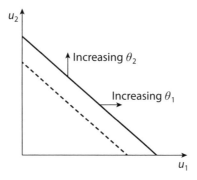

Figure 5.2. Pareto frontiers in the Becker-Coase theorem.

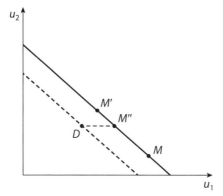

Figure 5.3. The Becker-Coase theorem.

would actually be better off divorcing. Indeed, in figure 5.3, if M denotes the initial division of welfare, one may suspect that θ_1 was large while θ_2 was small (or even negative); anyhow, agent 1 gains much whereas agent 2 would actually prefer the allocation in case of divorce (point D). However, divorce will not follow, at least if we assume efficient decisions: there exists a continuum of locations on the Pareto frontier when married that *both* agents prefer over divorce.

What, then, do we expect in that case? The answer depends on rules governing divorce, as well as on assumptions made about commitment. Assume, for instance, that divorce requires the mutual consent of both spouses; in that case, agents might well remain at M, since agent 1 will typically veto a divorce request made by agent 2. On the contrary, under unilateral divorce, M is not sustainable, because 2 would rather leave. Then the spouses will presumably change the allocation of the economic gain so as to reach a point (say M') that both agents prefer over divorce. De facto, agent 1, who benefits much from the marriage, "bribes" agent 2 into remaining married by offering a larger share of the surplus, therefore by compensating 2 for the low realization of θ_2. This is the second part of the Becker-Coase theorem: while laws governing divorce cannot change the divorce *decisions*, they certainly influence the surplus allocation between spouses.

Lastly, how will point M' be determined? Here is where commitment issues come into play. In the absence of any form of commitment, a natural solution is to refer to cooperative game theory and use Nash bargaining (or any other solution concept), with divorce providing the threat point. Assume, on the contrary, that agents can, at the date of marriage, make binding agreements, the latter being only restricted by the fact that agents cannot legally commit not to divorce. Then the optimal contract involves the minimal change compatible with individual rationality; in practice, the spouses will choose a point such as M'', for which 2 is just indifferent between divorcing and remaining married. For a precise discussion of these issues, the interested reader is referred to the survey by Chiappori and Mazzocco (2017).

5.5.2   Extensions

I now briefly discuss two extensions to this basic setting.

Violations of the Becker-Coase Theorem

First, what happens when the two crucial assumptions (TU when married and QLUS) are relaxed? As I said before, QLUS can be slightly relaxed at no cost. Essentially, what is needed is that utility be transferable both when married and after divorce; note, however, that it must be the case that the two Pareto frontiers are, in both situations, straight lines with slope -1 *for the same cardinalization of individual utilities*. In practice, however, this property is quite difficult to obtain outside of quasilinearity; again, the interested reader is referred to Chiappori, Iyigun, and Weiss (2016).

Now, what if this feature is violated? The crucial insight is that, depending on the realization of the nonmonetary shocks, the two Pareto frontiers (while married and if divorced) may now *intersect*. A first consequence is that the Becker-Coase theorem no longer holds. Indeed, intersecting frontiers mean that some Pareto-efficient allocations imply divorce, whereas others require spouses to remain married. Then efficiency considerations, by themselves, do not determine the outcome; it all depends on which Pareto-efficient allocation will be selected— i.e., on how the surplus generated by marriage is allocated and how income would be split in case of divorce. Moreover, the legislation now becomes relevant: whether divorce is unilateral or requires mutual consent does affect divorce probabilities.

These features are illustrated in figure 5.4. In figure 5.4a, the allocation prevailing when married (described by point M) is more favorable to spouse 1,

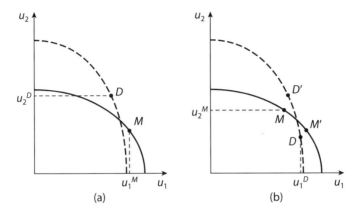

Figure 5.4. Divorce without Becker-Coase.

whereas divorce (point D) is better for spouse 2. Here, if mutual consent is required, then agents do not divorce. By threatening to decline to divorce, agent 1 can guarantee for himself a utility at least equal to u_1^M; but there is no point on the Pareto frontier under divorce that provides 1 with that level of utility, so 2 cannot offer a sufficient compensation to induce 1 to accept divorcing. If, however, agents can unilaterally decide to divorce, then 2 is entitled to receiving at least u_2^D. Now, there exist points on the Pareto frontier when married that provide 2 with that utility level; but these points are, from 1's perspective, worse than divorce, so 1 is unwilling to bribe 2 into remaining married. In particular, this is a situation in which a switch from mutual consent to unilateral would increase divorce probabilities. Note, however, that this conclusion crucially depends on the location of M (which, in turn, reflects not only the initial division of economic surplus, but also the realization of *both* nonmonetary shocks) and of D (reflecting, among other things, the postdivorce allocation of resources).

More surprising, perhaps, is the fact that in different contexts, switching from mutual consent to unilateral may sometimes *discourage* divorce. Such a pattern is illustrated in figure 5.4b). For one thing, neither M nor D are efficient; therefore, none of them will ultimately be chosen. Under unilateral divorce, M is not sustainable, because 1 can claim at least u_1^D. But then both spouses can improve their situation by remaining married and agreeing on a point like M': it is even better than D for 1, and 2 will not oppose the move, since M', while worse than M, is nevertheless preferred to divorce. Consider, now, the mutual consent case. Now D is not reachable (2 would veto it); and while M can still be improved upon, it is only through divorce and a renegotiation settlement—since both spouses would rather get D' than M. In other words, the apparently common-sense claim that a switch from mutual consent to unilateral can only increase divorce frequency is incorrect; in a world where transfers are feasible, the actual outcome depends on the entire context, including not only existing legislation and economic context, but also the distribution of marital shocks.[10]

Remarriage

A second assumption that we may want to relax is that people remain single after divorce. In reality, remarriage is a massive phenomenon. More than half of divorcees remarry (with a clear gender gap, men being more likely to remarry). According to a recent report by the Pew Research Center,[11] in 2013 no less than 4 in 10 new marriages in the US involved at least one partner who had been married before.

However, modeling remarriage raises difficult problems. One is the exact definition of the "remarriage market". Broadly speaking, still considering the US in 2013, half of all marriages where at least one partner had been married before were first marriages for the other spouse—whereas for the other half, both spouses had previously been married. In other words, we do not see a clear separation between a market for first marriage and a distinct remarriage market; on the contrary, a significant fraction (around one-fifth) of first-married individuals tied the knot with a spouse who had already been married. In matching terms, we have a global marriage/remarriage market in which the list of previous marriages (if any), as well as the features of these marriages (e.g., the characteristics of the former spouse) are potentially among each partner's characteristics

Moreover, the introduction of remarriage prospects considerably complicates the analysis of the divorce decision. Indeed, when considering whether to divorce, many individuals consider remarriage as a possible (and sometimes even likely) outcome; in the previous formalization, divorce can be seen as an opportunity to "redraw" a new realization of the nonmonetary gains. Economic considerations, however, are probably at least equally important; the divorce decision is likely to be influenced, among other things, by the agent's expectations regarding not only remarriage probability, but also the characteristics of the (potential) new spouse, as well as the (potential) distribution of the generated surplus between the new spouses. However, both aspects are endogenous—they are clearly related to the number and characteristics of divorcees on the marriage/remarriage market, which themselves simply reflect (aggregate) divorce decisions. In a nutshell, the analysis, again, must rely on *equilibrium* considerations, whereby agents' expectations trigger behavior that may fulfill them ex post.

---

[10] For a more detailed discussion, see Clark (1999) and Chiappori, Iyigun, and Weiss (2016).

[11] See http://www.pewsocialtrends.org/files/2014/11/2014-11-14_remarriage-final.pdf.

Not much has been done on this topic, at least from a pure theory perspective, in the context of matching models. An interesting contribution, however, is due to Goussé, Jacquemet, and Robin (2016), who extend the search-matching model of the marriage market of Shimer and Smith (2000) to allow for labor supply, home production, match-specific shocks, and endogenous divorce. In particular, the authors estimate how equilibrium marriage formation affects the wage elasticities of market and nonmarket hours, and quantify the redistributive effect of intrahousehold resource sharing.

To summarize:

- In the simplest model of matching with divorce, a match between two agents generates a surplus involving a random component ("match quality") that is revealed after marriage. Then divorce obtains when realized match quality is poor enough to compensate for the economic gains of marriage.
- Under strong assumptions on preferences (utility must be transferable both during marriage and after divorce, and at the same rate), the Becker-Coase theorem obtains: legislation governing divorce does not affect divorce rates.
- However, these assumptions go well beyond efficiency and TU. In particular, in a standard model of divorce and remarriage under TU, the Becker-Coase theorem cannot be expected to hold in general.

6

Matching under Transferable Utility: Applications

I will now give two examples of applications of the techniques developed above to the analysis of economic phenomena. The first example deals with the legalization of abortion, and more specifically with an old claim of the feminist literature, whereby this crucial evolution empowered *all* women (as opposed to only the subset of women who were willing to actually use the newly legalized method). As we shall see, matching theory helps with understanding how the benefits of an innovation that initially concerns a fraction of the population can propagate to everyone via the equilibrium mechanisms at stake. The second example discusses the puzzle described in the introduction regarding the discrepancy between male and female demand for higher education over the last decades. The argument, here, is that the benefits of a college education and beyond are not only perceived on the labor market; education also affects marital prospects along a host of different dimensions. Unlike the labor market returns, which are essentially equivalent for men and women, these "marital returns" may notably differ between genders, and these differences may account for the asymmetries in observed behavior.

6.1   *Roe v. Wade* and Female Empowerment

Our first application deals with the impact of innovations in birth control that took place during the last decades of the twentieth century.[1] Their impact on modern societies has been abundantly discussed. The direct effect on demography, and especially on birth rates in specific social groups, has been clearly documented.[2] An additional, indirect effect operates through the reduction in uncertainty faced by couples and single women due to the increased ability to plan demographic phenomena. This fact has dramatically altered the context in which decisions regarding human capital accumulation were made. For instance, many authors have argued that the spectacular increase in women's education and participation in the labor market since the 1960s was largely due to these innovations.[3]

A third and relatively less studied consequence goes through a different channel—namely, the impact of the changes on the "balance of power" within

---

[1] This section is directly borrowed from Chiappori and Oreffice (2008).

[2] See for instance Levine et al. (1999), Klerman (1999), Angrist and Evans (1999), and Ananat, Gruber, and Levine (2004).

[3] See Michael (2000) and especially Goldin and Katz (2002).

the couple. The intuition, here, is that innovations in birth control technology, including the legalization of abortion, must have had a potentially huge effect on men's and women's respective decision rights within the household regarding such crucial issues as the number or timing of births. It is hard to believe that a shift of such magnitude would leave the balance of powers unaltered. This claim has been put forth by a number of sociologists,[4] but there is little in terms of an economic analysis of this phenomenon.

Oreffice (2007) has provided some econometric confirmation of these ideas. The change she considers is the legalization of abortion, which was initially introduced in some states[5] before being extended nationwide by the well-known US Supreme Court decision in *Roe v. Wade* (1973). She studies the impact of legalization on labor supply of married females in their fertile age. If, as is often argued, legalization actually improved the wife's bargaining situation within married couples, then she should have consequently received a larger share of household resources. By a standard income effect, the reform should thus decrease her labor supply and increase her husband's. As it turns out, the predictions of the model are confirmed by the data. A significant effect is observed on both male and female labor supply for married couples, but not for older couples nor for single males and females. She concludes that the "empowerment" effect of legalization was real.

However, the mechanism by which this empowerment occurs deserves some scrutiny. While it is not hard to convince oneself that *some* women (e.g., career-oriented women who want to delay fertility) will gain, whether *all* will is another matter. Women have heterogeneous tastes with respect to children (or different attitudes toward abortion); some, in particular, do not consider abortion as an option, either for religious or ethical reasons or because they do want children. Whether the legalization will benefit these women as well is not clear. From a general perspective, the new context will affect the matching process on the market for marriage, and in particular the way the surplus generated by marriage is shared between members. In principle, such "general equilibrium" effects could annihilate or even reverse the direct impact, particularly for those women who are unlikely to derive much direct benefit from the reform. Clearly, such an issue must be analyzed within a matching framework. This is done in a paper by Chiappori and Oreffice (2008, from now on CO).

---

[4] See, for instance, Williams (1994), Héritier (2002), or Coombs and Fernandez (1978).

[5] Six "repeal states" (Alaska in 1970, California in 1969, D.C. in 1971, Hawaii in 1970, New York in 1970, and Washington in 1970) had legalized first-trimester abortions under most circumstances; 13 "reform states" permitted abortion to preserve the physical or mental health of the mother, whereas the remaining nonreform states prohibited abortion for any reason except to save the life of the mother. See, for instance, Myers (2012).

6.1.1   The Model

Preferences and Budget Constraints

In the economy that CO consider, there exists a continuum of men and women who derive utility from one private composite good a and from children. For the sake of expositional simplicity, let us only consider the choice between having children or not, although the generalization to different numbers of children is straightforward. Let the dummy variable k denote the presence ($k = 1$) or the absence ($k = 0$) of children in the household; alternatively, k can be interpreted as the additional children that men and women may have at any given moment.

Men have identical, quasilinear preferences over consumption and children. To sharpen the analysis, let us assume that the utility of single men only depends on their consumption; i.e., men cannot derive utility from (and do not share the costs of) out-of-wedlock children due to the fact that they do not live in the same household. On the other hand, married men's utility is of the form $U_H(a_H, k) = a_H + u_H k$, where the parameter $u_H > 0$ is identical for all men in the economy. Note, in particular, that the utility of a married man does not depend on the identity of the person he married, but only on the fertility decision and on the share of composite good he receives.

Women differ in their preferences toward children. Specifically, female utility functions take the quasilinear form $U(a, k) = a + uk$. Here, each woman is characterized by the individual-specific taste parameter u, which is distributed according to the density f and the cumulative distribution function F over some support included in the interval $[0, U]$. This implies that utilities are transferable; also, note that matching is not based on income but on the preference parameter u.

Let us assume that any woman (single or married) who wants a child can have one. However, should she plan not to have children, unwanted births may still occur with some probability p, which depends on the technology available. The price of the private composite good is normalized to 1. Male income is denoted Y. Women initially receive an income y; however, if a woman has children, her income drops to z, with $z < y$, reflecting both the loss in her earning capacity due to childbearing and the cost of raising the child. Hence, a single woman without children consumes her income y; if she decides to have a child (or if an unwanted pregnancy occurs), she also consumes her income (which has dropped to z) and receives moreover the utility u from her child, which is independent of her marital status.

Regarding couples, let us assume that $u_H < y - z$, i.e. that the gain received by the husband from having a child does not offset by itself the loss in income experienced by the wife. This assumption implies, in this framework, that the couple's decision to have a child or not will also depend on the wife's preferences. Therefore, married women must agree with their husband on two issues. One is the fertility decision; i.e., they must decide whether to have kids or not, and the decision depends (in particular) on the wife's preferences towards children. The other decision relates to the distribution of resources within the household (i.e., the allocation of total income between male and female consumption of the composite good). Both decisions are ultimately determined by the equilibrium on the market for marriage.

Using this simplified framework, CO consider the impact of innovations in birth control technology. Specifically, they model the legalization of abortion (and generally the availability of some birth control technology) as an exogenous decrease in the probability p of experiencing an unwanted pregnancy. In particular, other benefits derived from the improved birth control technology (e.g., increased ability to plan and control human capital accumulation, or easier access to sexual activity before marriage) are disregarded in this stylized model.

Marriage Market

The marriage market is modeled as a frictionless matching process. Any individual gets married as long as the utility she/he can get from marriage is larger than or equal to the utility obtained from remaining unmarried. Because children are public goods, marriage generates a net surplus; hence it must be the case that either all men or all women are married. As is often the case with matching models, the qualitative properties of the stable match will crucially depend on which side is in excess supply. Let us normalize the mass of women to be 1, and let M denote the total mass of males on the market. Hence, one must distinguish two main cases, depending on whether the male population M is smaller or larger than 1, as well as several subcases.

6.1.2   Stable Matching on the Marriage Market

One can now characterize the main features of the equilibrium (or stable matching) reached on the marriage market.

Fertility Decisions

Let us first consider the fertility decisions of singles and couples, starting with single individuals. Single men do not make decisions: they consume their income and get a utility equal to Y. Single women, on the other hand, will decide to have children if and only if the benefit compensates for the income loss, i.e., if $u \geq y - z$, leading to a utility equal to $z + u$. In the alternative case when $u < y - z$, single women of type u choose not to have a child; any pregnancy will be involuntary and occur with probability p. Their expected utility will thus be equal to $y(1 - p) + p(z + u)$. In what follows, the threshold $y - z$ is

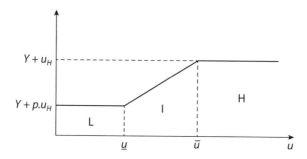

Figure 6.1. Male maximum possible utility by wife's preference u.

denoted $\bar{u}$; women whose parameter is larger than or equal to $\bar{u}$ will be said to be of "high" type.

Regarding couples, note, first, that in a transferable utility context the stable match must maximize total surplus. The total benefit, for a couple, of having a child is $u_H + u$, whereas the cost is $y - z$. It follows that a married couple will plan to have a child if $u \geq y - z - u_H$—then total utility is $Y + z + u_H + u$. The threshold $y - z - u_H$ is denoted $\underline{u}$; note that $\underline{u} < \bar{u}$. If $u < y - z - u_H$, only unwanted kids are born, leading to an expected total utility equal to $Y + (1 - p)y + p(z + u_H + u)$. Women whose parameter is smaller than $\underline{u}$ will be said to be of "low" type, while those between $\underline{u}$ and $\bar{u}$ will be called "intermediate".

In summary:

- Women of "high" type ($u \geq \bar{u}$) always choose to have a child.
- Women of "intermediate" type ($\underline{u} < u < \bar{u}$) choose to have a child only when married.
- Women of "low" type ($u \leq \underline{u}$) never choose to have a child.

The next step is to analyze the properties of the equilibrium. As said above, two cases must be distinguished.

Marriage Market with Excess Supply of Women

Consider, first, the case of an excess supply of women; i.e., assume that $M < 1$. Because women are in excess supply, they have to compete for marriage. An intuition of the driving force behind this competition is provided by Figure 6.1, which plots the maximum utility $\Phi(u)$ a man can achieve when marrying a woman of taste u (in other words, $\Phi(u)$ denotes his utility if he were to appropriate *all* the surplus generated by marriage). The function Φ is increasing; i.e., it is always better (for the husband) to marry a wife with a larger taste coefficient u.

More precisely, women whose parameter u is greater than $\bar{u}$ (the high type), and who would plan to have a child even when single, are the most attractive from the male's perspective. While they differ in taste, this difference is irrelevant from a husband's viewpoint, since they require the same compensation c_H for getting married (namely, to be left with a private consumption equal to their income with a child z). Women between $\underline{u}$ and $\bar{u}$ (the intermediate type) come next in males' preferences. They plan to have a child only when married, and the minimum compensation they require is equal to $c_I(u) = (y - u)(1 - p) + pz \geq z$. Note that this compensation decreases with the taste parameter; hence, men strictly prefer intermediate women with a higher parameter u. Finally, women with a u smaller than $\underline{u}$ (the low type) never plan to have a child. Again, these women are equivalent from a husband's perspective, since they require the same compensation for getting married, namely, their consumption as single, i.e., $c_L = (1 - p)y + pz$.

As is often the case in matching models, the properties of the stable match crucially depend on the identity of the marginal spouse (i.e., the "last" single woman or the "first" married woman). We denote by $u(M)$ the taste parameter of this marginal woman. Technically, $u(M)$ is defined by the fact that the measure of the set of women with a taste parameter larger than $u(M)$ is exactly M; i.e., the value $u(M)$ solves the equation

$$\int_{u(M)}^{U} f(t)dt = M,$$

or equivalently,

$$u(M) = F^{-1}(1 - M).$$

Competition between women on the marriage market implies that women who generate a larger surplus for their husband will be preferred. In particular, whenever a women belonging to the intermediate type is married, then all women with a larger taste parameter are married as well—this is the case depicted in figure 6.2. The intuition is that women with a larger preference for children have a comparative advantage: the compensation they need from their husband to accept marriage is smaller, because they value highly the prospect of having a child. In general, the category of this marginal woman depends on the location of $u(M)$ with respect to the two thresholds $\underline{u}$ and $\bar{u}$.

An obvious property of stable matches in this context is that *all males receive the same utility*; indeed, they are assumed identical, and the absence of friction implies that any difference of welfare between males would be competed away. Since the marginal woman is indifferent between being married or single, her husband gets all the surplus generated by the relationship, namely $\Phi(u(M))$. Then all other men receive the same utility. Graphically, this corresponds, in figure 6.2, to the horizontal dotted line going through $\Phi(u(M))$.

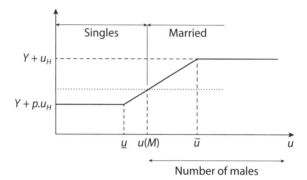

Figure 6.2. Excess supply of women.

A crucial insight, at this point, is the following. Take any woman with a taste parameter u larger than $u(M)$. Then *the difference $\Phi(u) - \Phi(u(M))$ represents the surplus received by this woman.*[6] In figure 6.4, for instance, the surplus received by any woman of high type is depicted by a bold arrow.

Using this geometric intuition, the characterization of the equilibrium is straightforward. Three cases should be distinguished:

- If $M \le \underline{W} = \int_{\tilde{u}}^{U} f(t)dt$, the excess supply of women is large, in the sense that there are fewer men than high-type women. Then $u(M) \ge \bar{u}$, and the marginal married woman belongs to the high type. Only (some of) these women are matched. Women of the same type who remain single decide to have a kid; all other women remain single and decide not to have children (although they may have one involuntarily). Regarding welfare issues, note that, in this case, married women receive no surplus from marriage; their consumption is the same as if single (Figure 6.3).
- If $\underline{W} < M < \bar{W} = \int_{\underline{u}}^{U} f(t)dt$ (intermediate excess supply of women, as depicted in figure 6.4), the marginal wife belongs to the intermediate type. All married women have a child and consume the same amount, which is such that the marginal wife is indifferent between getting married and remaining single. All married women (but the marginal one) get a positive surplus from marriage, and high-type women receive the maximal surplus.
- Finally, when the excess supply of women is small enough (technically, $M \ge \bar{W}$), the marginal wife belongs to the low type (i.e., $u(M) \le \underline{u}$—see

---

[6] If her husband's utility were $\Phi(u)$, he would get all the surplus generated by the marriage. Since his equilibrium utility is only $\Phi(u(M))$, the difference $\Phi(u) - \Phi(u(M))$ represents the part of the surplus appropriated by the wife.

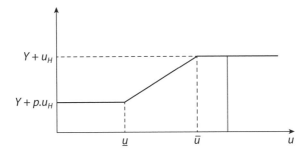

Figure 6.3. Large excess supply of women.

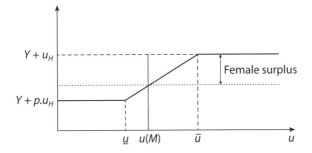

Figure 6.4. Intermediate excess supply of women.

Figure 6.5). Her fertility is the same with and without marriage—namely, no planned child. Stability requires that her consumption be also the same, i.e., equal to $(1 - p)y + pz$. The same conclusion applies to all married, low-type women. Other married women belong to the high or intermediate type, and hence decide to have a child; their consumption is defined by the fact that men, who are in short supply, must be indifferent between the various potential spouses. Again, this condition generates a positive surplus for all women of high and intermediate types; high-type women receive the largest surplus (Figure 6.5).

The equilibrium is technically not unique, because in the first and third situations the identity of married women is indeterminate. In the first case, high-type women are identical from the husband's perspective, and hence any subset of size M may be married at equilibrium; the same argument applies to low-type women in the third case. Note, however, that the respective consumptions are uniquely determined in each case; so are welfares, since in the first (resp. third) case, high-type (resp. low-type) women are indifferent between marriage and singlehood.

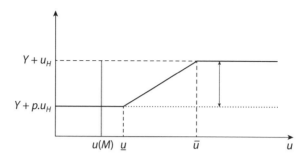

Figure 6.5. Small excess supply of women.

   The variation in women's utility across the three types of equilibria exhibits interesting patterns. Not surprisingly, the smaller the excess supply of women on the market, the higher the utility of each woman. However, when women's excess supply is either large or small, their welfare does not depend on the size of the imbalance. In the intermediate case, on the contrary, a marginal increase in the number of men continuously reduces the taste parameter $u(M)$ of the marginal woman, which ameliorates the welfare of all married women.

Marriage Market with Excess Supply of Men

The alternative case in which men are in excess supply on the marriage market is much simpler. All women are married; and stability requires that each married man be indifferent to remaining single. Since men have to be indifferent between marriage and singlehood, women leave them with whatever is needed for them to achieve their utility as single, namely Y. In particular, the utility men derive from having children is captured by women under the form of additional consumption.

Comparative Statics

Simple as it may be, the model still offers interesting insights on the role of several key parameters.

Incomes

Consider, first, the impact of female income on fertility and allocations. Not surprisingly, female utility always increases with both y (her income without a child) and z (her income with a child). However, the respective impact of the two incomes on a woman's welfare depends on the woman's type. For high-type women, for instance, an increase in z is always favorable, since they always have

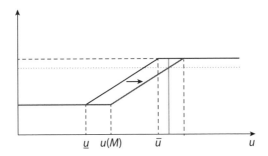

Figure 6.6. The impact of proportional income growth.

a child. Still, y may also matter for them; for instance, in the case of intermediate excess supply of women, the rent received by married women is positively related to the income of childless women. A similar logic prevails for women of the low type: y always matters (they will never *elect* to have a child), but so does z (because of unwanted pregnancies).

The situation is more complex when y and z do not increase by the same *amount*, because of the possible impact on the fertility decisions and the type of equilibrium finally reached. An interesting illustration obtains when both y and z are increased by the same *factor*. Then the difference $y - z$ increases proportionally, which reduces the number of high-type women and inflates the low-type population (the effect on the intermediate type depends on the distribution of tastes). In figure 6.6, one can see that income growth shifts the function Φ to the right. A first consequence is a negative impact on fertility. More interestingly, the type of equilibrium reached may switch, at least when women are in excess supply; indeed, the thresholds $\underline{u}$ and $\bar{u}$ are positively related to the difference $y - z$. For instance, a large excess supply of women (in the sense just defined) may become intermediate, and an intermediate case may switch to small.

We conclude that in a context of excess supply of women, a growth in female income reduces the severity of the excess supply phenomenon, which inflates their welfare gain beyond the change in income, and decreases male well-being accordingly. On the other hand, a variation in male income has no impact on fertility and on the equilibrium structure; only men's equilibrium payoffs will vary.

Smaller Male Population

Let us now study the impact of the size M of the male population. Not surprisingly, a variation large enough to switch from an excess supply of men to an excess supply of women will favor men and cost women. More interesting are changes taking place within the regime of excess supply of women. Assume, for instance, that the

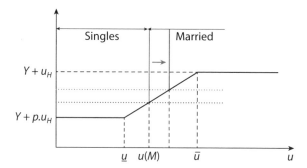

Figure 6.7. Reducing the male population.

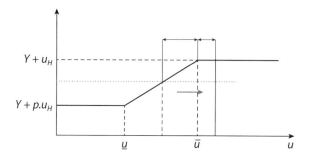

Figure 6.8. Changing regime.

initial situation is characterized by an intermediate excess supply of women (as depicted in figure 6.7).

All married women (but the marginal one) receive a share of the surplus generated by marriage. A reduction in the male population, assuming that the equilibrium remains an "intermediate excess supply" type, moves the threshold $u(M)$ to the right. Some women who were previously married are now single; they decide not to have children, which reduces total fertility, and they entirely lose the share of the marital surplus they initially received. Even women who are married in both cases receive a smaller share of the surplus in the second situation.

Assume, now, that the number of men is reduced below the threshold $\underline{W}$, so that the equilibrium switches to a large excess type (figure 6.8). Various consequences can be expected:

- In the initial situation, some of the intermediate-type women were married and had a child, while they are single and childless (except for unwanted pregnancies) in the new equilibrium; hence, *total fertility is smaller.*

- High-type women were all married and had a child in the initial equilibrium. Some of them are now single, but they still choose to have a child. The result is *higher out-of-wedlock fertility*.
- The welfare of *all* married women is decreased down to their reservation utility. Indeed, in the initial, intermediate excess supply equilibrium, married women receive a share of the surplus generated by marriage. In the new equilibrium, characterized by a large excess supply, men appropriate all the surplus, leaving married women at their reservation utility.
- The same analysis applies to those intermediate women who are married in the initial equilibrium but not in the new one. Again, all but the marginal one receive a fraction of the surplus when married, and therefore singlehood results in a welfare loss.
- In both cases, male utility is increased.

Finally, a similar analysis applies if the equilibrium switches from small to intermediate excess supply types. On the other hand, if the initial equilibrium was characterized by a large excess supply of women, or if their excess supply is small in both cases, welfare does not change in response to a reduction in M.

Single Parent Benefits

So far, we have assumed that the income of a woman with a child is z, whatever her marital status. We now allow for single-parent benefits, say b, and assume for simplicity that all single women are eligible. The income of a woman with a child is thus still z when she is married, but becomes $b + z$ when single. We assume, however, that $b \leq u_H$, i.e., that the surplus stemming from the public nature of children in case of marriage compensates for the (monetary) loss of the single-parent benefit. This condition is necessary in our simplified model for marriage to take place at equilibrium.

The case of an excess supply of men is of little interest: single parent benefits do not matter in that case, since all women are married and receive all the surplus created by marriage. We thus consider the alternative context of an excess supply of women.

The main changes with respect to the initial situation can be summarized as follows. First, the upper threshold $\bar{u}$ declines by b: more women are now willing to have children, even when single. It follows that when the excess supply of women is large, *out-of-wedlock fertility* increases. Note that, technically, an equilibrium initially classified as intermediate may now become large, since the number of high-type women has increased.

If we assume that the type of equilibrium does *not* switch, then women always gain from the introduction of the benefits. Specifically:

- In the case of a large excess supply of women, women of intermediate or low type are single and choose not to have a child. Still, they are entitled to the additional payment b in case of unwanted pregnancy, hence an increase in expected utility equal to pb. Women of the high type receive an additional gain equal to b when they are single, because they all have a child. But then equilibrium requires that they receive the same gain when married (their reservation utility has increased by b). We thus have the counter intuitive result that *the introduction of single-parent benefits profits all women*, and that married women (who do not receive the benefit) gain on average more (per capita) than most singles. Not surprisingly, men lose the same amount b.
- When the excess supply of women is either intermediate or small, all women (married or single) get an extra pb, and all men lose the same expected amount.

These conclusions should, however, be qualified for two reasons. First, when the initial excess supply of women is large, the number of potential spouses (i.e., women of the high type) increases. For a given supply of men, this decreases the probability that each one gets married; note, however, that since women are indifferent between getting married and remaining single, the resulting welfare loss is nil (at least in our model).

Secondly, a more complex situation arises when the change generates a change of equilibrium, the excess supply of women switching either from small to intermediate or from intermediate to large. Indeed, such a switch harms all women, because tougher competition on the marriage market results in smaller rents. The welfare comparison becomes somewhat intricate, because this loss should be traded off with the higher expected utility when single (which boosts married women's reservation point); intuitively, women perceive a smaller rent beyond a higher reservation utility. It can be shown that depending on the parameters, the introduction of the benefit may actually harm some married women.

Finally, if the distribution of these single-parent benefits is "too" generous, in the sense that $b > u_H$, then marriage becomes inefficient from the couple's viewpoint;[7] indeed, the surplus generated may be inferior to the opportunity cost in terms of lost income. Then welfare benefits would decrease (in our model, eliminate) marriage, fertility becoming exclusively an out-of-wedlock phenomenon.

---

[7] We assume that the single-parent condition can be enforced; i.e., we do not consider situations in which a man and a woman enjoy the benefits of parenthood through cohabitation while receiving the single-parent benefit.

The US Example

In practice, this simple model generates predictions that seem to fit fairly well the main stylized facts characterizing the marriage market in the US. Some predictions are fairly straightforward; for instance, the rise of female wages has had a negative impact on fertility. More interesting (and perhaps less expected) is the fact that a decline in the supply of "marriageable" males reduces total fertility but increases out-of-wedlock birth rate. Such a mechanism may have played an important role in specific submarkets. For instance, an overwhelming phenomenon that took place during the last few decades is the dramatic rise of incarceration rates for young, low-skilled black males. According to Western and Pettit (2000), the percentage of black male, high school dropouts in prison or jail reached 36% in 1996, up from 15% in 1982; as a comparison, the rate for white male, high school dropouts went only from 4% to 7% over the same period.[8] If we accept that the marriage market is largely assortative by race and education, the "submarket" of low-skilled black individuals has experienced a dramatic decline in male supply. According to our analysis, such a brutal change should induce a sharp rise in nonmarital fertility. Indeed, while the overall fertility rate of black female, high school dropouts aged 25 to 29 has slightly declined over the period (from 102.5 per mil in 1980 to 99.5 per mil in 2000), the fraction of women never married with children has risen from 3% in 1960 to 35% in 1990, as compared to 6% for white high school dropouts of the same age and for black women with a college education.[9] The results, on this point, are in line with earlier intuitions proposed by Neal (2004).

6.1.3   Changes in Birth Control Technology

We now come to the main implications of our model, namely the impact of a technological change in birth control.

Legalizing Abortion

We first consider the impact of innovations in birth control technology that reduce the probability of unwanted pregnancies, assuming that all women (including

---

[8] Similar effects can be observed on employment data. Among black high school dropouts aged 26–36, the percentage of individuals who worked at least 26 weeks during the poll year dropped from 80% in 1960 to 44% in 1990. For high school graduates, the drop is from 86% to 67% (Neal 2004, table 2). See also Wilson (1987).

[9] The effect may initially have been further boosted by the increased generosity of single-parent benefits during the 1960s and the early 1970s. Note, however, that this latter trend has largely reverted since then (Moffit 1992), while the increase in birth outside marriage has persisted, suggesting that the marriage market factor may have been dominant.

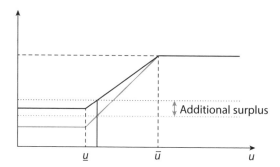

Figure 6.9. The impact of technological change (intermediate case).

singles) are given free access to the technology; a natural example could be the legalization of abortion that took place in the 1970s.

We start with the case of an excess supply of men. Then the innovation has no impact on behavior and has a straightforward impact on welfare. Before and after the change, all women are married. The welfare of women of the high and intermediate types does not change: since all are married and planning to have kids, the technology has no consequence for them. Couples in which the wife is of the low type are better off, but only because they do not plan to have a child, and the new technology improves their ability to reach that goal. Clearly, all the gains go to the wife.

The situation is drastically different in the alternative (and probably empirically more relevant) situation in which women are in excess supply. The situation is depicted in figure 6.9 (which, for expositional convenience, considers the case in which the risk of unwanted pregnancies goes to zero). The new technology decreases the maximum utility attainable by husbands of low- or intermediate-type women, resulting in a shifts downwards of the graph of the function Φ. This leads to the following conclusions:

- Not surprisingly, women who do not want to have a child (either because they belong to the low type or because they are single) benefit from the technology, precisely because unwanted pregnancies become less likely. In the extreme situation in which unwanted pregnancies are eliminated, the monetary gain is thus $p(y - z - u)$.
- More interesting is the fact that when the excess supply of women is not large (in the sense defined above), women who decide to have a child do also benefit from the technology, although to a lesser extent than singles. The intuition is that the intrahousehold distribution of resources is driven by the marginal women; for a small or intermediate excess supply

of women, the marginal woman is indifferent between getting married and remaining single *without a kid*. Her reservation utility is thus improved by the new technology. The nature of a matching game, however, implies that any improvement of the marginal agent's situation must be transmitted to all agents "above" the marginal one.

In practice, in the case of the intermediate excess supply depicted in figure 6.9, the benefit experienced by all married women, assuming the new technologies drive the risk of unwanted pregnancies to zero, is $p(y - z - u(M))$ (where, again, $u(M)$ denotes the taste parameter of the marginal married woman). This benefit continuously increases with the number of men M. When the excess supply is small, the gain is pu_H, still smaller than $p(y - z)$ (the gain for single women) but nevertheless positive.

- On the other hand, when the excess supply of women is large, married women do *not* benefit from the new technology, because the marginal woman does not use it. Hence, the impact of the new technology upon married women's welfare is intimately related to the situation that prevails on the marriage market.

Finally, men cannot gain from the introduction of the new technology. When the excess supply of women is large, their utility is not affected. When the excess supply of women is small, so that the marginal wife does not want a child, the total welfare of the household is increased, but so is the reservation utility of the wife; the husband is left with the same consumption, but loses the benefit he would have received from an unwanted birth. The intermediate case is even more spectacular. Here, all marriages result in a child being born, so the total surplus generated by marriage is not affected by the innovation. What changes, however, is the intrahousehold allocation of the surplus. The new technology improves the reservation utility of the marginal woman, hence her share of resources; stability requires this shift to be reproduced in all couples. All in all, the new technology results in a net transfer from the husband to the wife, equal to the expected gain of the marginal single woman, i.e., $p(y - z - u(M))$, without any change to the fertility of married couples (who actually do not use the new technology).

We thus conclude that in our model, an improvement in birth control technology, such as the legalization of abortion, generally increases the welfare of *all* women, including those who want a child and are not interested in the new technology. Note, however, that the mechanism generating this gain is largely indirect. The reason why even married women willing to have a child benefit from birth control technology is that the latter, by raising the reservation utility of single women, raises the price of all women on the matching market. However, this logic fails to apply in situations of a large excess supply of women.

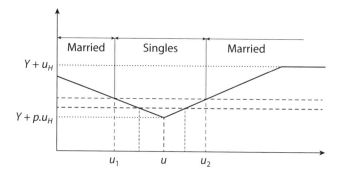

Figure 6.10. Innovation limited to married women.

As argued above, empirical evidence suggests that specific submarkets (e.g., low-skill African Americans) may exhibit the typical features of a large excess supply of women. In that case, our analysis suggests that married women belonging to this social group may have derived little benefit from the legalization of abortion, although the technology may be widely used in the subpopulation under consideration.

The Power Shift of the Pill

The previous argument shows clearly that an important channel through which the new technology benefits all women—what could be called *female empowerment*—is the rise in their reservation utility. In turn, the source of this change lies in the fact that single women can access the new technology. Consider, now, a situation in which a new technology of this type is introduced but exclusively available to married women. A typical illustration is provided by the pill, which became available first (in 1960) to married women only, and later (by the end of the 1960s) to single women as well (Goldin and Katz 2002).

The case of male excess supply is of little interest, since, in our simple model, all women marry in that case (so that the restriction is irrelevant). On the other hand, in the case of women in excess supply, our previous conclusions are drastically modified by the restrictions on access. In what follows, let $u(M)$ denote the preference parameter of the marginal woman *in the prereform equilibrium*. Although various cases can be considered, we only discuss here the most realistic (and interesting) one, represented in figure 6.10.

We see in figure 6.10 that making the new technology available only to married women has major and somewhat counterintuitive consequences. First, the selection of women into marriage is qualitatively different from the initial case, at least when the excess supply of women is not large. The key point is that the graph in figure 6.10 is no longer monotonic. Indeed, marriage may now also attract women with a very low taste for children—precisely because they view marriage as the only way to access birth control technology. Because of this new demand, the competition for marriage becomes tougher; it actually does if $u(M) \leq \frac{u}{1-p}$. Then some intermediate-type women are single, when otherwise they would have been married. Even for women who are married in both situations, welfare is lower with the new technology, because increased competition on the marriage market reduces their share of total surplus. The gainers from the new technology are (i) women with the lowest taste for children, and (ii) men.

The conclusion of this analysis is clear: reserving the new technology to married women essentially *reverses* the empowerment effect. The availability for marriage of women with a low taste for children, who are willing to accept a lower compensation from the husband for getting married and gaining access to the new technology, toughens competition for husbands. Women of the high or intermediate type are made worse off by the introduction of the new technology. Only women with a very low preference for children gain from the innovation.

This comparison emphasizes the complex and partly paradoxical welfare impact of a new technology. On the one hand, its effects can go well beyond the individuals who actually use it, or even consider using it. Our model suggests that a consequence of better birth control may have been a shift in the intrahousehold balance of powers and in the resulting allocation of resources, even (and perhaps especially) in couples who were not considering using the technology as an option. On the other hand, the new technology benefits all married women only because it is available to singles. A technological improvement which is reserved to married women will have an impact on their fertility, partly because it changes the mechanisms governing selection into marriage. But its impact on women's welfare is largely negative, except for a small fraction of women who choose marriage as an access to the new technology.

Our analysis thus suggests that as far as the intrahousehold balance of power is concerned, the introduction of the pill in 1960 (when it was available to married women only) may have had a *disempowerment* effect on most women. The true empowerment revolution came later; it was caused by the generalization of its availability for single women during the late 1960s, and strengthened by the legalization of abortion in the 1970s.

Obviously, this analysis is only partial, in that it omits other benefits of the pill (such as women's increased ability to plan their fertility and to achieve higher levels of education). These aspects, which have been intensively discussed in the literature, clearly favored all women, including married women. Still, the strong message of this analysis is that reserving the technology to married women makes an important difference, and, more surprisingly, that most married women are likely to *lose* from this exclusivity.

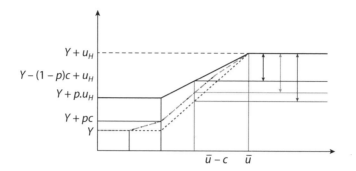

Figure 6.11. Costly access to the technology.

6.1.4   Extensions

Costly Access to the New Technology

Finally, we can consider a few extensions of the model. First we can introduce the assumption that access to the new technology is "costly". The cost, here, should be understood in a general way; it includes financial costs, but also the moral or ethical discomfort some women may experience with the new technology. The cost, denoted by c, is assumed for the moment to be identical for all women. Since, however, preferences for children differ, a uniform cost generates different responses over the population. Specifically, single women will use the technology only if the net cost of the child (i.e., the income loss minus the benefit u) is large enough to compensate for the abortion cost. Hence:

- A single woman with preference $u \leq \bar{u} - c$ will always abort; the probability of having a child is zero.
- For $\bar{u} - c < u < \bar{u}$, she will neither abort nor try to have a child; the probability of birth is then p.
- For $u \geq \bar{u}$, she has a child with probability one.

A similar argument applies to couples, $\bar{u}$ being replaced with $\underline{u}$.

The resulting equilibrium is depicted in figure 6.11. Here, the new male surplus curve (large dots) is located between the prereform one (continuous line) and the zero cost one (small dots).

The general conclusion is that under costly access,

- all women are better off than before the technology became available (unless the excess supply of women is large, in which case only low-type women are better off and the others are indifferent),

- but all women are worse off than if the technology was available at zero cost (except if the excess supply of women is very small, in which case there is no welfare change).

A clear policy implication is that *any legislative change that increases the cost of the technology generally reduces the welfare of all women, including those who would not use (or even consider using) the technology.* This analysis sheds a new light on the reforms affecting the accessibility to abortion, for instance, through Medicaid public funding.[10] In the first few years after the national legalization of abortion in 1973, abortion was eligible for Medicaid public funding; this provision was ruled out in 1976 by the Hyde Amendment, which generated many similar provisions at the state level. According to our analysis, these fluctuations in public funding not only modify women's actual use of abortion, but affect the gains generated by the legalization *for all women*—including those who are willing to bear the costs and those who are not interested in abortion in any case.

Heterogeneous Costs

In practice, different women face different costs. The psychological distress clearly varies between women; and even though the financial cost is more uniform, its relative impact on individual consumption and welfare is as heterogenous as individual incomes, a feature that our simplified model does not consider. To capture the idea of heterogeneous costs, we make the simple assumption that some women pay the full cost c discussed above, while for others the cost is nil. Also, we assume that the distribution of this cost among women is not correlated with marital status.[11]

To further sharpen our point, we consider the extreme case of an infinite cost. Hence, among women with identical preferences, some are willing to adopt the new technology while others do not (or cannot); and the respective proportion of the two classes (say, μ and $1 - \mu$) is identical for all values of the taste parameter u. Finally, we concentrate on the case in which women are in excess supply. Our results can readily be extended to a less restrictive framework (finite cost, nonzero correlation), as well as to the opposite context of male excess supply; this task is left to the reader.

In this new context, women who do not accept the new technology are in a weaker position on the market, because their reservation utility as single is lower. A first consequence is that these women are, everything equal, more likely to marry.

---

[10] Other examples include the provisions of mandatory counseling and parental consent for abortion for minors.

[11] Under the opposite extreme assumption, where abortion is costly for single women only, we are back to the case, studied above, of a technology exclusively available to married women.

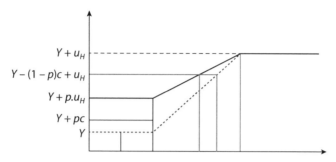

Figure 6.12. Heterogeneous costs.

Regarding the equilibrium structure, there are now five possible cases. First, when the excess supply of women is large in the previous sense, nothing is changed, since the marginal married woman belongs to the high type and wants children in all situations.

In all other situations, things are more complex. Indeed, married women may either be women with a large taste parameter or women unwilling to adopt the new technology (both being ready to accept a lower compensation). Depending on the size of male supply, four other cases may obtain:

- In the second case, there exist two marginal married women; both belong to the intermediate type, but one accepts the technology while the other does not, the taste parameter being larger for the former. In this situation (Figure 6.12), all low-type women are single, as are some intermediate-type women, and the marginal value of the taste parameter before the innovation, $u(M)$, is replaced with the two marginal values $u_N(M)$ (for women refusing the new technology) and $u_A(M)$ (for those accepting it; note that $u_A(M) > u_N(M)$). Stability requires the utility of the respective husbands be the same.
- In the third case, there are still two marginal women, but one (who rejects the technology) belongs to the low type, while the other is intermediate and accepts abortion.
- The fourth possible situation is such that all women who reject the technology (including the low-type ones) are married, whereas some intermediate women who accept the technology remain single; there is only one marginal woman, who belongs to the intermediate type and accepts abortion.
- Finally, if the supply of males is large enough, the only women remaining single (as well as the marginal married woman) are low-type women who accept the technology.

From a welfare point of view, it should be noted that no woman can possibly lose from the introduction of the new technology, even when some (possibly many) women reject its use. It is generally the case that all women gain from the introduction, including those who reject it, except when the excess supply of women is large (in which case there is no welfare change). Conversely, if we take as a benchmark the situation in which all women can access the technology, the introduction of costs that preclude its use by some women harms all women in general. Finally, all results are continuous and monotonic in the proportion μ of women willing to adopt the new technology. When μ is close to one, the welfare analysis is largely similar to the initial one; when μ is small, the introduction of the new technology makes little difference altogether.

Shotgun Marriages

In the discussion of the consequences of *Roe v. Wade*, the issue of shotgun marriages has attracted considerable attention. In an influential paper, Akerlof, Yellen and Katz (1996) have argued that abortion led to the disappearance of shotgun marriages, since women could avoid unwanted pregnancies, a fact that was known to (and potentially used by) men. They conclude that legalizing abortion may actually have harmed some women.

There Is No Such Thing as a Free Marriage

A first difference between the shotgun approach and ours reflects the emphasis we put on the intrahousehold allocation of resources as the endogenous outcome of equilibrium formation on the marriage market. In our model, a women being shotgun married is not necessarily better off than a woman remaining single, especially if she can use the new technology. The intuition is simply that in a context of excess supply of women, the surplus generated by marriage will be partly or fully appropriated by the husband; the woman will thus "pay" for the marriage by a low share of household consumption.

This argument stresses an important issue—namely, that shotgun marriage may not come for free. Whether forced marriages closely following an unwanted pregnancy really benefited women is at least debatable; after all, the resulting allocation of household resources was unlikely to favor women, and it is at least conceivable that the new wife's situation within such "shotgun couples" was no better than what it would have been had she been single. This is a case in which one would not want to postulate that the benefits, for the woman, of being married are exogenously given, unaffected by the reform, and such that women are always better off married than single.

The issue is difficult to assess empirically, if only because modifications of social norms are hard to document (let alone measure). Note, however, that a complete investigation *must* involve estimates of intrahousehold inequality. If our perspective is correct, neglecting changes in intrahousehold allocations resulting from the new technology may lead to erroneous conclusions. To take but one example, the idea of a "feminization of poverty" taking place in the 1970s should probably be considered with some caution. Insofar as available empirical evidence mostly relies on comparison *between* individuals and couples while failing to address the crucial issue of the allocation of individual well-being *within* couples, it may be largely misleading. Standard answers to this problem, based on equivalence scales, are inadequate. Relating the income of a single mother to half (or, for that matter, any fixed fraction) of the couple's income amounts to assuming that income is split within the couple according to some *exogenously given* rule. Matching models, simple as they may be, at least stress that economic theory in general, and equilibrium considerations in particular, tells us that the split is endogenous, driven by the environment, and responsive to technological changes as well as to market conditions in general. Should these effects be taken into account, the conclusions may be reversed.

In order to establish that some female pauperization resulted from the legalization of abortion, one has to compare the *individual* welfare of women before and after the change. The mere claim that the reform reduced the number of marriages directly implies that the comparison has to be between the well-being of married and single women. From a theoretical perspective, standard, unitary models of household are unable to help, since they do not allow one to recover individual utilities within the couple. The alternative, collective approach seems particularly well adapted to tackle the problem. Although available evidence is scarce, Oreffice's (2007) findings, already mentioned, suggest that the effects described in our model are well supported by the data.

Neal (2004) has provided a detailed discussion of the analysis shotgun marriage. Neal raises two questions. If one believes that the decline in shotgun marriages is the primary explanation for the rise in never-married motherhood, why should the impact be concentrated among the economically disadvantaged, and especially among less-educated black women? And how come the number of adoptions per nonmarital birth did not increase over this period? Note that our model provides simple answers for both phenomena. We relate the rise in out-of-wedlock fertility to the sharp decline in men's supply, a phenomenon specific to the population of black males with lower education. Moreover, in our model, the babies born out-of-wedlock were *wanted*, which explains the feeble rate of adoptions.

However, a second effect, which can readily be incorporated into our model, may reverse our conclusion. Specifically, assume, following Akerlof, Yellen, and Katz (1996) that (i) a fraction of the male population is not interested in marriage, but only in sexual activity, (ii) in the absence of birth control technology, social norms impose an implicit commitment from the male part, whereby sexual activity leading to pregnancy must end up in marriage, even against the male's initial intention, and (iii) the availability of abortion results in the disappearance of the social norm, in the sense that the father of an unwanted child no longer feels committed to the mother's decision to keep the child. Under such circumstances, the new technology may result in a *reduction in the supply of marriageable men*. According to the previous analysis, such a reduction may be harmful for women in two cases: when the initial equilibrium was characterized by an intermediate excess supply of women, and when the type of equilibrium changes because of the cut in male supply.

This interpretation has empirical implications that can be tested. In our framework, the "impoverishment of women" effect that would result would have to operate through a particular channel—namely, a significant fraction of the male population decides to remain single, while they would have chosen (or be forced) to get married before legalization. One way to empirically analyze this issue, hence, is to see whether legalization had a significant impact on the probability that a male will remain single. Casual observation does not seem to support this prediction. The proportion of single men in the male population does not seem to respond to legalization. A regression of the probability of being single on age, education, race, and fixed effect by year and state, as well as an abortion dummy on the male population aged 15 to 50 in the Current Population Surve March supplements 1968–1980, finds that the abortion dummy is not significant, and its point estimate is actually negative. The results seem robust to various specifications. Thus, the notion that a significant proportion of males decided to withdraw from the marriage market (hence remain single) following legalization, may not be supported by the data.

6.2   Gender and the Demand for Higher Education

Introduction

As a second application, let us reconsider one of the puzzles described in the introduction of this book: why did women's demand for higher education (particularly at the postcollege level) increase so much faster than men's in recent decades? One possible explanation, which I will describe more precisely in this subsection, was proposed by Chiappori, Iyigun, and Weiss (2009, from now on CIW). It is based on a very simple insight—namely, that acquiring education yields two different types of returns. First, education improves a person's opportunities in the labor market; educated people have a higher earning capacity, are less likely to be unemployed, receive higher wages, and have better careers. This impact has been abundantly studied. But it can hardly explain the gender difference that lies at the core of our puzzle, because it has evolved in a similar way for men and women; if anything, men have gained more, in particular since they still work more hours on average.[12]

A second type of returns, however, although crucially important, has attracted much less attention, at least from economists. What I have in mind is the return perceived in the marriage market. Education affects the probability of getting married, the characteristics of the future spouse, and the size and distribution of the surplus generated within marriage. If this impact happens to be quite different between genders, it may be sufficient to explain the observed discrepancies between incentives to invest.

The obvious problem with this explanation is that it is notoriously hard to test. Unlike the labor market return, the marital impact of education is difficult to assess, let alone quantify. Neither the size of the surplus nor its allocation are easily observable; and while the relationship between education and marriage patterns can readily be seen in raw data, the final impact on individual welfare is far from obvious. This is precisely why an explicit, formal model is needed. In practice, what we need is a simple equilibrium framework for the joint determination of premarital schooling and marriage patterns of men and women. Couples sort according to education and, therefore, changes in the aggregate supply of educated individuals affect who marries whom and the division of the gains from marriage. Conversely, this (perceived) impact may well be a crucial determinant of the decision to invest in education; that is precisely the channel that we want to explore.

An important aspect of education decisions is their social nature. The gains from schooling received within marriage strongly depend on the decisions of others to acquire schooling—how many of my potential mates (and of my potential competitors) will have acquired an education level similar to mine. However, since much of schooling happens before marriage, partners cannot coordinate their investments. Rather, men and women make their choices separately, based on the anticipation of marrying a "suitable" spouse with whom schooling investments are expected to generate higher returns. This is precisely why an equilibrium framework is required to discuss the interaction between marriage and schooling.

The basic ingredients of the CIW model are as follows. Consider a frictionless marriage market in which, conditional on the predetermined spousal schooling levels, assignments are stable: there are no men or women (married or single) who wish to form a new union and there are no men or women who are married but wish to be single. Assume that utility is transferable, that men and women can be divided into two schooling classes (high and low), and that the interactions between married spouses depend only on their classes. In particular, although

---

[12] See, for instance, Becker, Hubbard, and Murphy (2010, fig. 7) and Bronson (2014, fig 3.)

men and women have idiosyncratic preferences for marriage and investment in schooling, they all have the same ranking over spouses of the opposite sex, which depends only on their schooling. While highly simplified, such a framework is quite useful for investigating the issue under consideration. It implies that every educated man (woman) and every uneducated man (woman) has a host of perfect substitutes; as discussed before, such an absence of rents allows one to pin down the shares of the marital surplus of men and women in each schooling class based on competition alone. These shares, together with the known returns as singles, are in turn sufficient to determine the investments in schooling of men and women.

The model I just described—and that I will now present in more detail—is a highly simplified version of CIW. In particular, I shall omit individual marital preferences, which play a crucial role in CIW. The resulting "lite" model is much more tractable (in particular, it allows simple, graphical representations), while still providing a good intuition of some of the main messages of CIW.

6.2.1 The CIW Model

Men and women initially decide on some investment in education, the cost of which is individual-specific. By investing in schooling, agents can influence their labor market opportunities and their marriage prospects. Competition over mates determines the assignment (i.e., who marries whom) and the shares in the marital surplus of men and women with different levels of schooling, depending on the aggregate number of women and men who acquire schooling. In turn, these shares, together with the known market wages, guide the individual decisions to invest in schooling and to marry. The idea, therefore, is to investigate the rational-expectations equilibrium that arises under such circumstances.

There are two equally large populations of men and women to be matched; let i denote a particular man and j a particular woman. Individuals live for two periods. Investment in education takes place in the first period of life and marriage in the second period; it is lumpy and takes one period so that a person who invests in schooling works only in the second period, while a person who does not invest in schooling works in both periods. Lastly, investment in schooling is associated with idiosyncratic costs denoted by μ_i^i for person i. The distribution of these cost is gender-specific; let $G_g(\mu)$ denote the distribution of μ, where $g = m, w$.

When woman i and man j form a union, they generate some marital gain g_{ij}^i that they can divide between them. The exact nature of this gain can be of various types—consumption of private and public goods, leisure, domestic production, and many others—and could be derived from an explicit model of household behavior; for the time being, let us use a reduced form approach and simply consider them as given. Woman i alone can produce $g_{i\emptyset}^i$ and man j alone can produce $g_{\emptyset j}$. The *surplus* of the marriage is defined as

$$z_{ij} = g_{ij} - g_{i\emptyset} - g_{\emptyset j}. \qquad (6.2.1)$$

The key simplifying assumption is that both the gains and the material surplus generated by a marriage of woman i and man j depend only on the class to which they belong. That is,

$$g_{ij} = g_{I(i)J(j)} \quad \text{and} \quad z_{ij} = z_{I(i)J(j)}, \qquad (6.2.2)$$

where $I(i)$ represents the schooling level (class) of woman i ($I(i) = 1$ if i is uneducated and $I(i) = 2$ if she is educated), and similarly, the class of man j is denoted by $J(j)$, where $J(j) = 1$ if j is uneducated and $J(j) = 2$ if he is educated.

It is natural to assume that both the gains and the surplus rise with the schooling of both partners. More education means higher wages, therefore more consumption; in particular, more educated couples typically consume more public goods, which increases the marital surplus (see subsection 3.1.3 above). Similarly, let us assume that schooling levels of married partners complement each other (or, equivalently, that the surplus is supermodular); this implies assortative matching by education, a pattern clearly supported by the data.[13] Formally:

$$z_{11} < z_{12} < z_{22}, \qquad (6.2.3)$$

$$z_{11} < z_{21} < z_{22}, \qquad (6.2.4)$$

$$\text{and} \quad z_{11} + z_{22} > z_{12} + z_{21}. \qquad (6.2.5)$$

The per-period material utilities of woman i and man j as singles also depend on their education, and are denoted by $g_{i0} = g_{I(i)0}$ and $g_{0j} = g_{0J(j)}$; they are assumed to increase in $I(i)$ and $J(j)$. Thus, a more educated person has a higher utility, even as a single. Men and women who acquire no schooling and never marry have lifetime utilities of $2g_{10}$ and $2g_{01}$, respectively. A person that invests in schooling must give up the first-period utility and, if he/she remains single, the lifetime utilities are g_{20} for men and g_{02} for women. Thus, the (absolute) return from schooling for never-married men and women are $R^m = g_{20} - 2g_{10}$ and $R^w = g_{02} - 2g_{01}$, respectively. These returns depend only on the wages associated with each level of schooling and can be different for men and women if their wages differ. We shall refer to these returns as the *labor-market* returns to schooling.

In addition, those who marry perceive a second return from schooling investment in the form of an increased marital surplus, which can also be different for men and women, but is endogenously determined at equilibrium; they add up to the total surplus z. We refer to these additional returns as the *marriage-market returns* to schooling.

---

[13] A case in which spousal traits are substitutes is analyzed in Iyigun and Walsh (2007).

The Marriage Market

Any stable assignment of men to women must maximize the aggregate marital surplus (or output) over all possible assignments; and the maximization of the aggregate surplus is equivalent to the maximization of aggregate gain because the utilities as singles are independent of the assignments. As before, we denote by v_j for man j and u_i for woman i the individual payoffs, which obtains as the solutions to the dual of this linear programming problem. The stability condition requires that

$$z_{I(i)J(j)} \leq u_i + v_j, \tag{6.2.6}$$

with equality if i and j are married with positive probability. Equivalently,

$$u_i = \max\{\max_J[z_{I(i)J} - v_j], 0\}$$

$$\text{and} \tag{6.2.7}$$

$$v_j = \max\{\max_I[z_{IJ(j)} - u_i], 0\},$$

with the usual interpretation that $\bar{u}_i = u_i + g_{i0}$ and $\bar{v}_j = v_j + g_{0j}$ are the *total* utility levels that man j and woman i require to participate in any marriage. At equilibrium, a stable assignment is attained and each married person receives his/her reservation utility, while each single woman i receives g_{i0} and each single man j receives g_{0j}.

Our specification imposes a restrictive but convenient structure in which the interactions between agents depend on their group affiliation only, i.e., their levels of schooling. Assuming that, in equilibrium, at least one person in each class marries, the payoff for woman i in $I(i)$, married to j in $J(j)$, can, from Proposition 1, be written in the form

$$u_i = \max(u_{I(i)}, 0) \quad \text{and} \quad v_j = \max(v_{J(j)}, 0). \tag{6.2.8}$$

Here, u_I and v_j are the payoffs that the partners receive from the material surplus of the marriage; in our simple structure, all women of a given education I receive the *same* share u_I of the surplus no matter whom they marry, because all the agents on the other side consider them as perfect substitutes.

Lastly, remember that u_i and v_j represent shares of the marital *surplus*; i.e., they represent additional utility generated by marriage, over and above what the person would get as a single. Total utility of person i is, therefore,

$$U_i = u_i + 2g_{1\emptyset} \text{ if } i \text{ is not educated, and}$$

$$U_i = u_i + g_{2\emptyset} \text{ otherwise.}$$

Clearly, no man or woman marries if the marital surplus, $u_{I(i)}$ or $v_{J(i)}$, is negative; should u_I or v_J be negative, the material utility that agent $i \in I$ or $j \in J$ receives when married is lower than what he/she would get as single, and these agents would not marry. Let us assume, for the time being that $z_{I,J} > 0$ for all I, J, so that all individuals marry in equilibrium; the introduction of preferences for singlehood will be discussed later.

The Stable Matching

Although we assume equal numbers of men and women in total, it is possible that the equilibrium numbers of educated men and women will differ. I shall assume throughout that there are some uneducated men who marry uneducated women and some educated men who marry educated women. This means that the equilibrium shares must satisfy

$$u_2 + v_2 = z_{22}, \tag{6.2.9}$$

$$u_1 + v_1 = z_{11}. \tag{6.2.10}$$

Then three possible matching patterns may emerge, depending on the respective number of educated men and women. If there are more educated men than women among the married, some educated men will marry uneducated women; therefore, we shall have

$$u_1 + v_2 = z_{12},$$

while

$$u_2 + v_1 > z_{21}.$$

In the opposite case, there are more educated women than men among the married; then some educated women marry "down", and

$$u_1 + v_2 > z_{12},$$

while

$$u_2 + v_1 = z_{21}.$$

Lastly, in the case of an exactly identical number of educated men and women, then we have two inequalities:[14]

$$u_1 + v_2 \geq z_{12}$$

and

$$u_2 + v_1 \geq z_{21}.$$

---

[14] If the number of educated men and women were exogenously given, this would be a knife-edge case. However, they are endogenous, and therefore the case of equal populations will occur for an open set of parameters, as we shall see below.

Note, however, that it is impossible that all four conditions will hold as equalities, because this would imply

$$z_{22} + z_{11} = z_{12} + z_{21},$$

which violates the supermodularity assumption (6.2.3). Thus, either some educated men marry uneducated women or some educated women marry uneducated men, but not both.

When types mix and there are more educated men than educated women among the married, the previous conditions imply

$$u_2 - u_1 = z_{22} - z_{12}, \tag{6.2.11}$$
$$v_2 - v_1 = z_{12} - z_{11},$$

while in the opposite case,

$$v_2 - v_1 = z_{22} - z_{21}, \tag{6.2.12}$$
$$u_2 - u_1 = z_{21} - z_{11}.$$

One may interpret the differences $u_2 - u_1$ and $v_2 - v_1$ as the *returns to schooling in marriage* (or the *marital schooling premium*) for women and men, respectively. The quantity $z_{22} - z_{12}$, which reflects the contribution of an educated woman to the material surplus of a marriage with an educated man, provides an *upper bound* on the return that a woman can obtain through marriage, while her contribution to a marriage with an uneducated man, $z_{21} - z_{11}$, provides a *lower bound*. Analogous bounds apply to men. When types mix in the marriage market equilibrium, we see that the side that is in short supply receives the marginal contribution to a marriage with an educated spouse, while the side in excess supply receives the marginal contribution to a marriage with an uneducated spouse.

Investment Decisions

In equilibrium, individuals know (or rationally anticipate) u_I and v_J, which are sufficient statistics for investment decisions. Given these payoffs and knowledge of their cost of schooling μ, agents know for sure what utility they will get in the second period conditional on their choice of schooling in the first period.

Woman i chooses to invest in schooling if

$$g_{20} - \mu_i + u_2 \geq 2g_{10} + u_1. \tag{6.2.13}$$

The probability that woman i will invest—or, for a large population, the proportion of women investing—is therefore equal to

$$\Pr(\mu_i \leq g_{20} - 2g_{10} + u_2 - u_1) = G_w(g_{20} - 2g_{10} + u_2 - u_1). \tag{6.2.14}$$

Similarly, man j chooses to invest in schooling if

$$g_{02} - \mu_j + v_2 > 2g_{01} + v_1, \tag{6.2.15}$$

leading to a proportion of educated men equal to

$$\Pr(\mu_i \leq g_{02} - 2g_{01} + v_2 - v_1) = G_m(g_{02} - 2g_{01} + v_2 - v_1). \tag{6.2.16}$$

In other words, (6.2.13) and (6.2.15) describe how the dual utilities u_m and v_m ($m = 1, 2$) influence the investment decision, whereas the (second-stage) matching model described above determines how the dual utilities result from the agents' (aggregate) investment decisions.

6.2.2 Equilibrium

The equilibrium of the game can be found in two different ways. One is to explicitly solve the game as described, which implies finding four numbers u_1, u_2, v_1, and v_2 such that the investment behavior described by (6.2.13) and (6.2.15) which leads to the proportion of educated men and women characterized by (6.2.14) and (6.2.16), gives a matching problem for which the dual variables are exactly u_1, u_2, v_1, and v_2. Technically, this is not an easy task, because we must find a fixed point of a matching which is quite complex (it involves the relationship between the constraints on the primal program and the values of the dual solutions).

An alternative, and in this case much simpler, approach relies on the results described in section 5.1. Let us consider the fictitious game in which agents first match (based on their *exogenous* idiosyncratic characteristic, namely, their cost of education), then jointly (and efficiently) decide on their education choice. This is a standard matching problem, in which the marital gain is simply the maximum marital gain the couple can obtain over all possible education choices.

The Fictitious Game

As an illustration, assume that the cost of education μ are uniformly distributed on some intervals, say $[0, \bar{A}]$ for women and $[0, \bar{B}]$ for men. The proportion α of women investing is then

$$\alpha = \frac{g_{20} - 2g_{10} + u_2 - u_1}{\bar{A}}$$

if $(g_{20} - 2g_{10} + u_2 - u_1) \leq \bar{A}$, and 1 otherwise. Similarly, the proportion of educated men will be

$$\beta = \frac{g_{02} - 2g_{01} + v_2 - v_1}{\bar{B}}$$

if $g_{02} - 2g_{01} + v_2 - v_1 \leq \bar{B}$, and 1 otherwise. In practice, we assume that $\bar{A}$ and $\bar{B}$ are large (some people have very high costs of education), so that the proportions α and β are always smaller than 1.

Now consider, in the fictitious game, a couple (i, j), with respective costs of education (a, b) deciding on their joint education. There are four choices:

- $(1, 1)$ (none gets an education), then the total utility of the couple is

$$Z_{11} \equiv 2g_{10} + 2g_{01} + z_{11};$$

- $(2, 1)$ (only the wife is educated), for a total utility

$$Z_{21} - a \equiv g_{20} + 2g_{01} + z_{21} - a;$$

- $(1, 2)$ (only the husband is educated), for a total utility

$$Z_{12} - b \equiv 2g_{10} + g_{02} + z_{12} - b;$$

- $(2, 2)$ (they both invest), for a total utility

$$Z_{22} - a - b \equiv g_{20} + g_{02} + z_{22} - a - b.$$

Here, the notational convention is that a capital Z denotes total utility, whereas a small z denotes the corresponding surplus; the difference, obviously, being the sum of utilities as singles.

Education Decision

The optimal choice can be readily characterized; the outcome is summarized in figure 6.13, which has four zones, with two shifting points, denoted by P and Q, with

$$P = (Z_{21} - Z_{11}, Z_{22} - Z_{21}) \text{ and}$$
$$Q = (Z_{22} - Z_{12}, Z_{12} - Z_{11}).$$

Note that because of supermodularity, P must be located to the northwest of Q, as in figure 6.13.

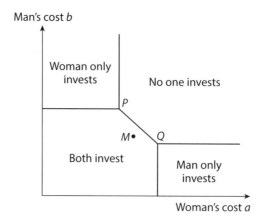

Figure 6.13. Investment decisions in the fictitious game.

The investment decisions of the couple are quite different from those of single individuals. In particular, consider the couple represented by point M, close to but slightly below the line PQ. One can readily check that if the corresponding individuals were singles, none of them would invest; because of the additional returns to education perceived on the marriage market, they both invest.

Matching in the Fictitious Game

We can now characterize the stable matching of the fictitious game. Note, first, that this matching is not unique. For instance, take any two couples in which all individuals have a very low investment cost (so that all will invest at any stable match). Then switching spouses between the two couples does not decrease total surplus, since the latter only depends on their education. That said, and because of the (weak) supermodularity of the model, it is simpler to concentrate on the perfectly assortative matching, in which for any two couples the higher cost man is always matched with the higher cost woman. Given the shape of the distributions, this gives a linear matching in which a woman with cost a is matched with a man with cost $b = a \times \bar{B}/\bar{A}$.

The corresponding line is drawn (in dashed line) in figure 6.14. We see that three patterns are possible.

- A first case is described by Figure 6.14a; it corresponds to the parameter values such that

$$\frac{\bar{B}}{\bar{A}} < \frac{Z_{12} - Z_{11}}{Z_{22} - Z_{12}}. \tag{6.2.17}$$

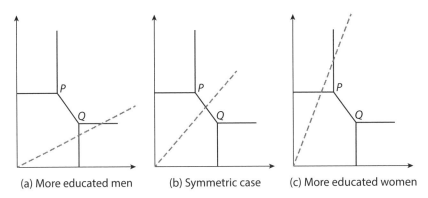

Figure 6.14. Matching patterns of the fictitious game.

Such a situation obtains when $\bar{A}$ is relatively large with respect to $\bar{B}$ (meaning that education costs are relatively higher for women than men on average), and/or when the difference $Z_{22} - Z_{12}$ (representing the gain in total utility stemming from the wife's education, when the husband is educated) is small with respect to the difference $Z_{12} - Z_{11}$ (representing the gain in total utility stemming from the husband's education, when the wife is uneducated). In other words, these are situations where there is a significant gain in the husband acquiring an education, but once this has been done the additional benefit stemming from the wife's education is meager.

In that case, three types of couples coexist. Two of them are assortatively matched, in the sense that both spouses have the same education; in couples of the third type, the husband is educated while the wife is not. Note that the right-hand-side expression in (6.2.17) is increasing in Z_{12}: this situation is more likely to occur when much utility is generated in mixed couples where he is educated and she is not.

- The opposite, polar case (Figure 6.14c) obtains when

$$\frac{Z_{22} - Z_{21}}{Z_{21} - Z_{11}} < \frac{\bar{B}}{\bar{A}},$$

suggesting that the cost of education is on average relatively smaller for women, and that the parameter Z_{21} (representing total utility of a mixed couple where she is educated and he is not) is large. Then we have again two sets of assortatively matched couples (in which both spouses have the same education), and a third set where the wife is more educated than the husband.

- Lastly, in the intermediate case (Figure 6.14b),

$$\frac{Z_{12} - Z_{11}}{Z_{22} - Z_{12}} < \frac{\bar{B}}{\bar{A}} < \frac{Z_{22} - Z_{21}}{Z_{21} - Z_{11}},$$

the game results in strictly assortative matching: the same proportion of men and women acquire an education. Obviously, this includes the case where genders are perfectly symmetric ($\bar{A} = \bar{B}$ and $Z_{12} = Z_{21}$). But, as mentioned above, it is also compatible with (some) asymmetry between genders: technically, it occurs whenever, from the perspective of the marginal man, the investment in education is worth the cost only if he can marry an educated wife (and conversely).

Other Equilibria

The results derived in section 5.1.5 above state that the solution I just described—i.e., the stable matching of the fictitious model—always constitutes a Nash equilibrium of the initial, two-stage framework. If all agents invest efficiently, none of them would benefit from deviating to some inefficient investment level. However, as mentioned above, other, inefficient equilibria may exist. This general conclusion can easily be illustrated in our simple model. Assume, for instance, that $Z_{11} = Z_{12} = Z_{21} \ll Z_{22}$; in other words, investment by one spouse is extremely profitable, but only if the partner invests as well. Then there exists an equilibrium in which no agent invests: if none of my potential spouses invests in equilibrium, the benefit of my unilateral investment would be nil, and is certainly not worth the cost. Note that such an equilibrium may entail any matching pattern, including one in which low-cost agents marry high-cost ones, a mismatch with respect to the efficient pattern. Alternatively, assume for a minute that $Z_{11} < 0$, $Z_{12} < 0$, $Z_{21} < 0$, and $Z_{22} \gg 0$—that is, no marriage is beneficial except one between educated people; then again we may be stuck in an inefficient equilibrium where agents do not invest (because they do not expect to find an educated partner), and therefore are better off as singles.

Fortunately, such situations are unlikely to occur in our model. Whatever the intracouple distribution of the marital surplus may be, there is still a private benefit to education (the $g_{2\emptyset}$ and $g_{\emptyset 2}$), which is perceived even by singles; this rules out a situation in which no one invests. In a more complex model, things may be more complicated. But at any rate, even if different (efficient and inefficient) Nash equilibria coexist in the two-stage game, it is natural to use a refinement to select some of them. If we agree that efficiency could be such a refinement, then the previous equilibrium does constitute at least a natural benchmark.

6.2.3 Preferences for Singlehood

A clear limitation of the model as I just described it is that all agents marry in equilibrium—not a very realistic pattern. CIW's initial contribution, indeed, considered a richer framework, in which agents are characterized by two idiosyncratic traits: the cost of acquiring an education *and* the agent's preferences for marriage. In practice, the natural way to introduce such preferences while keeping the model tractable is to import a Choo-Siow technology, as described in Section 4.2. That is, agent *i* has preferences for marriage, but these preferences do not depend on the particular partner she gets—only on the partner's education.[15] An interesting feature of this extension is the interdependence it introduces between marital preferences and education choices. For instance, two agents with identical cost of education may be driven by their idiosyncratic marital preferences to different investment decisions: individuals are more likely to invest if they are more eager to marry (since they are more likely to receive the additional, marital return to education), particularly if they would prefer an educated partner. Conversely, this intuition suggests that, in equilibrium, the distribution of marital preferences should vary between education classes (as observed ex post), if only because these preferences act as a selecting device into education. Moreover, introducing preferences for marital status allows us to model the decision to remain single as stemming from a trade-off between preferences for singlehood and the material gains generated by marriage. If we assume some stability in marital preferences, the percentage of singles informs us on the nature of the trade-off; for instance, a decline in the marriage rate typically corresponds to a reduction in total marital surplus. These interpretations play a crucial role in the empirical implementation of this approach; the interested reader is referred to CIW for a theoretical discussion and to Chiappori, Salanié, and Weiss (2017) and Chiappori, Costa Dias, and Meghir (2017) for empirical estimations.

6.2.4 Comparative Statics

The Traditional Model

It is tempting to reconsider the recent evolution of demand for higher education in America in the light of the previous model. Start from a "traditional" context, where, in the typical household, everyday living requires a large number of time-consuming chores to be accomplished. Assume, moreover, that these chores do not require much human capital to be accomplished, and that the domestic production

---

[15] In CIW, preferences are assumed to be uniform over education levels, but this assumption could readily be relaxed.

function is such that time spent by husband or wife are mostly substitutes (anyone can wash dishes, a task that does not require help from the other partner). Then, as argued by Becker (1991), it may be efficient for one spouse to specialize in domestic work while the other works mostly on the market. If there exists even a minor asymmetry between genders in terms of either cost of acquiring education or productivity in domestic work (say, because girls, due to prevailing social norms, are more familiar with domestic production technologies than boys), then the specialization pattern typically involves the husband as the breadwinner.

What would the technical translation of these assumption be in our reduced-form model? First, the coefficients Z_{12} and Z_{21} are probably quite high, indicating that the efficient living arrangement can pretty much be reached with only one spouse (the breadwinner) being educated. In practice, we therefore expect the difference $Z_{22} - Z_{12}$—representing the additional surplus generated by the wife's education when the husband is educated—to be rather small, whereas the difference $Z_{12} - Z_{11}$—representing the additional gain of an educated husband when the wife is uneducated—to be quite large (in the end, it represents the difference in welfare between families with a high- and a low-income breadwinner). These are exactly the conditions under which condition (6.2.17) is likely to hold, leading to an excess supply of educated males, as described in figure 6.14a.

Note that, in this case, the distribution of utility within the couple satisfies conditions (6.2.11), which, in terms of total utility, implies that

$$U_2 - U_1 = z_{22} - z_{12} + g_{2\emptyset} - 2g_{1\emptyset} \quad \text{and} \tag{6.2.18}$$
$$V_2 - V_1 = z_{12} - z_{11} + g_{\emptyset 2} - 2g_{\emptyset 1}.$$

Here, the first expression represents the total return to education for women, whereas the second is specific to men. The impact of the marriage market on investment decisions is clearly larger for men (since $z_{12} - z_{11}$ is large) than for women ($z_{22} - z_{12}$ being smaller).

A Revolution in the Second Half of the Twentieth Century

Let us now change some parameters of the model; our goal, here, is to capture, in our reduced-form approach, some of the deep societal changes that took place during the second half of the twentieth century. First, household technology is drastically affected by the introduction of what Greenwood, Seshadri, and Yorukoglu (2005) call "engines of liberation"—a series of labor-saving consumer durables and products, from washing machines to frozen food and from ready-made clothes to vacuum cleaners. The change was gradual, starting as early as 1920 for washing machines and lasting at least until the 1980s (with the introduction of microwaves and the development of frozen food; see also Albanesi and Olivetti 2009). From our perspective, the obvious consequence of these technological innovations is a considerable reduction in the time needed for the type of time-consuming, unskilled chores in which women used to specialize.[16]

A second change affects the costs of acquiring education, particularly for women. Several authors (Michael 2000; Goldin and Katz 2002) have argued that progress in birth prevention technology (from the pill to the legalization of abortion) has enabled women to better plan their fertility, thus significantly reducing the cost of investing in higher education. A related but different argument has been proposed by Low (2014), who argues that the sharp change in desired family size by the mid 1970s has drastically reduced the opportunity costs of postponing childbearing (see subsection 6.2.6 below).

Lastly, starting in the 1980s, the labor market returns to education have increased sharply. Empirical estimates suggest that the college premium, representing the gain in expected income generated by a college degree, has basically doubled since 1970.[17] As expected (and as confirmed by equations (6.2.18)), this boosts incentives to invest for both genders, in a way that, according to the data, is largely symmetric. Since total marital gain is typically convex in family income,[18] we expect the increase in welfare to be particularly high for couples where both spouses receive high wages. More importantly, and given the increasing returns to education, parents, especially educated ones, invest more in their children, which implies, in particular, spending more time with them.

The Changing Nature of Household Production

In summary, the second half of the twentieth century has witnessed a dramatic change in the nature of household production. The time needed for basic chores has been drastically reduced; simultaneously, time spent on children has increased over recent decades. There is a crucial difference between the two types of domestic productions—basic chores versus child care. Washing dishes and cleaning up the house do not require much education; these are tasks that can be performed by basically anyone; and, as mentioned above, husband's and wife's *time are typically substitute*. Parent's education, on the other hand, has been documented to be an important input in the process of educating children; there is both a direct

---

[16] Greenwood, Seshadri, and Yorukoglu note that in 1900 the average household spent 58 hours a week on housework (meal preparation, laundry, and cleaning); this compares with just 18 hours in 1975. They also give the specific example of a farm wife in 1945: "[…] it took her about 4 h to do a 38 lb load of laundry by hand, and then about 4–5 h to iron it using old-fashioned irons. By comparison it took 41 minutes to do a load of the laundry using electrical appliances and 1.75 h to iron it." (2005, p. 112).

[17] See, for instance, Bronson (2014).

[18] See section 3.1.

impact (see, for instance, Currie and Moretti 2003), and an indirect one since educated parents tend to be wealthier and spend more on children (as shown by Carneiro, Meghir, and Parey 2012, among others). Moreover, and although definitive evidence is hard to obtain, many economists agree that maternal and paternal times are more complement than substitutes (as is the case, for instance, with the Cobb-Douglas form adopted by Del Bocca, Flinn, and Wiswall 2014). This suggests that the advantages of the traditional model, whereby one spouse specializes in domestic production and is less likely to invest in higher education, have largely disappeared.

Reduced-Form Translation

These changes, in turn, alter the structure of our reduced-form model in a significant way. For one thing, the contribution of women's education to total surplus is boosted, particularly in couples where the husband is educated. In practice, the difference $Z_{22} - Z_{12}$ is now much larger. Secondly, the distribution of education cost for women has shrunk. In our uniform approximation, the translation is a sharp reduction in the parameter $\bar{A}$. Both changes imply that condition (6.2.17) is now much less likely to be satisfied. Depending on the value of the various parameters, we may be in case b, or possibly in case c. Regarding the latter hypothesis, Becker, Hubbard, and Murphy (2010) remark that in primary and secondary school, girls typically perform better than boys on average (although the variance is larger for boys). This seems to suggest that the cost of acquiring a high level of human capital may be smaller for girls, which would favor case c.

6.2.5   Empirical Implementation: What Do Data Say?

Raw Data: Some Interesting Patterns

A simple look at data confirms the patterns just described. Start with domestic production and child care. Table 6.1 is borrowed from Browning, Chiappori, and Weiss (2014), and describes variations in domestic time use for various countries over 25 to 30 years (in hours per day). Two patterns emerge. First, regarding domestic production, we see a clear decline in women's time, while men's increases. This pattern is largely due to the net increase in women's education, wage, and (market) labor supply over the period; and it strongly suggests that regarding domestic chores, male and female time, seen as inputs to the domestic production process, are probably substitutes rather than complements. The story is, however, totally different when we consider time devoted to child care. Here, both male and female time increases over the period, often in a spectacular way (it more than doubles in many countries); this pattern is all the more striking considering that the average number of children per couple has decreased over the period. This

Table 6.1. Time Spent on Home Production and Child Care.

	USA		Canada		UK		Norway	
Year of survey	1975	2003	1971	1998	1975	2000	1971	2000
Home production								
Married men, child 5–17	1.18	1.52	1.56	1.63	0.97	1.70	1.61	1.93
Married women, child 5–17	3.63	2.83	4.55	3.29	4.01	3.37	5.48	2.75
Married men, child <5	1.10	1.38	1.83	1.66	0.90	1.42	1.37	1.64
Married women, child <5	3.67	2.64	4.79	3.03	4.13	3.03	5.03	2.65
Child care								
Married men, child 5–17	0.20	0.57	0.14	0.41	0.06	0.26	0.23	0.32
Married women, child 5–17	0.65	1.13	0.64	0.77	0.30	0.58	0.65	0.59
Married men, child <5	0.40	1.24	1.21	1.47	0.28	1.04	0.54	1.23
Married women, child <5	1.63	2.67	2.16	2.97	1.28	2.57	2.08	2.61
Source: Browning, Chiappori, and Weiss (2014).								

seems to support the views that the value of children's education has increased over time and that the mother's and father's times tend to be complement when it comes to child care.

Moreover, the time spent varies by race and education. Table 6.2, borrowed from Phillips (2011), shows that educated moms spend significantly more time with their children, particularly when it comes to human-capital enhancing activities. Again, this conclusion obtains despite the fact that the opportunity cost of these mothers' time is much higher; moreover, these numbers do not take into account additional time spent by tutors, nannies, or teachning aides, which is also much higher in wealthy and more educated families. This confirms that the trend towards higher investment in children's human capital is specific to the top of the educational distribution.

The decline of the traditional model, whereby the husband works full time in the labor market and the wife (partly or totally) specializes in domestic production, can be seen in figure 6.15. Traditional households represented more than 60% of the total in 1970; in 2005, this proportion is down to 40%, while in another 40% of households husband and wife both work full-time.

Lastly, the evolution of marital patterns over this period is particularly interesting. Figure 6.16, borrowed from Chiappori, Salanié, and Weiss (2017), describes the matching patterns by education for two generations, respectively, born in the early 1940s and the mid-1960s. The graphs consider five education

Table 6.2. Time Spent with Children by Mother's Education.

Mother's education	Less than HS	High school	College	College+
Activity				
Being read to by mom (hrs/wk)				
0 to 2	0.09	0.41	0.9	0.51
3 to 5	0.16	0.25	0.69	0.74
6 plus	0.01	0.09	0.15	0.18
Talking with mom (hrs/wk)				
0 to 2	5.93	6.56	6.24	7.08
3 to 5	7.13	9.49	10.83	9.93
6 plus	7.78	7.36	7.87	7.61
Doing literacy activities (hrs/wk)				
0 to 2	0.94	1.58	2.45	2.3
3 to 5	1.27	1.64	2.33	2.89
6 plus	0.89	1.44	1.86	2.83

Source: Phillips (2011).

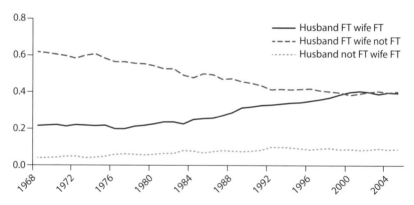

Figure 6.15. Work patterns of husbands and wives (aged 40–60). Source: Browning, Chiappori, and Weiss (2014).

levels—high school dropout, high school graduate, some college, college, and more than college; for each level, the colored bars indicate the spouse's education, whereas the total length of the bar represents the percentage of individuals who are married at age 45. We first observe a striking decrease in marriage rates, particularly for less-educated people; for instance, the proportion of male high

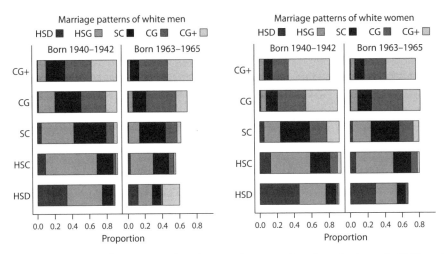

Figure 6.16. Matching patterns by education for generations born in the early 1940s and the mid-1960s. Source: Chiappori, Salanié, and Weiss (2017).

school dropouts who are married at 45 drops from more than 90% in the older generation to less than 40% in the younger one. In our formal model, the translation would be that surplus Z decreases significantly over the period, particularly for low education levels (typically, Z_{11} is much lower for the younger generation).

Regarding marital patterns, however, the evolution is clearly gender-specific. For men, the probability of marrying a more-educated spouse does not decrease over the period. Conditional on marriage, it actually increases for all education levels; for instance, the proportion of married men with some college whose wife has a post graduate degree increases by more than half. The story is quite different for women. For the older generation, higher education appears to decrease marriage probability; this pattern is much less visible for the younger crowd. Even more striking is the sharp decline in the probability of "marrying up"; for women with some college, for instance, the chances of marrying a husband with a postgraduate degree have almost halved over the period. In other words, marital prospects for less-educated women have significantly deteriorated over the period. This is not surprising: in a world of assortative matching, when more women are educated, a lower education level becomes a serious handicap in the marriage market.[19] One can expect the consequence to be a boost in the marital

---

[19] As a lady economist born in the 1930s put it during a private conversation: "In my time, a nurse had good chances of marrying a surgeon. But now there is too much competition from female doctors."

returns to education. Interestingly, this phenomenon is fully women-specific. This fits the CIW story, according to which the difference between male and female demand for higher education is triggered by differential returns in the marriage market.

An Explicit Estimation: Chiappori, Salanié, and Weiss (2017)

Consistent as these empirical arguments may sound, they cannot be fully convincing as such. To mention just one issue, marital prospects cannot be fully summarized by the probability of marrying up; crucially important are both the size of the surplus generated by such a marriage—which has changed over time—and its allocation between spouses. Both aspects are endogenous to the model and not directly observable in the data. Therefore, a (semi-) structural model is needed to evaluate them.

That is precisely the purpose of a paper by Chiappori, Salanié, and Weiss (2017). Their theoretical framework generalizes CIW in several dimensions. In particular, they consider five levels of education, therefore six-dimensional vectors of marital preferences (including singlehood), and study the marriage market of various races. The stochastic structure is separable à la Choo-Siow; regarding intertemporal variations, they allow for nonparametric gender- and education class-specific trends, plus a linear trend in the supermodular core (i.e., the difference $Z_{IJ} - Z_{I'J} - Z_{IJ'} + Z_{I'J'}$ for any education levels i, J, I', J'), which allows them to test the assumption that "preference for assortativeness"—as measured by the supermodular core—have changed over the period. The model is estimated and tested on US data, for men born between 1940 and 1967 and women born between 1941 and 1968—a total of 28 cohorts.

Their findings can be summarized as follows. First, the joint surplus generated by marriage declines for most couples—which directly translates into a decline in the number of marriages. However, the decline in surplus is always smaller for more educated couples; in fact, surplus increases in couples formed by women with college or postgraduate education, at least when the wife is at least as educated as the husband. These findings are fully consistent with the increased preferences for assortativeness at the top of the distribution. Secondly, the intrahousehold distribution of the surplus also varies significantly. The share of the wife increases for matches between equally educated individuals. Things are more complex for couples where spouses have different levels of education. The share received by educated women who marry down tends to decrease; on the other hand, less educated women who marry up benefit from a significantly larger share of a joint surplus which has become smaller over the years.

Finally, the structural framework of CSW allows one to aggregate these various effects into a measure of individual marital welfare—the Us and Vs of my formal model—and evaluate their evolution over cohorts. By differencing the values corresponding to various levels of education, one can get an estimate of the corresponding *marital education premium*; for instance, the marital college premium for women can be measured by the difference $V_I - V_J$, where category I denotes college education and category J high school graduates. The most striking conclusion is that the *marital* gain generated by accessing the highest education level (5, corresponding to postcollege degree) has significantly increased for women over the period, whereas it remains roughly constant for men.

6.2.6   The Low Model

Corinne Low (2014) has proposed a related but slightly different explanation for this asymmetry. Her main insight is that investing in higher education (essentially postcollege training), by delaying marriage and childbearing, has a higher cost for women, whose biological clock runs much faster. Women's fertility drops sharply after the age of 35, and is close to zero after 45; the cost of acquiring a postgraduate degree should therefore be understood in terms of potentially lower fertility, which negatively affects the situation of women on the marriage market.

In order to model these effects, Low considers a matching model in which men differ by one characteristic (that can be interpreted as income, education, or social status), whereas women differ by two traits—innate ability *and* fertility. In Low's model, innate ability can be boosted by access to graduate education, resulting in a larger stock of human capital and higher income; however, this requires postponing childbearing, at the cost of a discontinuous drop in fertility.[20] She then studies the stable equilibrium of the model (in which, technically, one side is one-dimensional while the other is two-dimensional), and shows that it can be of either of two forms, depending on the parameters. When returns to human capital are large and the cost in terms of fertility loss is low, stability translates into standard, assortative matching on human capital; skilled women invest in higher education and marry the "best" men on the market. In the opposite situation, things are more complex. While the most able women still invest, they are matched to husbands of intermediate quality; top income men prefer less skilled but more fertile women. Low argues that the evolution of the US marriage market in recent decades can be interpreted as a shift from an equilibrium of the second type to one of the first.

To support her claim, Low makes two empirical remarks. First, there is no doubt that returns to human capital (and particularly to graduate education) have increased drastically over the period. Regarding the cost of postponing childbearing, she argues that it crucially depends on the desired family size.

---

[20] In Low's model, higher education results in a deterministic drop in fertility. The framework has been extended by Chiappori, McCann, and Pass (2016), who allow for a continuous joint distribution of human capital and fertility, the two traits being negatively correlated. The conclusions are similar.

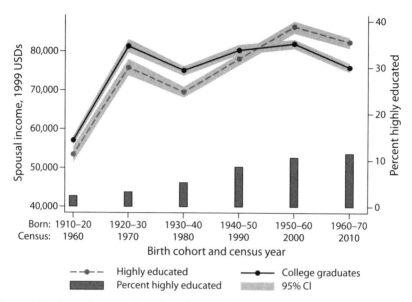

Figure 6.17. Spousal income by wife's education level, white women aged 41–50. Source: Low (2014).

Marrying after the age of 30 does not significantly reduce a woman's chances of having one or two children; but things are quite different if the aim is a family of six. Now, what data show is that a dramatic change in desired family size took place in the late 1960s–early 1970s. According to the Pew Research Center, in 1965 almost 45% of couples considered the ideal number of children for a family to be four or more; ten years later, the proportion is down to about 15%, while more than half the sample prefer two children.

Finally, do we observe the predicted shift in matching patterns? Figure 6.17, borrowed from Low (2014), shows that we do. For cohorts born before 1950, husbands' income is lower for highly educated wives than for college graduates; the trend is reversed for the later cohorts.

Matching under Imperfectly Transferable Utility

Transferable utility models have obvious advantages in terms of simplicity and tractability. Yet they exhibit some weaknesses, which may make them unsuitable for the study of specific problems. Chief among these is the fact that, under TU, couples behave as a single decision maker (the "representative consumer"), maximizing the sum of individual utilities. In particular, all Pareto-efficient allocations correspond to the same demand for public goods, which no intrahousehold redistribution of resources or power can affect. In some cases, this feature can be quite unsatisfactory. For instance, I have argued above that the balance of power within the couple may have significantly evolved over the recent decades. Still, in a TU framework, this evolution cannot possibly influence, say, household expenditures on children.[1] For some policy issues, such a priori restrictions on observable behavior may be inappropriate. Then one needs to generalize the TU approach by relaxing the representative consumer property, while maintaining the other features of the model (no restriction on transfers, frictionless competition, notion of stability, etc.). This is precisely the purpose of ITU models.

7.1 Basic Notions

7.1.1 Theoretical Framework

We start with the framework described in chapter 2. The Pareto set generated by the matching of Mrs. x and Mr. y is defined by the equation

$$u = H(x, y, v),$$

where u (resp. v) denotes the utility of x (y). A matching is therefore defined as a measure h and two payoff functions u, v such that

$$u(x) = H(x, y, v(y)) \quad \forall (x, y) \in \text{Supp}(h), \tag{7.1.1}$$

---

[1] Of course, other evolutions—such as changes in income or assortative matching—will have an impact even in a TU context.

where Supp(h) denotes the support of the measure h. Stability requires

$$u(x) \geq H(x, y, v(y)) \quad \forall (x, y) \in X \times Y, \tag{7.1.2}$$

which is equivalent to

$$u(x) = \max_y \{H(x, y, v(y))\} \quad \text{and} \quad v(y) = \max_x \{H^{-1}(x, y, u(x))\}. \tag{7.1.3}$$

At this stage, the main difference with the TU framework is that we have lost the equivalence between stability and surplus maximization. Actually, the mere notion of aggregate surplus is no longer well defined: absent the TU property, we no longer have a common metric for comparing (or adding) individual utilities.

A first consequence is that existence of a stable matching cannot be derived from a maximization argument; one must use a different approach. Various (related) paths can be borrowed here. One can refer to a variant of the standard Gale-Shapley algorithm applied to a discretized utility space, along a line initiated by Kelso and Crawford (1982). Alternatively, Legros and Newman (2007) and Chiappori and Reny (2016) use a result by Kaneko (1982) on central assignment games. In all cases, however, the number of agents was assumed finite; a generalization to a continuum would have to take limits. Secondly, uniqueness can simply not be expected to obtain in this setting, even in a generic sense—pretty much as in the NTU case.

However, some of the techniques used in the TU case readily extend to an ITU framework. We shall only consider here the one-dimensional case, although many of the results below extend to a multidimensional framework. We shall see that the Spence-Mirrlees condition, which is sufficient for positive assortative matching (PAM), can be generalized to the ITU case, although the interpretation is slightly more subtle. Moreover, it is still possible to recover individual utilities (up to a constant, as in the TU case), using techniques which are essentially similar to their TU counterpart.

7.1.2   Recovering Individual Utilities

Let's start with individual utilities. We have seen in chapter 2 that stability conditions, in the ITU case, become

$$u(x) = \max_z \{H(x, z, v(z))\} \quad \text{and} \quad v(y) = \max_z \{H^{-1}(z, y, u(z))\}. \tag{7.1.4}$$

Assuming that u, v, and H are differentiable, first-order conditions give, for an interior solution,

$$\frac{\partial H}{\partial y}(x, y, v(y)) + v'(y) \frac{\partial H}{\partial v}(x, y, v(y)) = 0, \tag{7.1.5}$$

from which we get

$$v'(y) = -\frac{\frac{\partial H}{\partial y}(x, y, v(y))}{\frac{\partial H}{\partial v}(x, y, v(y))}. \tag{7.1.6}$$

As before, first-order conditions give a differential equation (DE) in v—although this DE is more complex than in the TU case. Nevertheless, should the matching be known—say $x = \phi(y)$, assuming purity—then the PDE becomes

$$v'(y) = -\frac{\frac{\partial H}{\partial y}(\phi(y), y, v(y))}{\frac{\partial H}{\partial v}(\phi(y), y, v(y))}, \tag{7.1.7}$$

which determines v up to a constant; for each value of the constant, u can directly be recovered from

$$u(x) = H(x, \psi(x), v(\psi(x)),$$

where ψ is the inverse function of ϕ.

It is easy to see that condition (7.1.7) is an immediate generalization of what we had in the TU case. Under TU, indeed, we have

$$H(x, y, v) = S(x, y) - v;$$

therefore $\partial H/\partial y = \partial S/\partial y$, $\partial H/\partial v = -1$ and we get the usual condition $v'(y) = \partial S/\partial y$. As we have seen, this equation had a natural interpretation under TU: if a given individual (here a man) manages to increase his trait y by some infinitesimal amount, he will receive the entire additional surplus that this change has generated—his wife does not receive any of it.

What about the ITU case? Here, the additional term $\partial H/\partial v$ is simply *the slope of the Pareto frontier* at the point under consideration. Intuitively, it represents the exchange rate between his and her utility. In the TU case, this exchange is constantly equal to 1 and can therefore be omitted. In the ITU context, however, it must be taken into account. And the interpretation is similar: if y manages to marginally increase his trait, he will receive the entire gain generated—his wife's utility u will remain constant. Technically, indeed, if $u = H(x, y, v(y))$ then,

$$\frac{\partial u}{\partial y} = \frac{\partial H}{\partial y} - v'(y)\frac{\partial H}{\partial v} = 0.$$

7.1.3   Positive Assortative Matching

However, first-order conditions are necessary but not sufficient for the point under consideration to be an interior (local) optimum; we still need to check the second-order conditions, stating that the maximand is locally concave around the optimum. Differentiating (7.1.5) in y, the condition requires that

$$\frac{\partial}{\partial y}\left(\frac{\partial H}{\partial y}(\phi(y), y, v(y)) + v'(y)\frac{\partial H}{\partial v}(\phi(y), y, v(y))\right) \leq 0. \qquad (7.1.8)$$

This is not a very pleasant expression, if only because it involves the second derivative of the unknown function v. However, an old trick, directly borrowed from standard adverse selection theory, can help us out. Define function G by

$$G(x, y) = \frac{\partial H}{\partial y}(x, y, v(y)) + v'(y)\frac{\partial H}{\partial v}(x, y, v(y)),$$

so that the second-order condition simply requires that

$$\frac{\partial G}{\partial y}(\phi(y), y) \leq 0.$$

The key point, now, is that the functions G and ϕ are such that

$$G(\phi(y), y) = 0$$

for all y—this is just a restatement of the first-order optimality condition. Differentiating:

$$\phi'(y)\frac{\partial G}{\partial x} + \frac{\partial G}{\partial y} = 0 \quad \forall y;$$

therefore,

$$\frac{\partial G}{\partial y} \leq 0 \Leftrightarrow \phi'(y)\frac{\partial G}{\partial x} \geq 0.$$

Here,

$$\frac{\partial G}{\partial x} = \frac{\partial^2 H}{\partial x \partial y} + v'(y)\frac{\partial^2 H}{\partial x \partial v};$$

therefore,

$$\phi'(y)\frac{\partial G}{\partial x} \geq 0 \ \Rightarrow \ \phi'(y)\left(\frac{\partial^2 H}{\partial x \partial y} + v'(y)\frac{\partial^2 H}{\partial x \partial v}\right) \geq 0.$$

Now, when do we get positive assortative matching? Well, PAM requires that $\phi'(y) \geq 0$, and the second-order conditions then impose that

$$\frac{\partial^2 H}{\partial x \partial y} + v'(y)\frac{\partial^2 H}{\partial x \partial v} \geq 0, \tag{7.1.9}$$

which, using (7.1.6), can be written as

$$\frac{\partial^2 H}{\partial x \partial y} - \frac{\partial H/\partial y}{\partial H/\partial v}\frac{\partial^2 H}{\partial x \partial v} \geq 0. \tag{7.1.10}$$

Two remarks can be made here. First, this condition is a generalization of Spence-Mirrlees. Indeed, in the TU case, we have $\partial^2 H/\partial x \partial v = 0$, and (7.1.9) boils down to $\partial^2 S/\partial x \partial y \geq 0$. Second, the interpretation of condition (7.1.9) directly extends the intuitive interpretation of Spence-Mirrlees in the TU case—namely, that (if x and y denote, say, income) while everyone prefers a wealthier husband, the difference wealth makes is particularly large for wealthy wives (so they will be willing to bid more for him). Here, this notion is still present and is expressed by the term $\partial^2 H/\partial x \partial y$. However, a second effect must be taken into account: the impact of changes in (her) wealth on the exchange rate. Specifically, we know that $\partial H/\partial v < 0$; let us assume that $\partial H/\partial y \geq 0$, $\partial^2 H/\partial x \partial y \geq 0$, and that, in addition, $\partial^2 H/\partial x \partial v \geq 0$. The latter condition implies that the slope of the Pareto frontier—which, remember, gives her utility as a function of his—is flatter for wealthier wives. In other words, the wealthier the wife, the less costly it is for her (in terms of her own utility) to provide a given boost to her husband's well-being. In the bidding game that is implicitly at the core of the matching mode, wealthy women therefore enjoy a double advantage: they are willing to bid more, and their cost of bidding (expressed in utility terms) is lower. No surprise that they should win—resulting in PAM. Note, however, that if $\partial^2 H/\partial x \partial y \geq 0$ but $\partial^2 H/\partial x \partial v \leq 0$, the two effects are in opposition: wealthier women are willing to bid more, but the exchange rate is against them—and the outcome is now ambiguous.

Conditions (7.1.9) are standard in the literature (see, for instance, Legros and Newman 2007). They have been applied to income, but also to preferences. For instance, Chiappori and Reny (2015) show that when individuals with different risk aversions match pairwise to share identically distributed risks, then matching is always negative assortative: the more risk averse the husband, the less the wife.

7.1.4   Econometrics

Lastly, how can ITU models be taken to data? Just as in the TU case, the main difficulty is to account for unobserved heterogeneity; in practice, this requires introducing a random component into the matching process, while keeping as much theoretical and empirical tractability as possible. As it happens, this can be done through a direct extension of the Choo-Siow method, as recently demonstrated by Galichon, Kominers, and Weber (2016). The intuition underlying their work can be summarized as follows. Assume, as before, that agents belong to a finite set of categories (say, education classes). Take a given woman i, belonging to category I, and a given man j, belonging to category J. The feasibility constraint limiting the pair $(u(i), v(j))$ of utilities that i and j could reach if matched together is now of the form

$$u(i) = H\left(I, J, v(j) - \beta_j^I\right) + \alpha_i^J, \qquad (7.1.11)$$

where the α_i^J and β_j^I are random coefficients, the interpretation of which is exactly the same as in the TU case. Note that, as in Choo-Siow, the random terms enter additively and satisfy a strong, separability property: α_i^J only depend on the category J of i's spouse, not on his identity, and the same holds for β_j^I. Also, the TU case is obviously nested in this framework. Indeed, if we assume that

$$H(x, y, v) = Z(I, J) - v,$$

then (7.1.11) becomes

$$u(i) = Z(I, J) - v(j) + \beta_j^I + \alpha_i^J,$$

or equivalently

$$u(i) + v(j) = Z(I, J) + \beta_j^I + \alpha_i^J = z(i, j),$$

which is exactly the Choo-Siow model.

Now, we have the following result:

Proposition 1 *There exists* $2 \times K^2$ *numbers,* U^{IJ} *and* V^{IJ}, $I, J = 1, \ldots, K$, *such that:*

- *For all* I, J,

$$U^{IJ} = H(I, J, V^{IJ}).$$

- *If $i \in I$ is married to $j \in J$ at the stable matching, then the payoffs are*

$$u_i = U^{IJ} + \alpha_i^J \quad and \quad v_j = V^{IJ} + \beta_j^I.$$

Proof Assume that i and i', both in category I, are respectively matched with j and j', both in category J. Stability conditions imply that

$$u(i) - \alpha_i^J = H(I, J, v(j) - \beta_j^I)$$
$$u(i') - \alpha_{i'}^J \geq H(I, J, v(j) - \beta_j^I)$$
$$u(i) - \alpha_i^J \geq H(I, J, v(j') - \beta_{j'}^I)$$
$$u(i') - \alpha_{i'}^J = H(I, J, v(j') - \beta_{j'}^I).$$

Substracting the first equation from the second and the fourth from the third gives

$$u\left(i'\right) - u(i) - \left(\alpha_{i'}^J - \alpha_i^J\right) \geq 0 \text{ and}$$
$$u(i) - u\left(i'\right) - \left(\alpha_i^J - \alpha_{i'}^J\right) \geq 0.$$

It follows that

$$u(i) - \alpha_i^J - \left(u(i') - \alpha_{i'}^J\right) = 0,$$

which in turn implies that the difference $u(i) - \alpha_i^J$ does not depend on i, but only on the categories I and J. We can therefore write that

$$u(i) - \alpha_i^J = U^{IJ},$$

and by the same token

$$v(j) - \beta_j^I = V^{IJ}.$$

This proves the second part of the proposition. Moreover, plugging these two values into (7.1.11) directly gives the first part. ∎

Again, under the separability assumption, the matching model boils down to a series of standard, discrete choice models at the individual level.

7.2   Examples

We now present two examples of applications of ITU techniques.

7.2.1   Matching on Wages

The Model

We start with a basic but important variation on the models developed in the TU case: we now assume that the trait on which agents match is not their income but their income-generating capacity, i.e., on their wages. Specifically, let us consider a very simple collective model of labor supply where individual utilities are Cobb-Douglas:

$$u_i(L_i, Q) = L_i Q^\alpha.$$

Here, L_i denotes leisure and Q is some public expenditure, the price of which is normalized to 1.

We assume efficient decisions; therefore, the household maximizes a weighted sum of utilities:

$$\max_{L_1, L_2, Q} L_1 Q^\alpha + \mu L_2 Q^\alpha$$

(where the Pareto weight μ typically depends on wages), under household budget constraint:

$$Q + w_1 L_1 + w_2 L_2 = (w_1 + w_2) T,$$

where T denotes total time available. Assuming interior solutions, first-order conditions in L_1 and L_2 give

$$Q^\alpha = \lambda w_1 = \frac{\lambda}{\mu} w_2,$$

where λ is the Lagrange multiplier of the budget constraint. It follows that

$$\mu = \frac{w_2}{w_1},$$

so that the household maximizes the sum

$$w_1 u_1(L_1, Q) + w_2 u_2(L_2, Q) = (w_1 L_1 + w_2 L_2) Q^\alpha$$

under the budget constraint. In practice, the solution is

$$Q = \frac{\alpha}{1+\alpha} (w_1 + w_2) T \text{ and}$$

$$w_1 L_1 + w_2 L_2 = \frac{1}{1+\alpha} (w_1 + w_2) T,$$

giving the weighted sum of utilities:

$$w_1 u_1 (L_1, Q) + w_2 u_2 (L_2, Q) = \frac{\alpha}{(1+\alpha)^2} (w_1 + w_2)^2 T^2.$$

As in the TU case, the Pareto frontier is a straight line, defined by the equation

$$u_1 = H(w_1, w_2, u_2) = -\frac{w_2}{w_1} u_2 + \frac{\alpha}{(1+\alpha)^2} \frac{(w_1+w_2)^2}{w_1} T^2. \tag{7.2.1}$$

However, and unlike TU, the slope is now the wage ratio. In particular, if we keep the cardinalizations of utilities unchanged, this slope depends on the traits of both individuals—which is not compatible with the TU property.

Assortative Matching

Still, the previous approach directly applies. Let's start with the conditions for assortative matching. We have

$$\frac{\partial H(w_1, w_2, u_2)}{\partial w_2} = -\frac{1}{w_1} u_2 + \frac{2\alpha}{(1+\alpha)^2} \frac{w_1 + w_2}{w_1} T^2, \quad \frac{\partial F}{\partial u_2} = -\frac{w_2}{w_1}$$

$$\frac{\partial^2 H(w_1, w_2, u_2)}{\partial w_1 \partial w_2} = \frac{1}{w_1^2} u_2 - \frac{2\alpha T^2}{(1+\alpha)^2} \frac{w_2}{w_1^2}, \quad \frac{\partial^2 H}{\partial w_1 \partial u_2} = \frac{w_2}{w_1^2}$$

and (7.1.10) becomes

$$\frac{\partial^2 H}{\partial w_1 \partial w_2} - \frac{\partial H/\partial w_2}{\partial H/\partial u_2} \frac{\partial^2 H}{\partial w_1 \partial u_2} = \frac{2\alpha T^2}{w_1 (\alpha + 1)^2} \geq 0, \tag{7.2.2}$$

which is always satisfied. We conclude that matching is indeed positive assortative. The matching patterns can therefore be derived from male and female distributions, as in subsection 3.4 (see equation 3.3.4); that is, Mrs. i, with wage w_i, marries Mr. j with wage w_j (which we denote with $w_i = \phi(w_j)$ as above) if and only if the number of married women with wage above w_i equals the number of married men with wage above w_j.

Individual Utilities

Lastly, individual utilities can be derived from the DE:

$$u_2'(w_2) = -\frac{\partial H/\partial w_2}{\partial H/\partial u_2} = \frac{-u_2 + \frac{2\alpha}{(1+\alpha)^2}(\phi(w_2) + w_2)T^2}{w_2},$$

which gives

$$u_2(w_2) = \frac{K}{w_2} + \frac{1}{w_2}\int_1^{w_2}\frac{2\alpha T^2}{(1+\alpha)^2}(\phi(t) + t)dt.$$

As expected, u_2 is defined up to a constant K; note, however, that, unlike the TU case, the constant is not additive. Still, it can be pinned down using conditions on the "last married woman," just like in subsection 3.4. Then u_1 is defined by the Pareto frontier equation (7.2.1).

The Linear Shift Case

If we assume that male and female wage distributions satisfy the linear shift assumption (3.4.2) defined in section 3, there is a linear relationship between his and her wage:

$$w_1 = \phi(w_2) = \lambda w_2,$$

where $\lambda < 1$ if male wages are (still) higher than female ones on average. Then,

$$u_2(w_2) = \frac{K}{w_2} + \frac{\alpha(\lambda + 1)T^2}{(\alpha + 1)^2}\frac{w_2^2 - 1}{w_2} \tag{7.2.3}$$

and

$$u_1(w_1) = -\frac{1}{\lambda}u_2 + \frac{\alpha T^2}{(1+\alpha)^2}\left(\frac{1+\lambda}{\lambda}\right)^2 w_1 \tag{7.2.4}$$

$$= -\frac{K}{w_1} + \frac{\alpha(\lambda + 1)T^2}{\lambda(\alpha + 1)^2}\frac{w_1^2 + \lambda}{w_1}$$

Also, let us assume, to keep things simple, that there are (very slightly) more women than men, so that some women (at the very bottom of the wage distribution, near the lowest female wage w_0) have to remain single. The utility of a single woman with wage w is given by

$$\max_{L,Q} L\, Q^\alpha \text{ s.t. } Q = w(T - L);$$

therefore,

$$L = \frac{T}{1 + \alpha}, \quad Q = \frac{\alpha w T}{1 + \alpha} \quad \text{and} \tag{7.2.5}$$

$$u_1^S = \alpha^\alpha \left(\frac{T}{1 + \alpha}\right)^{1+\alpha} w^\alpha.$$

The last married woman is indifferent between marriage and singlehood; therefore,

$$\alpha^\alpha \left(\frac{T}{1 + \alpha}\right)^{1+\alpha} w_0^\alpha = -\frac{K}{w_0} + \frac{\alpha\,(\lambda + 1)\,T^2}{\lambda\,(\alpha + 1)^2}\frac{w_0^2 + \lambda}{w_0}$$

and

$$K = \frac{\alpha(\lambda + 1)T^2}{\lambda(\alpha + 1)^2}(w_0^2 + \lambda) - \alpha^\alpha \left(\frac{T}{1 + \alpha}\right)^{1+\alpha} w_0^{\alpha+1}.$$

Labor Supplies

The equilibrium conditions allow one to recover individual labor supplies. Indeed, the utility of a wife with wage w_1 is equal to $L_1 Q^\alpha$, where $Q = \frac{\alpha}{1+\alpha}(w_1 + w_2)T$. Therefore,

$$L_1 \left(\frac{\alpha T(1 + \lambda)}{(1 + \alpha)\lambda}\right)^\alpha w_1^\alpha = u_1\,(w_1)\,,$$

which gives

$$L_1 = w_1^{-\alpha-1} \left(\frac{\alpha T(1 + \lambda)}{(1 + \alpha)\lambda}\right)^{-\alpha} \left(-K + \frac{\alpha(\lambda + 1)T^2}{\lambda(\alpha + 1)^2}\,(w_1^2 + \lambda)\right) \tag{7.2.6}$$

and similarly,

$$L_2 = w_2^{-\alpha-1} \left(\frac{\alpha T(1 + \lambda)}{1 + \alpha}\right)^{-\alpha} \left(K + \frac{\alpha(\lambda + 1)T^2}{(\alpha + 1)^2}\,(w_2^2 - 1)\right). \tag{7.2.7}$$

An interesting point is that, in our simple Cobb-Douglas setting, a single's labor supply is constant (as can be seen in equation (7.2.5)). The interpretation is that a change in wages generates an income and a substitution effect that exactly offset each other. In other words, according to this model, agents faced with different wages would choose basically the same labor supply; this is a typical (and somewhat unrealistic) consequence of the Cobb-Douglas assumption. But couples, even with these simple preferences, behave differently; labor supplies vary with wages in a complex manner, as expressed by equations (7.2.6) and (7.2.7). The intuition is that wages also affect Pareto weights, therefore affecting the distribution of power within the couple and, as a result, the respective amounts of leisure consumed by the spouses.

One last point: the functional form studied here has only an illustrative purpose; it does not aim at realism in any sense. One can readily see, for instance, that in the presence of uncertainty, such preferences would imply, for at least one spouse, a corner solution (i.e., no leisure or no participation) for almost all wage realizations. A realistic model—i.e., one that could be taken to data—would require a richer functional form, and the introduction of uncertainty complicates the analysis of assortative matching. It is certainly doable, though; the interested reader is referred, for instance, to Chiappori, Costa Dias, and Meghir (2017).

7.2.2   Endogenous Pareto Weights

Although the previous example did not belong to the TU family, it shared with the TU framework a very specific feature; namely, the Pareto weights within a couple exclusively depend on the characteristics of the spouses (here, on their wages), but not on the distribution of characteristics in the population. Clearly, matching patterns depend on that distribution: under assortative matching, the wage w_j of Mrs. w_i's husband depends on the mass of women (resp. men) with a wage larger then w_i (resp. w_j). However, for given values of w_i and w_j, the slope of the Pareto frontier equals minus the wage ratio, irrespective of the wage distributions above and below w_i and w_j.[2]

Such a situation, however, is largely atypical in the ITU context. We now consider an example due to Chiappori (2009), which, although quite specific, Pareto weights are fully endogenous and depend on the entire wage distribution. My presentation, here, exactly follows that of Browning, Chiappori, and Weiss (2014).

---

[2] A consequence of this point is that although the model does not belong to the TU family, it is still characterized by a close relationship between stability and some adequately defined optimal transportation problem. See, for instance, Chiappori, Costa Dias, and Meghir (2017).

Preferences

In this example, there is a continuum of males whose income y is distributed over $[b, B]$ according to some distribution v, and a continuum of females whose income x is distributed over $[a, A]$ according to some distribution μ. To simplify, we consider the linear shift case, where the matching functions are given by $\phi(x) = (x + \beta)/\alpha$ and $\psi(y) = \alpha y - \beta$; therefore, under assortative matching (see below), we would have

$$\alpha = \frac{A - a}{B - b}, \quad \beta = \frac{Ab - Ba}{B - b}.$$

Also, in order to pin down the constant, we assume that the number of female is almost equal to, but slightly larger than that of men, so that in couples at the bottom of income distribution the husband receives all the surplus (although other normalizations, such as equal splitting of the surplus for the poorest couple, would obviously be possible).

Males have identical preferences, represented by the Cobb-Douglas utility:

$$u_m = c_m Q, \tag{7.2.8}$$

where c_m denotes his consumption of some private, Hicksian composite commodity, and commodity Q is publicly consumed within the household; all prices are normalized to 1. Similarly, women all share the same preferences, characterized by some minimum level of consumption $\bar{c}$, beyond which private and public consumptions are perfect substitutes:

$$u_f\left(c_f\right) = -\infty \quad \text{if } c_f < \bar{c}$$
$$= c_f + Q \quad \text{if } c_f \geq \bar{c}.$$

In particular, if a woman is single, her income must be at least $\bar{c}$; then her utility equals her income. In other words, private and public consumption are complements for men and perfect substitutes for women. This (admittedly rather extreme) assumption is aimed at capturing the notion that women care more about children than men: while males would allocate an additional dollar to both private and public consumptions, women do not mind it to be *entirely* spent on children (provided she receives at least the minimum level $\bar{c}$).

We further assume that household income is always larger than $\bar{c}$; then female utilities are of the quasilinear form $c_f + Q$. In particular, any efficient solution involves $c_f = \bar{c}$, because beyond $\bar{c}$, spending a dollar on private consumption for the wife is inefficient: spent on the public good, the same dollar is as valuable for the wife and strictly better for the husband.

Efficient Allocations

We first characterize the set of efficient allocations. An efficient couple solves the program:

$$\max c_m Q \tag{7.2.9}$$

under the constraints

$$c_m + c_f + Q = x + y \tag{7.2.10}$$

$$u_f = c_f + Q \geq U, \tag{7.2.11}$$

where $x + y$ is household total income and U is some arbitrary utility level for the wife.

A first point is that at any efficient allocation, the utility parameter U cannot fall below $((x + y) + \bar{c})/2$. The reason for that is that as the wife receives the same consumption $\bar{c}$ in any efficient allocation, her utility varies only with the amount of the public good Q. Now, once $\bar{c}$ has been spent, the husband's maximal utility obtains when he receives his optimal bundle of private and public consumption, namely $Q = c_m = ((x + y) - \bar{c})/2$; this choice generates a wife's utility of $((x + y) + \bar{c})/2$, and this value is thus a lower bound of what she can get, since it represents what she would get if her decision power were nil. There are, however, efficient allocations where she gets more than the minimum—i.e., such that $U > ((x + y) + \bar{c})/2$. Then providing her with U requires more resources to be spent on the public good (and less on the husband's private consumption) than what the husband would choose by himself; the constraint (7.2.11) is now binding, reflecting the fact that his utility could be increased by a reduction of U. Therefore, the Pareto frontier is given by

$$u_m = H((x + y), u_f) = \left(u_f - \bar{c}\right)\left((x + y) - u_f\right), \tag{7.2.12}$$

where $u_f \geq \frac{(x+y)+\bar{c}}{2}$. We can readily compute the corresponding consumptions, namely, $Q = u_f - \bar{c}$ and $c_m = (x + y) - u_f$. Figure 7.1 displays the shape of this Pareto frontier.

Note, in particular, that a single man and a single woman, whatever their incomes, would always be better off as a couple than when single. Indeed, a man with income y chooses $Q = c_m = y/2$ for a utility of $y^2/4$, while a single woman with income $x > \bar{c}$ achieves a utility that equals x. Now, by marrying, they achieve an income $(x + y)$. If $x \leq y + \bar{c}$, he can achieve $(y + (x - \bar{c}))^2/4 > y^2/4$, while she gets $\bar{c} + (x + y)/2 > x$. If, on the contrary, $x > y + \bar{c}$, then he can achieve

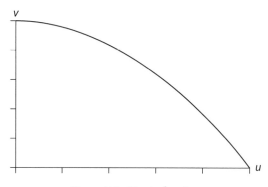

Figure 7.1. Pareto frontier.

$(x - \bar{c})y > y^2/4$, while she remains at x. Therefore, in our frictionless setting, either all women or all men marry: singles can only be on one side of the marriage market. Under our assumption, thus, all men marry and an infinitesimal fraction of women remains single.

Assortativeness

The Pareto frontier just derived has a particularly tractable form. Indeed, let us analyze the stability conditions along the lines previously described. For $v \geq \frac{(x+y)+\bar{c}}{2}$, we get

$$\frac{\partial H (x + y, v)}{\partial(x + y)} = v - \bar{c}, \quad \frac{\partial H (x + y, v)}{\partial v} = - (2v - (\bar{c} + (x + y))), \quad (7.2.13)$$

implying that

$$\frac{\partial^2 H (x + y, v)}{\partial(x + y)^2} = 0 \quad \text{and} \quad \frac{\partial^2 H (x + y, v)}{\partial(x + y)\partial v} = 1 \quad (7.2.14)$$

As we have seen above, these conditions are sufficient for the existence of a unique stable match involving assortative matching.

Intrahousehold Allocation of Welfare

We now turn to the allocation of welfare within the couple. Equation (7.1.6) becomes

$$v'(x) = -\frac{\frac{\partial H}{\partial x}(\phi(x) + x, v(x))}{\frac{\partial H}{\partial v}(\phi(x), x, v(x))}$$

$$= \frac{v(x) - \bar{c}}{2v(x) - (\bar{c} + x + \phi(x))}$$

$$= \frac{\alpha v(x) - \alpha\bar{c}}{2\alpha v(x) - (\alpha + 1)x - (\alpha\bar{c} + \beta)}. \tag{7.2.15}$$

Recovering the wife's utility requires solving this differential equation. For that purpose, we may, since v is strictly increasing, define the inverse function ω by

$$v(x) = v \Leftrightarrow x = w(v).$$

Then equation 7.2.15 becomes

$$\frac{1}{\omega'(v)} = \frac{\alpha v - \alpha\bar{c}}{2\alpha v - (\alpha + 1)\omega(v) - (\alpha\bar{c} + \beta)},$$

or

$$\omega'(v) + \frac{(\alpha + 1)}{\alpha v - \alpha\bar{c}}\omega(v) = \frac{2\alpha v - (\alpha\bar{c} + \beta)}{\alpha v - \alpha\bar{c}},$$

which is a standard first-order linear differential equation. The general solution is

$$\omega(v) = K(v - \bar{c})^{-\frac{\alpha+1}{\alpha}} + \frac{2\alpha}{2\alpha + 1}v - \frac{\beta + \bar{c}\alpha + 2\alpha\beta}{(\alpha + 1)(2\alpha + 1)},$$

where K is an integration constant.

To find K, we consider the marginal couple in which the wife receives the lowest female income a and the husband receives the lowest male income $b = (a + \beta)/\alpha$. Since we assumed that the number of women exceeds that of men, the utility of the marginal woman must be at its minimum level, namely, $((b + a) + \bar{c})/2$. Thus, we have

$$\omega(a) = K(a - \bar{c})^{-\frac{\alpha+1}{\alpha}} + \frac{2\alpha}{2\alpha + 1}a - \frac{\beta + \bar{c}\alpha + 2\alpha\beta}{2\alpha^2 + 3\alpha + 1} = \frac{1}{2}\left(\frac{a + \beta}{\alpha} + a + \bar{c}\right),$$

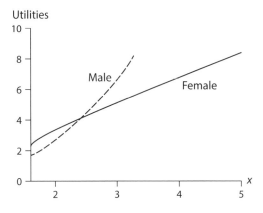

Figure 7.2. Utilities (female = solid, male = dashed).

which yields

$$K = \left(\frac{1}{2} \left(\frac{a + \beta}{\alpha} + a + \check{c} \right) - \frac{2\alpha}{2\alpha + 1} a + \frac{\beta + \check{c}\alpha + 2\alpha\beta}{(\alpha + 1)(2\alpha + 1)} \right) (a - \check{c})^{\frac{\alpha+1}{\alpha}}.$$

To illustrate, suppose that $\beta = 0$, $\alpha = .8$, $b = 2$, $a = 1.6$, $\check{c} = 1$. Then

$$K = 0.65$$

and

$$\omega(v) = 0.615v + \frac{0.65}{(v - 1)^{2.25}} - 0.171,$$

while the husband's utility is

$$u = F(x + y, v)$$

$$= (v - \check{c})(2.25\omega(v) - v).$$

The resulting utilities are plotted in figure 7.2. The horizontal line indicates the wife's income x. The wife's utility is represented by the solid line, while the husband's is dashed. As one moves up the assignment profile, the total income of the couples and utilities of both husband and wife rise.

Pareto Weights and Consumptions

Figure 7.3 gives the consumption of the public good $Q = v - \check{c}$ (thin line) and the husband's private consumption c_m (thick line).

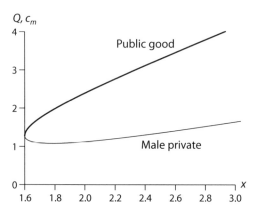

Figure 7.3. Consumptions.

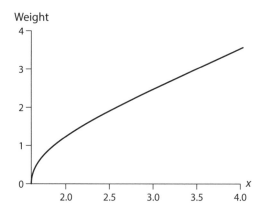

Figure 7.4. Wife's Pareto weight.

As argued before, the private consumption of the wife remains constant at $\bar{c} = 1$. The consumption of the public good rises; however, the private consumption of the husband c_m first declines and then rises.

The latter feature is quite remarkable and specific to an ITU framework. Husband's preferences are Cobb-Douglas; therefore, all goods are normal, and a wealthier person always consumes more of every good. The initial decline in private consumption while the couple's income increases would therefore be totally unexpected, both in a unitary framework and under TU. Here, however, it reflects the simultaneous change in Pareto weights that takes place as one moves upwards along the income distribution. Indeed, Figure 7.4 gives the wife's Pareto weight as a function of her income (the husband's being normalized to 1). For the poorest couple, her weight is zero, in line with our assumption that he gets all the

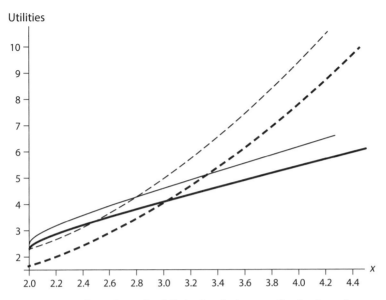

Figure 7.5. Impact of a rightwards shift in female income distribution of women on husband's and wife's utilities.

surplus. But the wife's weight increases sharply after that point, which explains the decline in husband's private consumption.

Comparative Statics

Finally, some comparative statics exercises are informative. For instance, suppose that we keep $\bar{c} = 1$ and $b = 2$ but shift the income distribution of women to the right so that $\alpha = 1$ and $a = 2$ (so that men and women now have the same income distribution). Then, $K = 1.12$ so that

$$\omega(v) = 1.12(v - 1)^{-2} + \frac{2}{3}v - \frac{1}{6},$$

while his utility is still

$$u = (v - 1)(2\omega(v) - v).$$

The husband's and the wife's utilities for these two cases are displayed in figure 7.5, where couples are indexed by male income (which remains invariant). For $\alpha = 0.8$, we represent, as before, the wife's utility with a thick solid line and the husband's with a thick dotted line. Thin lines (dashed for males and solid for females) represent u and v when $\alpha = 1$.

We see that the shift of the female distribution to the right benefits both men and women. More interesting are the spending patterns. Figure 7.6 displays public

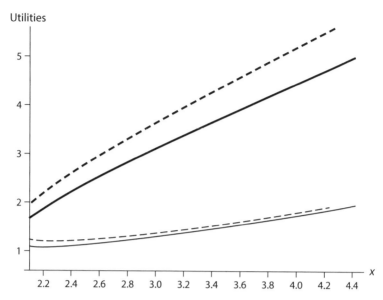

Figure 7.6. Impact of a rightwards shift in female income distribution of women on public consumption and the husband's private consumption.

(thick) and husband's private (thin) consumptions, both before (solid) and after (dashed) the shift. We see that most of the additional income is spent on the public good; increases in the husband's private consumption are quantitatively small and tend to shrink with income. In other words, while the husband does benefit from the increase in the wife's income, most of his gain stems from a higher level of public consumption (which actually benefits both partners).

Also, it is interesting to note the opposite features exhibited by cross-sectional and dynamic data. We have seen that in a cross section of couples, starting from the poorest, the husband's consumption initially declines with the couple's income. However, when income dynamics result in an increase of all incomes (including those at the bottom of the distribution), husband's consumption would increase in all couples, as can be seen on the graph (where the thin dashed line, which represents his consumption after the wife's income shift, is always above the thin solid one).

We conclude that in this model, unlike the TU case, changes affecting the wife's situation do affect the structure of consumption; moreover, improving the wife's status boosts public spending within the couples—a fact that has been abundantly confirmed by empirical investigation, especially if we think of children as a primary example of public consumption.

8

Conclusion

Matching models were designed to analyze markets for heterogeneous products and consumers; as such, they apply to a host of situations in economics, among which marriage markets are a prominent example. Since the initial contributions of Koopmans and Beckman (1957), Shapley and Shubik (1972), and Becker (1973), much progress has been made on both the theoretical and the empirical front.

Regarding theory, we understand better the power, but also the limits of the transferable utility model, particularly in its most general version (which involves multidimensional heterogeneity and unobservable characteristics). The TU framework can (admittedly under specific assumptions on preferences) encompass most aspects of family economics, from fertility to domestic production and from risk sharing to the consumption of public commodities. In particular, we now precisely understand which assumptions are required for preferences to be compatible with TU.[1] While strong, these assumptions are much less demanding than could have been expected a few decades ago (when matching models under TU mostly assumed quasilinear preferences and/or a unique consumption good). The links between matching under TU and optimal transportation, as well as those between matching and hedonic models, have been explicitly worked out. Last but not least, the basic structure of multidimensional models—and in particular the role of so-called twist conditions, which directly generalize supermodularity and single crossing properties à la Spence-Mirrlees—has been clarified; tractable methods are now available for solving multidimensional matching problems, both in closed form and numerically.

On the empirical side, the econometrics of matching models have seen several crucial advances. An important tool is the Choo-Siow model, in which the surplus is the sum of a deterministic component and a separable random term; a major advantage is that the stochastic distribution of the dual variables (i.e., individual utilities) can be readily recovered. This model has been fully characterized, and its comparative statics have been worked out. In particular, this model is exactly identified under the (strong) assumption that the distributions of the random terms are fully known. Testable generalizations must involve either richer data or a multimarket approach. In the first case, the idea is to independently observe

---

[1] Essentially, static (ex post) preferences must admit a cardinal representation such that conditional indirect utilities are affine with identical coefficients for the sharing rule, and (in an expected utility framework) VNM utilities must belong to the ISHARA family (see section 3.1.3).

either the surplus or the transfers. Observing transfers is easier in some cases (such as models of the labor market where wages are observed, or hedonic models in which the price schedule can typically be identified independently), much harder in others (such as family economics). Observing the surplus, on the other hand, appears to be a very promising solution in household economics, particularly since, under the TU assumption, household consumption and labor supply can be analyzed within a unitary framework, and identifying household utility— a problem to which a huge empirical literature has been devoted—allows one to directly recover the surplus function. Alternatively, matching models can be identified in a robust and testable way from matching patterns only when several markets (e.g., cohorts of agents) are observed. We must, however, keep in mind that such an approach must rely on specific assumptions regarding the variation of surplus across time, and that any empirical test is a joint test of the matching structure *and* these auxiliary assumptions.

A great strength, but also a serious weakness of the TU assumption is its main implication—namely, that once married, couples behave like single individuals and maximize a unique price- and income-independent utility. In a TU model, while intrahousehold allocation of resources depends on the distribution of power within the couple, aggregate household behavior is driven by the maximization of the sum of individual utilities. On the positive side, this property greatly simplifies the analysis by allowing one to disentangle behavioral patterns from redistributive issues. In many cases, such a simplification is welcome, in the sense that the insights thus provided are worth the loss in generality. If we primarily want to understand the role of assortative matching in the increase of intrahousehold inequality, or the importance of incentives produced by the marriage market for some crucial, premarital investment decisions (education, human capital acquisition, etc.), then a TU framework is certainly an excellent starting point.

These advantages come, however, at a price: some crucially important questions (how the allocation of power within the household impacts investment in children's education or health, to mention just one example) simply *cannot* be fully understood in a TU context. The natural solution, in that case, is to refer to ITU models. The main cost of shifting from TU to ITU is that an important and quite useful property of TU models—the equivalence between stability and surplus maximization—is lost; as a result, even basic issues like existence and especially uniqueness or purity become more intricate. Still, many of the tools developed in the TU framework can be extended to ITU models; I expect these models to attract more and more attention in the future.

Lastly, what do matching models teach us about reality? Obviously, I have to be quite careful here; after all, our models, as I said before, greatly simplify the infinite complexity of social life, and the conclusions they generate are only valid insofar as these simplifications remain acceptable. Still, some insights emerge from this literature; let me just point out a few of them that I find particularly important.

First of all, a host of social issues, particularly those related to the impact of policy changes, can only be analyzed from a general equilibrium perspective; a local approach is doomed to miss potentially crucial consequences. Take the case of *Roe v. Wade*, i.e., the Supreme Court's ruling that de facto legalized abortion in the US, as discussed in section 6.1. A superficial analysis may suggest that such a drastic change in the legal landscape can only benefit some women, namely those who are willing to actually use the newly legalized procedure; for those who are not going to resort to abortion—whether for religious or moral reasons, or simply because they do not need it—the change can at best be neutral and at worst detrimental. A more careful investigation concludes differently. A matching model that concentrates on this specific source of heterogeneity across women (i.e., differences in attitudes towards children and contraception) suggests that the benefits received by women who are ready to use the procedure tend to propagate to the whole population, precisely because a change in the allocation of power in some couples does, through the equilibrium mechanism, ultimately affect the allocation in all couples. Specific as this example may be, it illustrates a general issue—namely, that whenever a change affects a large fraction of the population, its general equilibrium effects cannot be disregarded, and will often result in a completely different outcome than what a "partial" (or local) analysis would suggest. In situations of this type, matching models are likely to be of major help.

Secondly, let me come back to my two motivating examples of chapter 1. Start with the asymmetry between male and female demand for higher education. Let me first say that, from an economic perspective, the current situation—in which women are more educated than men on average—is no more surprising (actually probably less) than what prevailed half a century ago, when women were less likely to invest in higher education and more likely to specialize in domestic production. The argument for intrahousehold specialization is pretty clear: if some basic chores require a large fraction of total time available, efficiency may require one spouse to specialize in domestic production while the other concentrates on market work.[2] But the asymmetry between genders remains puzzling: there is a priori no reason to expect it will always be the wife who remains at home. Empirical studies estimating the distribution of innate ability typically find that women are slightly above men on average (although their variance is smaller). That gifted young women may fail to fully exploit their productive potential appears as a clear inefficiency. In fact, in a situation where chores are a dominant constraint on people's time use, what our models would predict, as noted by Becker himself, is *negative* assortative matching: skilled individuals, male or female, should match with an unskilled partner who would specialize in domestic production. The fact that we do not

---

[2] Note, however, that whether specialization is efficient depends on the nature of the domestic production technology; see, for instance, Pollak and Wachter (1975), Pollak (2013) and Chiappori, Salanié and Weiss (2016).

observe such an outcome—in fact, positive assortative matching has always been a feature of matching patterns, at least in Western societies of the last century— suggests that much more was going on than chores-driven specialization, and that human capital investment has always been a key determinant.

Still, we need to explain the changes in economic incentives that drove the surge in female demand for higher education. The argument proposed by CIW is that the economic benefits provided by higher education are twofold, and that most of the literature has concentrated on the first while ignoring the second. On the one hand, more human capital improves an individual's situation in the labor market: lower unemployment probability, higher wages, steeper careers, better jobs, etc. These benefits have been abundantly studied, and their importance remains undisputed. Yet they are essentially symmetric across genders (several authors actually argue that, if anything, they are slightly larger for men, if only because men still work more hours); therefore, they can hardly explain the observed asymmetry. On the other hand, benefits from education can also be perceived on the marriage market; more human capital implies on average a more educated spouse, a larger surplus, and a larger share of the surplus. Unlike the former, the latter types of benefits have hardly been considered by empirical studies. Indeed, they are more difficult to measure: neither the size of the surplus nor its distribution between spouses is directly observable. Still, CIW argue that they may be quite sizeable— important enough, actually, to play a significant role in human capital investment decisions. Moreover, there is no reason to expect that they will be symmetric between spouses; indeed, empirical estimates, imperfect as they may be, strongly suggest they are significantly larger for women.

While many explanations can be given for the asymmetry, let me just emphasize one of the most convincing ones (I think), which was provided by Low (2014). Investment in higher education has two types of benefits, but also two types of opportunity costs: postponing entry into the labor market (the cost of which is measured in foregone wages), as well as, quite often, postponing childbearing. While, again, the first cost is mostly similar for both genders, the second is not: the biological clock does not run at the same speed for men and women. Low argues that 50 years ago, the return on human capital investment was lower, and the desired family size was large, resulting in a high opportunity cost of postponing the first birth; as a consequence, educated women had a comparative disadvantage on the marriage market, at least from the point of view of high-income potential spouses. Nowadays, returns are high and optimal family size is much smaller, leading to full assortative matching on human capital. This significant reduction in opportunity cost is specific to women, and may explain at least part of the surge.

Whatever the specific mechanism, though, analyzing an effect operating through the marriage market is possible only to the extent that we can assess the ultimate impact on *the individual's own welfare*. What matters, when I decide on my investment, is not so much how much additional surplus the investment will generate for my future household, but rather how much of it I will personally receive. Here, the usefulness of matching models is clear. The equilibrium condition states that individual returns equal social returns, suggesting that investments, although decided noncooperatively, still tend to be set at an efficient level. More importantly, the same condition allows one to fully characterize these returns, therefore the marital incentives to invest. In other words, although marital returns to education cannot be directly observed, they can be recovered from existing data (i.e., from matching patterns, preferably enriched by observed labor supply). Providing this link is clearly a major advantage of matching models.

Last but by no means least, let me come to the relationship between assortative matching and inequality. The mere fact that people marry more assortatively now than they used to is far from obvious; the issue, here, boils down to the precise definition of "more assortatively," a notion that would be clear if the gender distributions under consideration (education, income, or human capital) were fixed, but becomes much more complicated when they vary over time.[3] The first and obvious advantage of an explicit model is that it provides a formal definition of this concept, together with a tractable way of quantifying the various effects. This definition is certainly not indisputable; after all, the model does rely on strong assumptions that people may or may not be willing to accept. But at least these assumptions are clearly stated, which is a prerequisite for any structured discussion. The work of CSW, whose approach, relying on an extension of the Choo-Siow model, has been described in section 6.2, provide such a definition. If we accept it, then their empirical findings depict a complex picture. In particular, assortative matching did increase structurally (i.e., beyond the mechanical effects of the gender-specific variations in education over the period), but only at the top of the education distribution.

How can this trend be explained? While a host of justifications may come to mind, the mechanism described by CSW leads to important concerns. The key determinant, in their story, is the increased importance of human capital, particularly at the top of the distribution, combined with the specific aspects of human capital production. They argue that the major gains from marriage lie less and less in one spouse's specialization and more and more in the production of children's human capital (to use a Beckerian vocabulary), which requires human capital from both parents. For the most educated part of the population, investing in their children's human capital has become increasingly profitable, at least in terms of the child's future well-being; indeed, they devote more and more time to such activities, even though the opportunity cost of their time has surged over the period. CSW's model predicts that this trend should unambiguously lead to more

---

[3] For instance, the increase in assortativeness has to reconciled with the fact that the proportion of marriages where husband and wife have the same education remains roughly constant over the period.

assortative matching, although only at the top of the distribution of income and education.

These movements, however, generate serious concerns regarding the evolution of inequality over the coming decades. Recent work by Jim Heckman and coauthors[4] found that human capital formation requires a number of factors—e.g., the child's innate ability, formal education through the schooling system, but also both parents' time and investment—and that these factors tend, at least after early childhood, to become *complements*: a larger stock of one factor tends to *increase* the marginal productivity of the others.[5] Add to these characteristics of human capital production the CSW prediction that assortative matching must increase, and you reach the conclusion that inequality will inescapably grow, through a mechanism whereby parents endowed with a high level of human capital tend to match together and invest a lot of time, effort, and resources in their children's human capital, producing (on average) even more skilled individuals for the next generation.

Clearly, such a mechanism would tend to reinforce and exacerbate existing inequalities. These inequalities, moreover, affect not only the children's income, but more importantly their opportunities: kids born to a less educated family are at risk of receiving less investment, of lower quality, and later on of being less likely to marry educated spouses, thus perpetuating the initial handicap. This logic of human capital reproduction may have a serious impact on social mobility.[6]

The "inequality spiral" I have just described will be all the more difficult to alleviate (let alone reverse) in that it follows a logic of economic efficiency. After all, given what we know about human capital production, investing in children coming from an educated family generates higher returns, precisely because of factor complementarity; and the same can be said about assortative matching at the top of the distribution. Past history tends to show that government may (at least in some cases) be effective in correcting market failures, thereby improving efficiency; however, reversing evolutions that obey a strict efficiency logic is much more problematic, especially when they operate at the level of the entire economic system and when the stakes are of such a magnitude.

---

[4] See in particular Heckman and Krueger (2004), Heckman (2006), Cunha and Heckman (2007), Cunha, Heckman and Schennach (2010), and Almond and Currie (2010) for a general presentation.

[5] In addition, there is some evidence that the negative, long-term impact of various health shocks is stronger for poorer families (Currie and Hyson 1999).

[6] Recent work tends to show that intergenerational mobility is much less in the US than in Northern Europe, as well as in the UK (Black and Devereux 2010) and Canada. Over time, Chetty et al. (2014) find that while transition probabilities between deciles did not change much in the US, "the consequences of the "birth lottery"—the parents to whom a child is born—are larger today than in the past" (p. 141), reflecting the increase in inequality over the period.

The best chance of correcting the trend seems therefore to intervene quite early in children's lives—before the complementarity settles in. Our best hope, from this perspective, is provided by the literature I just mentioned, which also tends to find that early in a child's life, the factors driving the production of human capital are substitutes instead of complements; in other words, a public intervention may reduce or even avoid the inequality spiral, provided that it takes place early enough. This point has been vocally made by several authors, especially by Jim Heckman,[7] who emphasizes the very high social return of investing in early childhood.

As I said in the introduction, the matching literature is currently booming, and a host of new paths will be explored in the future. To conclude, let me just mention two directions that I find particularly promising. First of all, if we take seriously (as I think we should) the idea that assortative matching reflects fundamental economic features of human capital production, then we should model the *joint* decision of matching and investing in children, and take such models to data. On the theory side, effective as the TU framework has been so far, we may want to relax some of its implications—particularly the fact that household investment decisions do not depend on the allocation of power within the couple; for that purpose, ITU models seem fully appropriate. On the empirical side, we would definitely need better data; ultimately, we would like to be able to pair a detailed model of human capital formation at the household level with a global matching model—the former providing key information regarding the surplus function driving the latter. One can hope that the type of data needed for this purpose will be available shortly.

Secondly, most matching models developed so far were essentially static. There is no doubt, though, that the dynamic of the marital relationship(s) is crucially important. A dynamic extension of the existing matching models seems therefore needed. Clearly, such an extension would raise delicate issues. As always, dynamic models rely on specific assumptions regarding commitment. While some basic ideas have already been developed, particularly in the collective literature,[8] applying them to a matching context largely remains to be done. In addition, and as discussed above,[9] modeling remarriage is likely to raise challenging difficulties: the distributions prevailing on the remarriage market depend on divorce decisions, which in turn depend on the equilibrium that will prevail on the remarriage market. One can only hope that this book may direct the attention of younger economists to these issues.

---

[7] See, for instance, Heckman (2006, 2011, 2014).

[8] See, in particular, the recent survey by Chiappori and Mazzocco (2017).

[9] See section 5.5.

References

[1] Abdulkadiroglu, A., and T. Sonmez (2003), "School Choice: A Mechanism Design Approach," *American Economic Review* 93: 729–747.

[2] Acemoglu, D. (1996), "A Microfoundation for Social Increasing Returns in Human Capital Accumulation," *The Quarterly Journal of Economics* 111(3): 779–804.

[3] Akerlof, G., J. Yellen, and M. Katz (1996), "An Analysis of Out-of-Wedlock Childbearing in the United States," *Quarterly Journal of Economics* 111(2): 277–317.

[4] Albanesi, S., and C. Olivetti (2009), "Home Production, Market Production and the Gender Wage Gap: Incentives and Expectations," *Review of Economic Dynamics* 12: 80–107.

[5] Alderman, H., P.-A. Chiappori, L. Haddad, J. Hoddinott, and R. Kanbur (1995), "Unitary versus Collective Models of the Household: Is It Time To Shift the Burden of Proof?," *The World Bank Research Observer* 10(1): 1–19.

[6] Alkan, A., and D. Gale (1990), "The Core of the Matching Game," *Games and Economic Behavior* 2(3): 203–212.

[7] Almond, D., and J. Currie (2010), "Human Capital Development Before Age Five," NBER Working Paper 15827, http://www.nber.org/papers/w15827.

[8] Ananat, E. O., J. Gruber, and P. B. Levine (2004), "Abortion Legalization and Lifecycle Fertility," NBER Working Paper No. 10705.

[9] Angrist, J., and W. Evans (1999), "Schooling and Labor Market Consequences of the 1970 State Abortion Reforms," in *Research in Labor Economics* 18, S. Polachek, ed, Greenwich: JAI Press.

[10] Atakan, A. E. (2006), "Assortative Matching with Explicit Search Costs," *Econometrica* 74 (3): 667–680.

[11] Attanasio, O., and V. Lechene (February 2014) "Efficient Responses to Targeted Cash Transfers," *Journal of Political Economy* 122(1): 178–222

[12] Becker, G. (1973), "A Theory of Marriage: Part I," *Journal of Political Economy* 81: 813–846.

[13] Becker, G. (1974), "A Theory of Marriage: Part II," *Journal of Political Economy* 82: S11–S26.

[14] Becker, G. (1991), *A Treatise on the Family*, Cambridge and London: Harvard University Press.

[15] Becker, G., W. Hubbard, and K. M. Murphy (2010), "The Market for College Graduates and the Worldwide Boom in Higher Education of Women," *American Economic Review* 100 (2): 229–233.

[16] Bergstrom, T., and R. Cornes (1983), "Independence of Allocative Efficiency from Distribution in the Theory of Public Goods," *Econometrica* 51: 1753–1765.

[17]   Binmore, K., A. Rubinstein, and A. Wolinsky (1986), "The Nash Bargaining Solution in Economic Modelling," *RAND Journal of Economics* 17(2): 176–188.

[18]   Black, S., and P. Devereux (2010), "Recent Developments in Intergenerational Mobility," NBER Working Paper 15889.

[19]   Blundell, R., P.-A. Chiappori, and C. Meghir (2005), "Collective Labor Supply with Children," *Journal of Political Economy* 113(6): 1277–1306.

[20]   Bronson, M. A. (2014), "Essays in Labor Economics on Marriage, Education, and Labor Supply," *The Journal of Economic Perspectives* 4(4): 65–84.

[21]   Browning, M., F. Bourguignon, P.-A. Chiappori, and V. Lechene (1994), "Incomes and Outcomes: A Structural Model of Intra–Household Allocation," *Journal of Political Economy* 102: 1067–1096.

[22]   Browning, M., and P.-A. Chiappori (1998), "Efficient Intra-household Allocations: A General Characterization and Empirical Tests," *Econometrica* 66: 1241–1278.

[23]   Browning, M., P.-A. Chiappori, and Y. Weiss (2014), *Economics of the Family*, Cambridge, UK: Cambridge University Press.

[24]   Carneiro, P. C. Meghir, and M. Parey (2012), "Maternal Education, Home Environments, and the Development of Children and adolescents," *Journal of the European Economic Association* 11: 123–160.

[25]   Chetty, R., N. Hendren, P. Kline, E. Saez, and N. Turner (2014), "Is the United States Still a Land of Opportunity? Recent Trends in Intergenerational Mobility," *American Economic Review: Papers & Proceedings* 104(5): 141–147.

[26]   Cherchye, L., T. Demuynck, and B. De Rock (2014), "Is Utility Transferable? A Revealed Preference Analysis," *Theoretical Economics*, 10: 51–65.

[27]   Chiappori, P.-A. (1988), "Rational Household Labor Supply," *Econometrica*, 56: 63–89.

[28]   Chiappori, P.-A. (1992), "Collective Labor Supply and Welfare," *Journal of Political Economy* 100: 437–67.

[29]   Chiappori, P.-A. (2010), "Testable Implications of Transferable Utility," *Journal of Economic Theory* 145: 1302–1317.

[30]   Chiappori, P.-A. (2016), "Equivalence versus Indifference Scales," *Economic Journal* 126(592): 523–545.

[31]   Chiappori, P.-A., M. Costa Dias, and C. Meghir (2017), "The Marriage Market, Labor Supply and Education Choice," *Journal of Political Economy*, Special issue in honor of Gary Becker, forthcoming.

[32]   Chiappori, P.-A., O. Donni, and I. Komunjer (2012), "Learning From a Piece of Pie," *Review of Economic Studies* 79(1): 162–195.

[33]   Chiappori, P.-A., and I. Ekeland (2006), "The Microeconomics of Group Behavior: General Characterization," *Journal of Economic Theory* 130(1): 1–26

[34]   Chiappori, P.-A., and I. Ekeland (2009a), "The Micro Economics of Efficient Group Behavior: Identification," *Econometrica* 77(3): 763–99.

[35]   Chiappori, P.-A., and I. Ekeland (2009b), *The Economics and Mathematics of Aggregation*, Foundations and Trends in Microeconomics, Hanover Now Publishers.

[36]   Chiappori, P.-A., A. Galichon, and B. Salanié (2016), *On Human Capital and Team Stability*, Mimeo, Columbia University.

[37]   Chiappori, P.-A., and E. Gugl (2015), "Transferable Utility and Demand Functions: A Complete Characterization," Mimeo, Columbia University.

[38] Chiappori, P.-A., M. Iyigun, and Y. Weiss (2008), *An Assignment Model with Divorce and Remarriage*, Mimeo, Columbia University.

[39] Chiappori, P.-A., M. Iyigun, and Y. Weiss (2016), "The Becker-Coase Theorem Reconsidered," *Journal of Demographic Economics* 81(2): 157–177.

[40] Chiappori, P.-A., J. Lafortune, M. Iyigun, and Y. Weiss (2015), "Changing the Rules Midway: The Impact of Granting Alimony Rights on Existing and Newly-Formed Partnerships," *Economic Journal*, forthcoming.

[41] Chiappori, P.-A., and M. Mazzocco (2017), "Static and Intertemporal Household Decisions," *Journal of Economic Literature*, forthcoming.

[42] Chiappori, P.-A., R. McCann, and L. Nesheim (2010), "Hedonic Price Equilibria, Stable Matching, and Optimal Transport: Equivalence, Topology, and Uniqueness," *Economic Theory* 42(2): 317–354.

[43] Chiappori, P.-A., R. McCann, and B. Pass, "Multi- to One-Dimensional Transportation," *Communications on Pure and Applied Mathematics*, forthcoming.

[44] Chiappori, P.-A., R. McCann, and B. Pass (2016), *Multidimensional Matching*, Mimeo, Columbia University.

[45] Chiappori, P.-A., and C. Meghir (2015), "Intra-household Inequality," in *Handbook of Income Distribution*, A.B. Atkinson and F. Bourguignon (eds.), Amsterdam: Elsevier.

[46] Chiappori, P.-A., R. Nguyen, and B. Salanié (2015), *Matching with Random Components: Simulations*, Mimeo, Columbia University.

[47] Chiappori, P.-A., and S. Oreffice (2008), "Birth Control and Female Empowerment: An Equilibrium Analysis," *Journal of Political Economy* 116(1): 113–140.

[48] Chiappori, P.-A., S. Oreffice, and C. Quintana-Domeque (2012), "Fatter Attraction: Anthropometric and Socioeconomic Matching on the Marriage Market," *Journal of Political Economy* 120(4): 659–695.

[49] Chiappori, P.-A., S. Oreffice, and C. Quintana-Domeque (2017), "Bidimensional Matching with Heterogeneous Preferences in the Marriage Market," *Journal of the European Economic Association*, forthcoming.

[50] Chiappori, P.-A., N. Radchenko, and B. Salanié (2016), "Divorce and the Duality of Marital Payoff," Mimeo, Columbia University.

[51] Chiappori, P.-A., and P. Reny (2016), "Matching to Share Risk," *Theoretical Economics* 11(1): 227–251.

[52] Chiappori, P.-A., and B. Salanié (2016), "The Econometrics of Matching Models," *Journal of Economic Literature*, forthcoming.

[53] Chiappori, P.-A., B. Salanié, and Y. Weiss (2012), *Partner Choice and the Marital College Premium*, Mimeo, Columbia University.

[54] Chiappori, P.-A., B. Salanié, and Y. Weiss (2017), "Partner Choice, Investment in Children, and the Marital College Premium," *American Economic Review*, forthcoming.

[55] Choo, E., and A. Siow (2006), "Who Marries Whom and Why," *Journal of Political Economy* 114: 175–201.

[56] Clark, S. (1999), "Law, Property and Marital Dissolution," *The Economic Journal* 109: 41–54.

[57] Cole, H., G. Mailath, and A. Postlewaite (2001), "Efficient Non-Contractible Investments in Large Economies," *Journal of Economic Theory* 101(2): 333–373.

[58] Coombs, L., and D. Fernandez (1978), "Husband-Wife Agreement about Reproductive Goals," *Demography* 15(1): 57–73.

[59] Crawford, V., and E. Knoer (1981), "Job Matching with Heterogeneous Firms and Workers," *Econometrica* 49: 437–450.

[60] Cunha, F., and J. Heckman (2007), "The Technology of Skill Formation," *NBER Working Paper 12840.*

[61] Cunha, F., J. Heckman, and S. Schennach (2010), "Estimating the Technology of Cognitive and Noncognitive Skill Formation," *Econometrica* 78(3): 883–931.

[62] Currie, J., and R. Hyson (1999), "Is the Impact of Shocks Cushioned by Socioeconomic Status? The Case of Low Birth Weight," *American Economic Review* 89(2): 245–250.

[63] Currie, J., and E. Moretti (2003), "Mother's Education and the Intergenerational Transmission of Human Capital: Evidence from College Openings," *The Quarterly Journal of Economics* 118(4): 1495–1532.

[64] Dagsvik, J. (2000), "Aggregation in Matching Markets," *International Economic Review* 41 (Feb): 27–57.

[65] Dauphin, A., and B. Fortin (2001), "A Test of Collective Rationality for Multi-Person Households," *Economic Letters* 71: 211–216.

[66] Decker, C., E. Lieb, R. McCann, and B. Stephens (2011), *Unique Equilibria and Substitution Effects in a Stochastic Model of the Marriage Market,* Mimeo, University of Toronto.

[67] Del Boca, D., and C. Flinn (2014), "Household Behavior and the Marriage Market," *Journal of Economic Theory* 150: 515–550.

[68] Del Boca, D., C. Flinn, and M. Wiswall (2014), "Household Choices and Child Development," *The Review of Economic Studies* 81(1): 137–185.

[69] Duflo, E. (2003), "Grandmothers and Granddaughters: Old Age Pension and Intrahousehold Allocation in South Africa," *World Bank Economic Review* 17(1): 1–25.

[70] Dupuy, A., and A. Galichon (2014), "Personality Traits and the Marriage Market," *Journal of Political Economy* 122(6): 1271–1319

[71] Edlund, L., and E. Korn (2002), "A Theory of Prostitution," *Journal of Political Economy*, 110(1): 181–214.

[72] Ekeland, I. (2010), "Existence, Uniqueness and Efficiency of Equilibrium in Hedonic Markets with Multidimensional Types," *Economic Theory* 42: 275–315.

[73] Ekeland, I. (2010), "Notes on Optimal Transportation," *Economic Theory* 42(2): 437–459.

[74] Ekeland, I., J. Heckman, and L. Nesheim (2004), "Identification and Estimation of Hedonic Models," *Journal of Political Economy* 112(S1): S60–S109.

[75] Gale, D., and L. Shapley (1962), "College Admissions and the Stability of Marriage," *American Mathematical Monthly* 69: 9–15.

[76] Galichon, A. (2015), *Optimal Transport Methods in Economics,* Princeton: Princeton University Press.

[77] Galichon, A., S. Kominers, and S. Weber (2016), *Costly Concessions: An Empirical Framework for Matching with Imperfectly Transferable Utility,* Mimeo, New York University.

[78] Galichon, A., and B. Salanié (forthcoming), "Cupid's Invisible Hand: Social Surplus and Identification in Matching Models," *Review of Economic Studies.*

[79]   Gersbach, H., and H. Haller (1999), "Allocation among Multi-Member Households: Issues, Cores and Equilibria," in A. Alkan, C. Aliprantis, and N. Yannelis (eds.), *Current Trends in Economics: Theory and Applications (Studies in Economic Theory, 8)*, New York: Springer-Verlag Berlin Heidelberg.

[80]   Goldin, C., and L. Katz (2002), "The Power of the Pill: Oral Contraceptives and Women's Career and Marriage Decisions," *Journal of Political Economy* 110(4): 730–770.

[81]   Goldin, C., and L. Katz (2008), *The Race Between Education And Technology*, Cambridge: Harvard University Press.

[82]   Goussé, M., N. Jacquemet, and J.-M. Robin (2016), "Marriage, Labor Supply, and Home Production: A Longitudinal Microeconomic Analysis of Marriage, Intra-Household Bargaining and Time Use Using the BHPS, 1991–2008," *Cahier de recherche/Working Paper 16-01*, CIRPEE, Quebec.

[83]   Graham, B. (2011), "Econometric Methods for the Analysis of Assignment Problems *in the Presence of Complementarity* and Social Spillovers," in *Handbook of Social Economics*, J. Benhabib, M. Jackson, and A. Bisin (eds.) Amsterdam: North-Holland, Vol. 1B, 965–1052.

[84]   Greenwood, J., N. Guner, G. Kocharkov, and C. Santos (2014), "Marry Your Like: Assortative Mating and Income Inequality," *NBER Working Paper No. 19829*.

[85]   Greenwood, J., A. Seshadri, and M. Yorukoglu (2005), "Engines of Liberation," *Review of Economic Studies* 72: 109–133.

[86]   Gretsky, N., J. Ostroy, and W. Zame (1992), "The Nonatomic Assignment Model," *Economic Theory* 2(1): 103–127.

[87]   Grossbard-Shechtman, S. (1993), *On the Economics of Marriage: A Theory of Marriage, Labor, and Divorce*, Boulder: Westview Press.

[88]   Haag, B. R., S. Hoderlein, and K. Pendakur (2009), "Testing and Imposing Slutsky Symmetry in Nonparametric Demand Systems," *Journal of Econometrics* 153(1): 33–50.

[89]   Haddad, L., and R. Kanbur (1992), "Intrahousehold Inequality and the Theory of Targeting," *European Economic Review* 36: 372–378.

[90]   Hatfield, J., and S. Kominers (2011), "Stability and Competitive Equilibrium in Matching Markets with Transfers," *ACM SIGecom Exchanges* 10(3): 29–34.

[91]   Hatfield, J., and P. Milgrom (2005), "Matching with Contracts," *American Economic Review* 95(4): 913–35.

[92]   Heckman, J. (2006), "Skill Formation and the Economics of Investing in Disadvantaged Children," *Science* 312(5782): 1900–1902.

[93]   Heckman, J. (2011), "The Economics of Inequality: The Value of Early Childhood Education," *American Educator* 35: 31–47.

[94]   Heckman, J. (2014), "Invest in Early Childhood Development: Reduce Deficits, Strengthen the Economy," http://heckmanequation.org.

[95]   Heckman, J., and A. Krueger (2004), *Inequality in America—What Role for Human Capital Policies?* Cambridge: The MIT Press.

[96]   Heckman, J., R. Matzkin, and L. Nesheim L. (2010), "Nonparametric Identification and Estimation of Nonadditive Hedonic Models," *Econometrica* 78(5): 1569–1591.

[97]   Høritier, F. (2002), *Masculin/Fóminin II*, Paris: Odile Jacob.

[98]   Iyigun, M., and R. Walsh (2007), "Building the Family Nest: Pre-Marital Investments, Marriage Markets and Spousal Allocations," *Review of Economic Studies*, 74(2): 507–535.

[99]   Kalai, E., and M. Smorodinsky (1975), "Other Solutions to Nash's Bargaining Problem," *Econometrica* 43(3): 513–518.

[100]   Kaneko, M. (1982), "The Central Assignment Game and the Assignment Markets," *Journal of Mathematical Economics* 10(2–3): 205–232.

[101]   Kantorovich, L. (1942), "On the Translocation of Masses," Dokl. Akad. Nauk SSSR 37(7–8): 227–229. Reprinted in *Journal of Mathematical Sciences* 133(4): 1381–1382 (2006).

[102]   Kantorovich, L. (1948), "On a Problem of Monge," Uspekhi Mat. Nauk 3:225–226 (in Russian). English translation in *Journal of Mathematical Sciences* 133(4): 1383 (2006).

[103]   Kapan, T. (2010), *Essays in Household Behavior*, PhD Dissertation, Columbia University.

[104]   Kelso, A., and V. Crawford (1982), "Job Matching, Coalition Formation, and Gross Substitutes," *Econometrica* 50: 1483–1504.

[105]   Kenworthy, L., and T. Smeeding (Jan 2013), *Growing Inequalities and Their Impacts in the United States*, Country Report for the United States, gini-research.org/CR-United-States.

[106]   Klerman, J. (1999), "US Abortion Policy and Fertility," *American Economic Review* 89(2): 261–264.

[107]   Koopmans, T., and M. Beckmann (Jan 1957), "Assignment Problems and the Location of Economic Activities," *Econometrica*, 25(1): 53–76.

[108]   Lauermann, S., and G. Noldeke (2014), "Stable Marriages and Search Frictions," *Journal of Economic Theory* 151(5): 163–195.

[109]   Legros, P., and A. F. Newman (2007), "Beauty Is a Beast, Frog Is a Prince: Assortative Matching with Nontransferabilities," *Econometrica* 75(4): 1073–1102.

[110]   Levine, P., D. Staiger, T. Kane, and D. Zimmerman (1999), "Roe vs. Wade and American Fertility," *American Journal of Public Health* 89(2): 199–203.

[111]   Lewbel, A. (1995), "Consistent Nonparametric Hypothesis Tests with an Application to Slutsky Symmetry," *Journal of Econometrics* 67(2): 379–401.

[112]   Lindenlaub, I. (2015), *Sorting Multidimensional Types: Theory and Application*, Mimeo, Yale University.

[113]   Liu, Q., G.J. Mailath, A. Postlewaite, and L. Samuelson (2014), "Stable Matching with Incomplete Information," *Econometrica* 82: 541–587.

[114]   Low, C. (2014), *Essays in Gender Economics*, PhD dissertation, Columbia University.

[115]   Lundberg, S., and R. Pollak (1993), "Separate Spheres Bargaining and the Marriage Market," *Journal of Political Economy* 101(6): 988–1010.

[116]   Lundberg, S., and R. Pollak (2003), "Efficiency in Marriage," *Review of Economics of the Household* 1: 153–167.

[117]   Manser, M., and M. Brown (1980), "Marriage and Household Decision Making: A Bargaining Analysis," *International Economic Review* 21(1): 31–44.

[118]   Mazzocco, M. (2004), "Saving, Risk Sharing, and Preferences for Risk," *American Economic Review* 94: 1169–1182.

[119] McElroy, M. B., and M. J. Horney (1981), "Nash Bargained Household Decisions: Toward a Generalization of the Theory of Demand," *International Economic Review*, 22(2): 333–349.

[120] Michael, R. (2000), "Abortion Decisions in the U.S," in , E. Laumann and R. Michael, (eds.), *Sex, Love and Health: Public and Private Policy*, University of Chicago Press.

[121] Moffitt, R. (1992), "Incentive Effects of the US Welfare System: A Review," *Journal of Economic Literature* 30(1): 1–61.

[122] Monge, G. (1781), "Mémoire sur la Théorie des Déblais et des Remblais," in *Histoire de l'Académie Royale des Sciences de Paris*, 666–704.

[123] Mourifié, I., and A. Siow (2014), *Cohabitation versus Marriage: Marriage Matching with Peer Effects*, Working Paper, University of Toronto.

[124] Myers, C. (2012), "Power of the Pill or Power of Abortion? Re-Examining the Effects of Young Women's Access to Reproductive Control," IZA DP No. 6661.

[125] Myerson, R. B. (1991), *Game Theory: Analysis of Conflict*, Cambridge MA: Harvard University Press.

[126] Neal, D. (2004), "The Relationship between Marriage Market Prospects and Never-Married Motherhood," *Journal of Human Resources* 39(4): 938–957.

[127] Nöldeke, G., and L. Samuelson (2015), "Investment and Competitive Matching," *Econometrica* 83(3): 835–896.

[128] Oreffice, S. (2007), "Did the Legalization of Abortion Increase Women's Household Bargaining Power? Evidence from Labor Supply," *Review of Economics of the Household* 5(2): 181–207.

[129] Phillips, M. (2011), "Parenting, Time Use, and Disparities in Academic Outcomes," in *Whither Opportunity? Rising Inequality, Schools, and Children's Life Chances*, Greg J. Duncan Richard J. Murnane (eds.) Russell Sage Foundation, 207–28.

[130] Pollak, R. (2013), "Allocating Household Time: When Does Efficiency Imply Specialization?" *NBER Working Paper 19178*.

[131] Pollak, R., and M. Wachter (1975), "The Relevance of the Household Production Function and Its Implications for the Allocation of Time," *The Journal of Political Economy* 83: 255–278

[132] Roth, A. (1984), "The Evolution of the Labor Market for Medical Interns and Residents: A Case Study in Game Theory," *Journal of Political Economy* 92: 991–1016.

[133] Roth, A., and E. Peranson (1999), "The Redesign of the Matching Market for American Physicians: Some Engineering Aspects of Economic Design," *American Economic Review* 89: 748–779.

[134] Roth, A., and M. Sotomayor (1990), *Two-Sided Matching: A Study in Game-Theoretic Modeling and Analysis*, Cambridge University Press.

[135] Rubinstein, A. (1982), "Perfect Equilibrium in a Bargaining Model," *Econometrica* 50: 97–109.

[136] Saez, E. (2013), *Striking It Richer: The Evolution of Top Incomes in the United States (updated with 2012 preliminary estimates)*, Mimeo, University of California, Berkeley.

[137] Schulhofer-Wohl, S. (2006), "Negative Assortative Matching of Risk-Averse Agents with Transferable Expected Utility," *Economics Letters* 92(3): 383–388.

[138]   Shapley, L., and M. Shubik (1972), "The Assignment Game I: The Core," *International Journal of Game Theory* 1: 111–130.

[139]   Shore, S. (Aug. 2010), "For Better, For Worse: Intrahousehold Risk-Sharing Over The Business Cycle," *The Review of Economics and Statistics* 2010, 92(3): 536–548.

[140]   Shimer, R., and L. Smith (2000), "Assortative Matching and Search," *Econometrica* 68(2): 343–369.

[141]   Thomas, D. (1990), "Intra–Household Resource Allocation: An Inferential Approach," *Journal of Human Resources* 25: 635–664.

[142]   Townsend, R. (1994), "Risk and Insurance in Village India," *Econometrica* 62: 539–591.

[143]   Weiss, Y. (1977), "The Formation and Dissolution of Families: Why Marry? Who Marries Whom? and What Happens upon Divorce," in *Handbook of Population and Family Economics*, M. Rosenzweig and O. Stark (eds.) Amsterdam: Elsevier.

[144]   Western, B., and B. Pettit (2000), "Incarceration and Racial Inequality in Men's Employment," *Industrial and Labor Relations Review* 54: 3–16.

[145]   Williams, L. (1994), "Determinants of Couple Agreement in US Fertility Decisions," *Family Planning Perspectives* 26(4): 169–173.

[146]   Wilson, W. (1987), *The Truly Disadvantaged: The Inner City, the Underclass, and Public Policy*, Chicago: University of Chicago Press.

Index

The Gorman Lectures in Economics

Richard Blundell, Series Editor

Terence (W. M.) Gorman was one of the most distinguished economists of the twentieth century. His ideas are so ingrained in modern economics that we use them daily with almost no acknowledgment. The relationship between individual behavior and aggregate outcomes, two-stage budgeting in individual decision making, the "characteristics" model which lies at the heart of modern consumer economics, and a conceptual framework for "adult equivalence scales" are but a few of these. For over fifty years he guided students and colleagues alike in how best to model economic activities as well as how to test these models once formulated.

During the late 1980s and early 1990s, Gorman was a Visiting Professor of Economics at University College London. He became a key part of the newly formed and lively research group at UCL and at the Institute for Fiscal Studies. The aim of this research was to avoid the obsessive labeling that had pigeonholed much of economics and to introduce a free flow of ideas between economic theory, econometrics, and empirical evidence. It worked marvelously and formed the mainstay of economics research in the Economics Department at UCL. These lectures are a tribute to his legacy.

Terence had a lasting impact on all who interacted with him during that period. He was not only an active and innovative economist, but he was also a dedicated teacher and mentor to students and junior colleagues. He was generous with his time and more than one discussion with Terence appeared later as a scholarly article inspired by that conversation. He used his skill in mathematics as a framework for his approach, but he never insisted on that. What was essential was a coherent and logical understanding of economics. Gorman passed away in January 2003, shortly after the second of these lectures. He will be missed, but his written works remain to remind all of us that we are sitting on the shoulders of a giant.

Richard Blundell, University College London and
Institute for Fiscal Studies

Biography

Gorman graduated from Trinity College, Dublin, in 1948 in Economics and in 1949 in Mathematics. From 1949 to 1962 he taught in the Commerce Faculty at the University of Birmingham. He held Chairs in Economics at Oxford from 1962 to 1967 and at the London School of Economics from 1967 to 1979, after which he returned to Nuffield College Oxford as an Official Fellow. He remained there until his retirement. He was Visiting Professor of Economics at UCL from 1986 to 1996. Honorary Doctorates have been conferred upon him by the University of Southampton, the University of Birmingham, the National University of Ireland, and University College London. He was a Fellow of the British Academy, an honorary Fellow of Trinity College Dublin and of the London School of Economics, and an honorary foreign member of the American Academy of Arts and Sciences and of the American Economic Association. He was a Fellow of the Econometric Society and served as its President in 1972.